HOW TO
WIN AS A
STOCK MARKET
SPECULATOR

Alexander Davidson

KOGAN
PAGE

London and Philadelphia

To dear Acel
You have a great future
This book is for you

Publisher's note
Every possible effort has been made to ensure that the information contained in this book is accurate at the time of going to press, and the publishers and author cannot accept responsibility for any errors or omissions, however caused. No responsibility for loss or damage occasioned to any person acting, or refraining from action, as a result of the material in this publication can be accepted by the editor, the publisher or the author.

First published in Great Britain in 2004
First published in paperback in Great Britain in 2006
Reprinted in 2006

Kogan Page Limited
120 Pentonville Road
London N1 9JN
United Kingdom
www.kogan-page.co.uk

525 South 4th Street, #241
Philadelphia PA 19147
USA

© Alexander Davidson, 2004

British Library Cataloguing-in-Publication Data

A CIP record for this book is available from the British Library.

ISBN-10   0 7494 4494 0
ISBN-13   978 0 7494 4494 5

Typeset by JS Typesetting Ltd, Porthcawl, Mid Glamorgan
Printed and bound in Great Britain by MPG Books Ltd, Bodmin, Cornwall

Contents

Acknowledgements

At Kogan Page, my strong thanks to Jon Finch, my editor, for guiding the course of my books so astutely, and to Martha Fumagalli for working miracles with publicity over the years.

My great thanks to ShareScope for providing the excellent charts for this book and, in particular, to Angela Lopez for untiring patience and help extended to not the most technical of persons.

I am in a nostalgic mood. Thanks to all the guys at Harvard Securities in my youth, so many years ago, who taught me so much about how the stock market really works and about trading, and to Nicholas Pine at Scope Books who launched my writing career.

Last but by no means least, a special big thank you to my tens of thousands of readers, Web site visitors and clients who have made me feel that my work as a writer is worth while. Repay me by making money on the stock market, and never give up.

Wealth warning
Strategies covered in this book have worked spectacularly well for some in the past, but are not suitable for everybody. Also, market conditions vary enormously, and you must adapt accordingly. If you speculate on the stock market, it is at your own risk.

Those who live amongst wolves must learn to howl like wolves.
Russian proverb

Introduction

Make money speculating on the stock market, whether it is up or down

Speculating on the stock market is one of the last ways possible to get rich quickly and without spending time in proportion to the results achieved. It is possible even if you cannot initially afford to leave your job.

Traders who are starting out, or have a little experience, are faced with a bewildering range of advisers, books and courses. If you believe the gurus, you will need thousands of pounds of software, expensive training, vast amounts of start-up capital, Internet subscription services galore, and more hours than are in the day. This is even before you start speculating.

It is to rectify such misleading ideas that I have written *How to Win as a Stock Market Speculator*. Simple methods of stock market speculation work best, and are all that you need to make profits.

Expect no magic solution from this book. Instead, you will find out about methods that City professionals use for their own trading. Some of these have worked spectacularly well in the past. This is not in itself enough to make you rich as no one speculator stands exactly in the shoes of another, but it will take you a long way.

In the pages that follow, I will show you how to build your own stock market trading system. You must test it as you go, for it is only in this way that you will come to trust it.

Your system must be soundly based on money management. As part of this, you must preserve and protect your trading capital. Apportion your capital over a number of trades and limit your losses through a stop loss system, while you let your profits run.

To learn how to trade successfully, you must want to make money from it. At least half of stock market speculators do not. They think it is like having a flutter on the horses, or the National Lottery. Truth is, speculation, if it is to have any chance of long-term success, is not gambling. It is about narrowing the odds.

As a speculator, you need cast-iron self-discipline and to maintain a critical view of the markets. This book should help you to make the leap. You will find in its pages advice in such areas as these:

▌ What investment software you really need, and why. Almost nobody answers this question, until you have spent tens of thousands.

▌ Which parts of technical analysis work best and why.

▌ How to detect creative accounting tricks.

▌ Games market makers play.

▌ How to making money in falling markets.

▌ New issues, and the trading opportunity.

▌ How to speculate on penny shares.

▌ How to use tip sheets, message boards, newspapers and magazines.

▌ How to select and use derivatives.

If you are a beginner, this book will take you from knowing nothing to a high level of competence within a short period of time. Should you be an experienced speculator, it will help you build on your knowledge at an accelerated pace.

The first lesson of stock market speculation is that you will never have something for nothing. To get the most out of this book, you will need to commit your time.

The text is divided into four parts, incorporating a total of 21 seminars, together with this introduction and a final word. This order of presentation, in my experience, works well with starting speculators. The book will also serve you as a work of reference.

All great artists learn best by osmosis, absorbing through their pores the techniques they observe or read about elsewhere. Read *How to Win as a Stock Market Speculator* at least three times, and its substance will have started filtering through to your deepest subconscious. Use a highlighter pen to emphasis points that you particularly want to remember.

On your way forward, you will experience some difficult moments. Sometimes, you will lose money. The book shows you how to limit your losses, but you may find in the early days that the theory does not always work in practice.

As a former share dealer who has also worked in investment banking, a financial author, journalist and broadcaster, and trainer, there is little that I have not come across in the past 25 years. Feel free to contact me with comments and queries via my Web site, or care of my publisher, and I will respond.

As German author Johan Wolfgang von Goethe said, 'Whatever you can do or dream you can, begin it. Boldness has genius, power and magic in it.'

The stock market can bring you riches beyond your wildest dreams, but you have got to learn how to reach out for them. Investing in this book is your first step.

Alexander Davidson
www.flexinvest.co.uk

Part One

How to start speculating

Seminar 1

The truth about stock market speculation

INTRODUCTION

Stock market speculation is more exciting and more dangerous than investing, but can be a way to make your fortune much more quickly.

In this seminar, we will look at your preliminary considerations.

BASIC PRINCIPLES

The speculating game

Speculators on the stock market are trying to make money from high-risk situations that promise extra returns although, unlike gamblers, they ensure that the odds are first in their favour.

In the main, speculators are short-term players. Like traders, they are often buying or selling quickly, as in takeover situations and short selling. They also, however, speculate for the long term, for example on penny stocks or in emerging markets.

Investors take less risk than speculators. On a medium- to long-term basis, they diversify their portfolios and may use derivatives for risk reduction. They may be more prone to invest for value or growth than on technical specifics, and to know more about the underlying companies in which they invest.

There is some overlap. For example, investors who sell and repurchase shares frequently in their long-term portfolio can make a lot more money than their counterparts who simply buy and hold. But they must exploit large temporary price falls and cover significant dealing costs.

Does this make it speculating, rather than investing? Probably, although we are getting into the grey areas. In this book, I will show you how to chase the big money available to speculators on the broadest definition of the concept.

Image and reality

Stock market speculating has a glamorous image in the media. If you saw the film *Rogue Trader*, you will recall Nick Leeson's wild celebrations in Singapore bars after a day's trading. In another film, *Wall Street*, insider dealing is glamorized.

Forget such romantic rubbish. Making money on the stock market is in itself usually quite mundane.

A methodical, systematic approach to speculating, as we shall see, makes more money in the long run than the devil-may-care approach, although there are bullish runs when the reverse seems true.

A professional mindset

To succeed as a stock market speculator, you need a thorough understanding of the basics, as well as access to analysis and news. The market is a game and, if you are to compete in it successfully, you need to be well informed.

The theory is, of course, not enough. You will also have to make and implement snap decisions in the throes of a shifting market, which is by definition without boundaries. To achieve this, I recommend that you develop a professional mindset.

This is the commitment and the drive to implement the rules outlined in this book, which are as applied by professionals. It is, after all, these with whom you will be competing.

SPECULATE FROM FINANCIAL STRENGTH

Get your finances in order

Stock market speculation is risky, and, before you dip your toe in the water, you should have enough cash in place for your needs. The amount will depend on your circumstances, but I suggest that it includes at least £5,000 emergency money available in an instant access account.

Start up a pension and, if you have a family, life assurance. Pay pension contributions regularly, and check the performance of the funds. If a financial scandal hits your pension provider, be prepared to transfer.

Beyond this, you should own your own home and, over the years, have steadily increasing equity in it. You should also maintain some medium- to long-term investments, including shares and, with less risk, bonds.

Against this steady financial backdrop, you will be well placed to speculate, although, as we shall see later in this book, it must be only with money that you can afford to lose.

As a speculator, you will often, although not exclusively, be coming in and out of trading positions quickly, exploiting short-term price movements. Your trading capital must be enough to cover your losses.

Your entry and exit points

What are your buying and selling criteria? A number of successful profes- sional traders believe that market movements are completely unpredictable and that everything known or knowable is discounted in the share price. On this basis, security analysts' forecasts would be useless.

Other traders believe that forecasts have some value. In the short term, all are agreed that share prices rise on sentiment, and not simply because the stock is cheap on fundamentals.

The message is clear. As a speculator, you should not spend too much time on fundamental analysis to the exclusion of other factors. Technical analysis may serve you better, not least because so many traders use it that it can now dictate markets. On this basis, the charts can help you on *timing* of your trades. See Seminar 7 for the basics of technical analysis, and subsequently for more advanced coverage.

You should also watch directors' dealings. If a director buys shares in his or her own company for more than his or her annual salary, this can be a positive sign. Watch particularly in the two months before a given company releases its results, as this is the directors' last chance to buy or sell shares before they enter the close period when they are barred from dealing.

How can you keep abreast? Directors' dealings must be reported to the London Stock Exchange within five days. The Stock Exchange Weekly Intelligence publishes this information. Besides this, various news media, including newspapers, newsletters and financial Web sites such as Citywire (www.citywire.co.uk), will keep you informed.

For trading purposes, you also need to keep an eye on macroeconomic forecasts. If the reality turns out different, the stock market will overreact, in which case, before it corrects itself, you will have an excellent trading opportunity.

To take full advantage, you need a broad understanding of macroecon- omics. To achieve this, you do not need formal schooling, according to Victor Sperandeo, the great Wall Street trader. The basics are common sense.

Interest rates, for example, are a macroeconomic weapon. The Bank of England can raise them to combat inflation, but this is *detrimental* to the stock market, because the return on shares compared with bonds will fall, and companies will find borrowing more expensive. In addition, a company's future cash flows will be discounted at a higher rate, and so seem less favourable.

Conversely, a reduction in interest rates, like a decline in the value of a country's currency, is, in theory, good for the stock market. In practice, other factors can prevail. In mid-2002, interest rates were very low, and yet world stock markets remained at depressed levels and showed no serious sign of long-term recovery.

Macroeconomic analysis aside, your trading positions will be affected, probably every day, by unexpected variables. Events such as terrorist attacks or war can create extreme uncertainty, which the market punishes more than anything.

As you may already have surmised, stock market speculation requires more ongoing time and attention than long-term investing. Note too that trading is a *zero* sum game as, for every winner, there is a loser. You will be competing against professionals.

You must develop your own trading system, and the only way is through trial and error. I will show you the ropes in Seminar 3. In many traders' view, the most important part of this system is money management as this enables you to control how much of a security you buy or sell, and when, and when you reverse your position. We devote the whole of Seminar 4 to the art of money management.

Part- or full-time

I have known some traders achieve spectacular success on the stock market while holding down full-time jobs. This, however, is not usual, and in every case the individual trader has paid a price.

If you are in this position, you may need to trade in the middle of the day, and this may make or save you more than your year's salary. If this means that you will extend your lunch break, or leave a meeting early, or sneak out of the office to use your mobile, so be it. Most employers will not look kindly on this.

I know of some stock market speculators who use their work computers to access news, analysis, stock prices, charts, and statistics. This is easier if your job requires access to such information. Financial journalists and, even more so, City professionals are so privileged.

Cut your losses and run your profits

You cannot expect every trade to be successful. Speculators who hope for this typically make the mistake of holding onto a losing trade for too long.

If you get your trading right four times out of ten, but run your profits and cut your six losses quickly, you will make money. You can get rich by repeating this formula *ad infinitum*.

Q I have tried a number of stock market trading systems without success. Will the methods described in this book work?

A The answer is, yes. By this, I mean that they will work more often than not, which is enough to make you money. But you need to apply our techniques correctly, and modify them to suit your own circumstances.

This means that you must develop your own system, which will never be exactly the same as anybody else's, although the underlying principles will be unchanged.

Do not expect regular profits to come until you have mastered the basic trading techniques. If you are to make money from trading the stock market, you need to take it as seriously as your job, your life, and your partner or spouse, or anything else important to you.

Brokers are two a penny

As a stock market speculator, do yourself a favour and become self-reliant. I urge you to aim for this even when you are just starting out. When I speak at investment conferences, I am always struck by the shining faith that investors have in their broker. It is often misplaced.

Your broker may nonetheless help you a great deal, particularly when you are starting out. But do not rely on this. For every good broker, there are at least 20 incompetents, and a fair few rogues, and it can be difficult to tell which is which. For advice on selecting the best broker, see Seminar 2.

Derivatives provide opportunity

The trading is made more flexible nowadays as more financial instruments are at your disposal. These include contracts for difference, spread betting and futures, covered warrants and options.

Some speculators just stick to shares, but others use such derivatives as well. We will explore the range critically in Seminars 14–18. At this stage, suffice it to say that derivatives provide *geared* trading. This means that you will put up only a proportion of the money that you will trade. If the instrument proves volatile, you can make huge percentage gains or losses on this initial margin.

Using derivatives, you can also profit from a falling market by taking a short position. This is the equivalent to selling shares that you do not own with a view to buying them back at a lower price before settlement. The practice was common directly with shares some years ago when the settlement system was different. For details on how to take a short position, see Seminar 13.

BECOME A STREETWISE SPECULATOR

Opportunism

If you want to make money from speculating on the stock market, please grasp that the market is not always about honesty and reliability, although parties with a vested interest will have you believe otherwise. It is about opportunism.

The point was brought home to me as I was speaking in a panel debate on whom to trust in the City at a recent *Investors Chronicle* investment summit.

I found here that my audience was mostly sceptical about the City. This is as it should be. What disturbed me was that everybody wanted an ultimate litmus test to distinguish the *bona fide* from the dubious.

My fellow panellists attempted to enlighten our audience. One, an international expert in white-collar crime, went so far as to suggest that all salespeople were liars. Even if this were true, it is beside the point.

If you spend too long trying to detect who in the City is sincere or not, you are wasting your time. Even should you in this way be able to avoid the sharp operator, you might lose as much money from a sincere but stupid adviser. Let's face it, many private client stockbrokers are not exactly Einstein.

SHAKE OFF YOUR BAD OLD HABITS

Adjust to a brave new world

Although it is not always true in our society that the harder and longer we work, the more money we receive, there is a correlation.

In stock market speculation, there is none. It rewards only successful action. You could spend weeks trying hard, and lose money. Conversely, you could make your fortune within minutes.

Some traders simply cannot make good. If they lose, they become resentful. If they gain, they feel dreadfully guilty, and may find a way to give their profits back to the market.

The more that you have allowed yourself to be conditioned by society's rules, the harder it may be to trade successfully.

Forget school

Many successful stock market speculators feel that the problems start in our schools. They may have worked the examination system well and, which is rarer, appreciated education for its own sake. But, *much of this was no real use to them as a speculator.*

Our education system has inculcated in its most successful consumers a lack of self-reliance, a strong need for approval, and a tendency to follow the herd, despite lip service paid to independent thinking.

In this way, our schools are geared to turning out good employees in a society that operates along well-defined guidelines. It teaches that hard work gets results, and you should strive for perfection. Mistakes are discouraged, even ridiculed. Certain types of workplace continue to instill this set of values.

As a speculator, forget this brainwashing. You are not after top marks. If you aim for this, you will fail and could become badly discouraged. It is OK to make some mistakes, but you must aim to be right more often, or for longer, than you are wrong.

Despite my criticisms, school has its uses for the wannabe speculator. First, it can develop your analytical skills, your numeracy, and your speed of reaction, all of which will stand you in good stead.

Second, school can prepare you for higher education, which is now essential if you plan on becoming a stock market trader for an investment bank as a stepping stone to working for yourself. Third, it develops your personality, which helps to decide what kind of speculator you will become.

But if your teachers said you are worthless and will never amount to anything, this need not stop you from succeeding as a stock market speculator. If you get it right, you can earn more from trading stock positions in a few weeks, or days, than any teacher does in a year.

Your way forward

In this first seminar, I have given you an overview of our programme. This will enable you to set the rest in context.

You should note the key trading rules as they are presented. Your time is valuable, and so I have summarized these rules at the end of every seminar.

As you read these rules, you should wholeheartedly visualize yourself carrying them out in a trading situation. In this way, you will be instructing your subconscious, and will find yourself eventually implementing the rules.

THE NEXT STEP

In Seminar 2, we will be looking at how to select, and get the most out of, your stockbroker.

SEMINAR 1 GOLDEN RULES

▌ Trade only with money that you can afford to lose.

▌ As a speculator, you may find technical analysis more useful than the fundamental approach.

▌ If a director buys substantial shares in his or her own company, this can be a positive sign.

▌ If macroeconomic figures turn out not as expected, the stock market will overreact, providing a trading opportunity.

▌ You can speculate on the stock market while you work full-time, but it requires careful time organization.

▌ If you make more from your right trades than you lose on your wrong ones, you will succeed.

▌ Become self-reliant as a speculator and do not place undue faith in your broker.

▌ As a speculator, do not expect your profits to come instantly, or until you have mastered basic trading techniques.

▌ Derivatives enable you to trade more flexibly, and with less capital, as well as to take a short position.

▌ Do not waste your time trying to detect sharp practice but, instead, become an opportunist.

▌ Success at speculating on the stock market is not directly related to how long or how hard you work.

Seminar 2

How to find a suitable stockbroker

INTRODUCTION

In this seminar, we will look at the different types of stockbroker, and which is best for you. I will explain how you can use your broker to its best advantage.

TYPES OF STOCKBROKER

The basics

As a stock market speculator, you will normally be using an execution-only broker. This type of firm executes deals on your instructions, via the Internet or telephone, but will not give specific investment advice except, perhaps, on an add-on pay-as-you-go basis.

The alternative is an advisory broker, which will recommend stocks and help you to run your portfolio. Such a broker will cost you more in commissions than its execution-only counterpart, every time that you deal. If you use a good firm, it can save you from some very expensive mistakes, but otherwise it can be disastrous for you.

As a third alternative, a discretionary broker will make investment decisions on your behalf. This is an expensive option but it might appeal if you lack the time, interest or skill to run your own portfolio even with help. The problem here is that your broker may be irresponsible or incompetent and, if so, you can lose your money quickly, particularly in a bear market and if you are not watching over his or her shoulder.

In the next few pages, we will look at these three types of stockbroker in more detail, and how you should select the firm that is best for you. We will also look at how you can get the best out of your broker.

Execution-only brokers

Overview

Execution-only brokers rely on high volume as their charges, owing to competitive pressures, are low. Business has suffered severely in the three years following March 2000 after a bear market set in. The regulatory environment is increasingly demanding.

In the never-ending quest to cut commissions and so attract clients, some brokers have skimped too much on service. I know of brokers that run a skeleton ship. I pity clients that deal with these firms, hooked by the bait of low commissions. If something goes wrong, as invariably it will when dealing is particularly busy, the staff are too ignorant and too sparse to cope effectively.

As a protective measure, you should use one of the larger and more reputable online brokers, even if this means that you will pay slightly higher commissions than are available elsewhere. If your Internet broker offers a telephone dealing service as a backup, this may provide an opportunity to trade or to sort out queries should the Web site crash, which has been known to happen. As a further backup, I strongly advise you to have an account with two or three online brokers simultaneously.

This is for emergencies. Do not make a habit of alternating too much between brokers. Switching nominee accounts generates paperwork and costs money. Some brokers will charge you heftily for transfer and administration, although others are more lenient and some will offer these services for free.

If the worst happens and your broker goes out of business, perhaps after a few failed attempts at merging with a stronger player, your cash and shares should be safe. This is because they are required to be held separately from the firm's own assets.

To survive, even some of the larger players are merging. Charles Schwab, Europe, a giant in the field, has been absorbed by Barclays. On a smaller scale, Jarvis Investment Management has bought Sharenet, and this has expanded its client base by almost three times. Other brokers are closing down.

Select the right broker

Up to a point, you get what you pay for. The cheapest type of broker offers you an e-mail service to place orders. This often means very slow trading. The firm will not work immediately on your behalf. It may also wait to amass orders, executing them only at specified times during the day. Unless you are only an occasional speculator, this is dangerous as you need to time your details precisely.

The browser-based brokers mostly offer more timely trading, and will serve all but the most active speculators well. Through such a firm, you can execute a trade yourself, rather than ask the firm to do it for you. You will deal at a price shown on a screen that is linked directly to the London Stock Exchange.

The broker's charges can vary widely. When using a good firm, expect to pay, on current rates, perhaps £15 commission on every deal. Sometimes, a firm will offer a cheaper commission, but do not be tempted by this unless the service is up to scratch, and the firm has adequate financial backing.

Make sure that the charging structure suits your level of trading. If the firm has no minimum charge, you will pay lower commissions on small trades, but more on large ones. This is fine only if you are a frequent trader of small deals. If the broker has a substantial minimum charge, this should be cost-effective if you place large orders, but not for small ones.

Note that a commission rate quoted may apply only if you are a substantial trader. At the time of writing, Self Trade charges a £12.50 quarterly management fee, and Barclays Stockbrokers £9.00, in both cases unless you deal once a quarter. This is no problem for regular traders but it penalizes inactivity.

The more frequently that you trade, the more limitations you will find in browser-based brokers. When Internet traffic gets heavy, the firm's service may slow down. The problem can become acute when, for instance, you are buying volatile high-tech stocks during a bull market. In such cases, it has sometimes turned out that the price that you pay for your shares can be higher than as quoted on a real-time basis by your broker. This is because orders ahead of you in the queue are executed, so bumping up the share price.

If you are a prolific trader, be sure to use an active trader broker. This type of firm's charging structure benefits only those who trade a significant number of deals. The active trader broker provides software that you can load onto your computer, which enables you to execute your trades quickly, and with a minimum of inconvenience. The firm will not expend valuable time requiring electronic confirmation of your order, as some browser-based brokers do.

Whatever your level of trading, costs are only part of your broker's profile. Make sure that the firm will assist in any specialist areas that you require. You will want it to offer limit orders (see Seminar 4), and perhaps out of hours trading. If, for instance, you plan to speculate on continental or US stocks, check that your broker is prepared to deal in these efficiently and competitively.

Some brokers offer a paper trading facility or dummy run. This supposedly enables you to get a feel for trading without risking hard cash. In practice, it is a more benign experience, helpful perhaps, but no substitute for the real thing.

Most brokers offer information services. The timeliness of news and quality of analysis provided are improving, thanks to superior technology and intense competition, but they still vary. It is also worth remembering that you have access to many such services elsewhere on the Web. The range of products on offer is another variable factor.

Open your online account

To open your online account is simple. Download the relevant form from your broker's Web site, or request a form to be sent to you by e-mail. Print the form off, fill it in and sign it by hand, and send it by snail mail (ordinary post) to the broker, enclosing the deposit required to open your account. The firm will hold this cash, usually at least £1,000, in an interest-bearing account until you make your first trade.

When you deal with your broker online, you can nowadays rely on absolute confidentiality. Your broker will use encryption software to ensure that information swapped is scrambled, so making it unintelligible to interceptors. This should be 128-bit encryption, which at the time of writing is the strongest type.

In addition, your broker should hold insurance to protect client accounts. For access to your account details, you will need to use a password. For security purposes, make this a complicated nonsense word and keep it secret. When you are using it on your broker's Web site, make sure that you are not being watched. Once you have completed a transaction, print off evidence of it. Always log out correctly.

How to trade through your online broker

To trade, go to your broker's Web site, and find the spread for the stock that interests you. The spread represents the range between the offer price, which is that at which you can buy the stock, and the bid price, at which you can sell.

To find the spread, you may need to put in the EPIC code for the stock, although brokers increasingly have facilities for you to put in the name of the underlying company instead. The EPIC code is a three- or four-letter symbol, which you should be able to look up for a given stock on your broker's Web site.

You can deal in quoted shares in at least the normal market size (NMS). This represents the minimum number of shares for which a small market maker must quote firm bid and offer prices. As a broad generalization, the smaller the stock, the smaller is the NMS, and the wider the spread.

When you place your order, be careful. It is incredibly easy to make a mistake. If you add a '0' in the wrong place, you could, of course, commit yourself to buying or selling far more shares than you had intended.

Some brokers enable you to cancel a trade that you have made, albeit only within a very limited time period. This provides a lot of reassurance.

Help can come still earlier in the trading cycle. Some brokers offer you a facility to ensure that you do not spend more on shares than you can afford. If you are starting out as a trader, this may help you to become more self-disciplined.

Settlement

Online brokers prefer that you settle electronically through the CREST computerized system. This matches trades with payments and informs the company's registrars of changes to the share register.

You will normally complete such settlement within three days (T+3), compared with ten days if you were to settle with paper share certificates. The period is sometimes negotiable. You will hold your shares in a pooled nominee account run by your broker, but will retain beneficial ownership.

The disadvantage of electronic settlement in this way is that you will forfeit the right to receive an annual report and accounts and full shareholder perks, including voting at shareholder meetings. As a speculator, you need not be concerned, as you will not usually be holding the shares long enough for these factors to matter.

More important for you is the main advantage. Electronic settlement is effective from as soon as you buy stock, and you can trade without waiting to receive share certificates.

Alternatively, you may have a CREST-sponsored member account. On this basis, when you trade shares, it will be your details, and not your broker's, that are passed electronically with the transaction.

Advisory stockbrokers

Stockbrokers, particularly in the private client sector, are often not well informed. They may also be incompetent.

Robert Beckman, an investment guru who achieved prominence in the 1980s, has little time for your average advisory stockbroker. In his seminars, he used to tell investors that, if they wanted to achieve the success that he had from trading shares, they should heed his advice. If they instead aspired to the more modest lifestyle of their stockbroker, they should heed his exhortations to trade stock indiscriminately.

As a City professional, I prefer not to tar all advisory stockbrokers with the same brush. When you are starting out, an advisory broker can be of use to you. But make sure that you pick an honest, competent firm, with an individual broker who is attuned to your trading needs.

Any advisory broker that you use should have a nose for a good share. If the firm has its own quality research, so much the better. But never rely too much on the firm. I know of so many people who trusted their broker too much and lost their life savings.

Do not pay too much attention to the broker's qualifications. A starting broker needs to pass the Securities Institute Certificate examination, but this is a simple multiple-choice paper, which is instantly forgettable. Some brokers have the Securities Institute Diploma, which takes around two years of study, but its possession is no guarantee of practical ability.

Dubious brokers

Dubious advisory brokers will stuff you into high-risk stocks that may not suit your needs. Incompetent ones might sell less hard, but can lose you as much.

Dubious brokers will present their buying case selectively. If a stock has performed poorly, they will represent it as undervalued. If it has outperformed in recent months, they will stress its relative strength.

If you try to sell your shares, this type of broker will be happy only if you reinvest the proceeds with them. This way, they will make two sets of commissions and will keep your money under their control.

Such a broker may start the ball rolling by attempting to churn your portfolio. This is when they take you out of one stock and into another with the sole aim of generating commission for themselves.

Such churning is barred under the Financial Services Act, but can be hard to prove. If brokers manipulate you into suggesting the stock switch yourself, after some subtle prompting, this will protect them against allegations of churning. Some firms tape all calls and, in the event of dispute, your words will be played back as evidence of your having initiated the deal. The dubious firms specialize in such disguised churning.

The worst offenders are sometimes the half-commission men, so-called because they split commissions earned on stock deals, perhaps on a 50:50 basis, with their firm through which they put business. If they don't sell shares, they don't eat, and desperation can lead to poor recommendations, sales pressure and general corruption. I know of City firms where this happens every day. Read also about dubious penny share promoters in Seminar 13.

If you are unfortunate enough to get entangled with the wrong firm, do not necessary expect help from the regulators. For legal reasons, they will be unable to discuss how the firm operates, even if they understand it. If they try to rescind or refuse authorization, the firm may appeal. The process is drawn-out, and in the meantime, the firm will carry on dealing.

For a list of advisory brokers that welcome smaller clients, visit the Web site of The Association of Private Client Investment Managers and Stockbrokers at www.apcims.org. Once you have chosen and started using a broker, do not make the mistake of remaining loyal if the service is not up to scratch.

Scamsters

One step beyond dubious stockbrokers are the scamsters. These outfits are typically unregulated, and may operate from secret locations abroad, using an accommodation address as a front. They will sell shares either in small unquoted companies that do not exist except on paper, or, apparently, in well-known, quoted companies. Either way, if you send in your money, they will simply steal it.

A favourite trick is to represent an unknown company as backed by a well-known large multinational company, but to claim that this deal is not yet widely known. Many investors, including corporate funds and high net worth individuals, will be too lazy or too trusting to check out this lie before they commit their money.

The US Securities & Exchange Commission has highlighted the risks. Visit the Web site at www.mcwhortle.com, which you will find represents McWhortle as an 'established and well-known manufacturer of biological defense mechanisms'.

Visitors to the Web site are encouraged to apply for the company's shares under an ostensible initial public offering. They are led through the proposed deal to a SEC message that reads: 'If you responded to an investment like this. . . You could get scammed.'

As this mock promotion illustrates, the Internet is a powerful outlet for the crooks. It is not, however, the only one. Salespeople still cold-call UK investors in their offices and homes and persuade them to part with thousands, sometimes tens of thousands of pounds on the basis of a five-minute telephone conversation. For City veterans, this is reminiscent of the share-pushing scandals of the 1980s.

Typically, the promoters buy huge quantities of stock cheap, then create demand by hard-selling the stock. When the share price is at its highest, they sell out their own holdings. The share price will crash, and sellers will flock, but too late to sell large quantities of shares at a decent price. The more desperate the sellers become, the faster the price plummets. This is the classic *pump-and-dump*.

Let me give you a golden rule. Should you take nothing else from this book, take this. If somebody from an unknown firm calls and tries to sell you shares, put down the phone. It is not always easy to make, say, £50,000. It is very easy to lose it.

Finally, if you lose money through dealing with a scamster, avoid throwing good money after bad in becoming a client of an equally dubious self-styled fund collection agency.

Such operations contact victims of share frauds and offer to help them recover funds in return for an upfront fee. If you pay any money over, you will simply be throwing it away as you will not receive any help. As a final sting in the tail, it often transpires that the collection agency is run by the perpetrators of the fraud.

Discretionary brokers

Discretionary stockbrokers choose which shares to buy and sell on your behalf. To use their services, you may need a portfolio of at least £100,000, although there are increasingly services to cater for smaller portfolios.

So many such brokers have made a complete mess of private client portfolios that I urge you to be really careful. A firm may be large and prestigious, but this need not stop it from losing 60 per cent or more of your money, perhaps within months. I have known these firms offload highly speculative stocks on discretionary clients only because the corporate finance department wants to get rid of them, perhaps to protect its own position.

If you want to hear a typical horror story, visit the Web site at www.my killikaccount.co.uk, where investors explain how they have lost large sums of money investing with a London stockbroker. I have contributed advice to the site.

In view of these caveats, if you plan to use a discretionary broker, make sure that the individual in charge of your portfolio is a high calibre person, not restricted too much by your firm, who understands your needs. Check his or her track record. All this is notoriously hard to assess, and, of course, what works for one investor may not for another.

Once you have appointed your firm, please follow these simple rules. Watch what your broker is doing with your money. Discuss your portfolio with him or her, and query transactions as you see fit.

Ask for monthly – rather than quarterly or half-yearly – statements. This not only enables you to keep better track of your money, but will impress on your broker that you are watching him or her closely.

Make sure that your broker has an effective strategy for selling loss-making stocks. Check that he or she is applying some kind of stop loss, by which he or she sells shares if they fall below a certain percentage level.

In declining markets, do not hesitate to intervene and insist that your brokers sell your shares. There is no harm in holding cash for a short period, and it can save you a fortune on declining shares in which you would otherwise have been invested.

HOW TO MAKE A COMPLAINT

Your strategy

If you have a complaint about your stockbroker, first make it to the firm, preferably in writing. If you discuss the matter on the telephone, keep a written note of what is said, when, and with whom.

If the firm fails to resolve the issue satisfactorily, take your complaint to the Financial Ombudsman. This is an independent organization that has statutory powers to address and settle individual disputes between consumers and financial firms. The service is financed by a levy on financial institutions.

You can telephone and ask for a complaint form, or download it from the Web site (www.financial-ombudsman.org.uk). Fill in and sign this, and then return it in the post. The Ombudsman can award you up to £100,000 in compensation. His decision is binding on the firms, but not on you. If you wish, you may take the matter to court.

In addition, you can always complain to the press about a firm, which, by arrangement with the journalist, could be on an anonymous basis. Go to national newspapers, where exposure will hit the firm hardest. Ideally choose the Sunday papers where the journalists have more time to dig around. Avoid the tabloids, as they will often distort the information that you give them.

If your stockbroker defaults, you will have access to the industry's compensation scheme. The first £30,000 of any proven claim will be met in full, and 90 per cent of the next £20,000 will be met – with £48,000 being the maximum compensation paid to any single claimant.

THE NEXT STEP

In the next seminar, we will focus on how to get started as a trader. Once you have grasped these basics, you will be well placed to use the more advanced techniques described later.

SEMINAR 2 GOLDEN RULES

▊ Avoid online stockbrokers that accept orders through an e-mail facility, as the service tends to be too slow.

▊ If you trade to a limited extent, use a browser-based online broker.

▊ If you are a substantial trader, use an active-trader online broker.

▊ Use a nominee account to hold your shares. Avoid paper share certificates as the transfer process can slow your trading.

▊ Be wary of dishonest or incompetent advisory stockbrokers. Ultimately, take responsibility for making your own investment decisions.

▊ Never buy from an unknown share salesman that operates from a firm of which you have never heard. Simply put down the telephone receiver.

▊ If you use a discretionary broker, watch your portfolio carefully and insist on monthly statements.

▊ Use the formal complaints procedures outlined in this chapter. In addition, you can take your complaint to the national press.

Seminar 3

How to get started as a trader

INTRODUCTION

Trading shares is a major part of speculating. In this seminar, we will look at how to get started, and the practicalities of developing your own trading system.

THE TRADING MENTALITY

The basics

Trading shares is the world's most exciting business that you can start from home. It is also one of the riskiest. You can make or lose thousands of pounds within minutes. The more volatile the market, the bigger the rewards, and risks. If you trade derivatives, the stakes are still higher.

As a securities trader, you are a speculator, which means that you will risk your capital when the odds are in your favour. The losers in this game are often gamblers who take a risk when the odds are *against* them, betting on hope.

What motivates the gambler? Freudian theory suggests that he is a victim of oedipal conflicts. The gambler feels guilty for demanding his mother's full attention, and so seeks as a penance to pay dues to a symbolic father.

The truth may be more mundane as most amateur traders have a gambling streak in them. They trade for the thrill of it, just as they play the National Lottery.

Such an approach must eventually fail. Trading is a business, and anybody who is serious always treats it as such, even when doing it part-time.

Made not born

Have you got what it takes to join them? Stuart Watson, who runs Reindeer Capital, a successful US-based trading operation, takes the view that anybody can trade shares, and you do not have to be born to it.

Richard Dennis, a legendary US trader, has proved the point. He set up a school for wannabe traders without experience, and turned many of these into outstanding professionals. As a result, Dennis won a bet with his partner who had not believed that it was possible.

Dennis had been selective when it came to recruiting from the many applicants to his program. The chosen few had in common a suitable attitude to risk.

Successful traders are risk takers. This is partly in their nature. It is because they are more motivated by the prospect of winning than the fear of losing. Money is the measure of their success, but not an end in itself. Traders who think only about money find that fear and greed adversely affect their professional judgement.

As a trader, you will make some mistakes. Most successful traders have at some point let their own rules slip and lost all their committed capital. Your losses are the price that you must pay for ultimate success, but you should still keep them as low as possible.

If you have the right personality and attitude, lack of age and experience will never hold you back. But you can improve with time. Renowned short seller Simon Cawkwell says of equity trading that it is as much fun as sex and football, but it is less short lived. After the age of 40, you will not be a great footballer. After 50, sex will take a back seat. But share trading can improve with experience, even into ripe old age.

Older traders, however, need to be cautious. They will perhaps have capital to play with, but there will be less time in which to retrieve losses.

Your timescale

Share trading breaks down into three broad categories: day, swing and position trading. Depending on your own mental framework, you can operate in any one or more of these categories.

▌ As a day trader, you close out your position every day. You will avoid the risk of holding shares overnight, but will also limit time for retrieving a position that has gone wrong.

▌ As a swing trader, you hold shares for between two and five days, which gives you more, sometimes too much, flexibility.

▌ As a position trader, you will hold shares for between one and two months, which makes it less imperative to watch the market minute by minute.

Even on the longest of these frameworks, you will not as a trader be able to rely on buying cheap on fundamentals and selling dear. Instead, you will be trading on the basis of how other traders and investors are reacting to a stock, regardless of whether this reflects intrinsic value.

Economist John Maynard Keynes compared the position of stock market traders to that of readers who try to pick the 5 prettiest girls out of 100 in a beauty contest held in their newspaper. The prize comes if you pick the contestants who receive the most votes from readers.

This way, readers would be required to pick the contestants that they think are most likely to be picked by other readers, and not give too much weight to their own taste. As Keynes puts it, the requirement is to anticipate 'what average opinion expects the average opinion to be'.

GET READY TO TRADE

Setting up

If you are *serious* about trading, you will require a dedicated office, with computer terminals and telephone to hand. The cheapest and most convenient way is from home.

Trading from home can be extremely lonely. The risk is that you will be tempted to discuss your position with your family. Avoid this as it creates too much pressure on you to succeed and, when trouble hits, you may be tempted to blame your loved ones.

There are solutions. You can liaise with trading buddies on the Internet. A good Web site that enables this through its message boards is at www. trade2win.co.uk.

If you need live company, you could work from a day trading centre. The technology here should be good, as should the support. But it works out expensive.

Become cost conscious

You will need some capital to start trading, but not necessarily much. Successful traders have often started small, honing their techniques through trial and error. Wealthy novice traders are often less careful and, as a result, achieve less.

Before you break into profit, you will need to cover dealing expenses involved, including the spread. Another expense is stamp duty, which is a 0.5 per cent tax that the government levies every time that you buy shares, although not when you sell them.

You will also pay a stockbroker's commission on the purchase or sale of stocks. The lower this is, the better, provided that the standard of service does not lapse. If you are a prolific trader, there are often discounted rates available. See Seminar 2 for details on selecting your broker.

Achieve balance

To trade successfully requires concentration and, once this starts waning, it is time to stop. Make time outside trading, however limited it is, for your family and friends. If you miss out on this and feel guilty, it may adversely affect your trading.

YOUR TRADING SYSTEM

Develop a system

To trade successfully, you will need a system. This is the rock on which you will build your future profits. It will be based on rules that all successful traders follow but will have its own secret sauce.

Your system should adjust to market conditions and cover every eventuality. It will reflect, for example, that in bull markets, you can trade less cautiously than in bear markets.

The most important part of your system will be money management. We will cover this skill in Seminar 4.

If your first attempts at creating a system fail, this is normal and you should not panic. Work at refining your system or creating another one. Be patient and remember that no method works all of the time.

Once your system is proven, stick with it. Do not be tempted to deviate in the throes of an unpredictable trading situation.

TRADING TIP

Be ready before the market opens. Read the morning's news. Check yesterday's major risers and fallers as this may give you clues for profitable trading today.

Mood control

Never trade for the sake of it. Traders typically do 10–15 per cent of their trades because they are bored. If you can't summarize why you should own a stock in four sentences, you probably should not own it, according to ex-fund manager Peter Lynch.

If you are having a bad trading run, take a break. Do the same after you have achieved success. In both cases, make sure that you have first closed out your positions.

I know of traders who have travelled abroad without doing this, and suddenly their mobile phone doesn't work, or their plane is delayed. This can cost them tens of thousands of pounds, if their trading position hits trouble.

Keep records

Keep meticulous records of your trades and use them to assess your successes and mistakes. Tweak your system accordingly.

Set goals

As part of your system, set trading goals. You may wish to change these as time goes on. Have broad goals for the next three to five years, broken down into each individual year, each month and each day respectively.

When you have achieved some significant goals, reward yourself. If you fail, remember that this is part of the learning process, but you must take responsibility and learn from your mistakes.

TRADING TIP

Keep a trading diary. This, coupled with your records, will provide a valuable log of your complete trading experience.

Keep this diary private, not least because if it falls into the wrong hands, it may horrify the readers.

Trade selectively

Once you are using a system, you will be trading stocks selectively according to its criteria. You will need to make judgements, which requires you to select the significant from a mass of information available.

As you assess this, do not assume that the most recent statistics and news items are the most important. This is not always the case.

Investor diversification

Stockbrokers typically advise investors to hold a diversified portfolio. They should hold shares in a mix of sizes and across sectors and in more than one geographical region, as well as in some other financial instruments.

The typical case would be that you should always have oils, pharmaceuticals and financials in your portfolio. Beyond this, your portfolio makeup and emphasis would vary with market conditions.

For instance, when the economy takes a downturn, you should increase the proportion of defensive stocks in your portfolio, including such areas as electricity, food and pharmaceuticals.

In the middle of a recession, just before the economy changes, is a good time to buy cyclical stocks in sectors such as transport, metals, chemicals, homebuilding, textiles, consumer hard goods and natural resources. You should not try to catch the tops and bottoms but simply hitch a ride. The cyclicals will lead market recovery as their depressed earnings return, but only for 12–18 months.

Convertible bonds offer a good yield that will help to keep their price stable. When the share price rises, the price of the convertible may rise too. You can convert the bond into stock. Convertible interest is payable before issuing dividends and, in the event of bankruptcy, convertibles have a superior claim to stock.

Unfortunately, the more diversified your portfolio, the more mediocre the performance as the winners will be dragged down by any also-rans and losers. Warren Buffett, the world's most successful investor, calls it a 'protection against ignorance'.

As a trader, do not make diversification your priority. Instead, focus on finding stocks that will make you money, regardless of size or sector. If you possess only a small number of stocks, perhaps five, you will be able to watch them more closely than if your portfolio is widely diversified. If you apply a stop loss, you will be able to sell out of any loser with minimum damage.

Games market makers play

Market makers as wholesalers of shares make their money from the spread between the bid and offer price of a stock, and not from share price movements. As a rule, they will have minimized their own position, and have covered any short position by buying stock from a rival firm or borrowing it.

They have responsibility to brokers, who are the retailers, as well as to the companies in whose shares they make a market, which are their clients, and to shareholders.

Throughout the day, market makers are obliged to trade shares in which they have a market at a quoted price in the normal market size. This in itself encourages liquidity, which the market makers can reduce by selling shares in bulk to large investors, or asking their client companies to reduce the flow of press releases.

The prices showing on screen are the best offered by any market makers at the time, which is why they change so often. The market makers do change their own spreads, but less often.

When you are watching how trading influences the best price, bear in mind that there can be delays in posting trades. In addition, some trades are not reported, particularly if small or arranged via a matched bargain or similar. Very large trades may be reported late.

Learn to recognize market makers' tricks and this will alert you to loss-making situations that you can take steps to avoid. The following two are particularly common:

Shaking the tree

In a rising stock market, market makers need to find sellers, so they *shake the tree*. They mark the share price down sharply, causing some shareholders to sell out in panic. The market makers then raise the price again, and recent sellers promptly repurchase the stock because they are emotionally attached to it.

Dead cat bounce

The *dead cat bounce* is when market makers move the share price down, and then sharply – but temporarily – up.

News flow

Track financial news on Web sites such as Bloomberg (www.bloomberg. co.uk) and Ample (www.ample.co.uk). Some sites will e-mail you news.

Do not expose yourself to an excess of information. As speculator Victor Niederhoffer suggests, checkers and chess are more useful to you as a trader than browsing the Internet.

Do not be influenced unduly by bulletin boards on financial Web sites as parties posting messages often have ulterior motives.

Learn before you earn

Winning traders learn more about their business at every opportunity.

This book will take you some way towards mastering the theory of stock market speculation. Also visit Flexible Investment Strategies at www.flex invest.co.uk. This is my own Web site, and you will find here some educational material that serves as a supplement to this book. Other interesting Web sites include Career Daytrader.com (www.careerday trader.com) and DayTraders.com (www.daytraders.com).

If you find that your emotions prevent you from trading dispassionately, consider undertaking neuro-linguistic programming. This shows you how to visualize your way to success and has worked well for some traders.

Reading and training will, of course, never be a substitute for actual trading experience. Do not become the John Doe who soaks up every book and training course like blotting paper, but never puts the theory into practice.

As trader Jesse Livermore often told his sons, the only way to get a real education in the market is to invest cash, track your trades, and study your mistakes.

THE NEXT STEP

In the next seminar, we will look at money management, which is arguably your most important skill as a trader.

SEMINAR 3 GOLDEN RULES

▌ Always treat trading as a business. Your losses are the price of success, but keep them as small as possible.

▌ Money is the measure of your trading success, but should not be an end in itself.

▌ Trade from a dedicated office, and stop working once your concentration has started to wander.

▌ Make time outside trading for your family and friends, and keep a sense of balance.

▌ Develop and refine your own trading system.

▌ Do not trade for the sake of it, but always have a reason.

▌ If you have had a bad (or a good) training run, take a break.

▌ Set trading goals for the short, medium and long term.

▌ Keep trading records, and a diary.

▌ Do not focus too much on diversifying your shares. Instead, pick likely winners.

▌ Avoid reacting to market makers' temporary movements of the share price to encourage buyers or sellers.

▌ Do not burden yourself with an information overload, and remember that messages on the bulletin boards of financial Web sites are often biased.

▌ Read about trading and do courses, but these are no substitute for practical experience.

Seminar 4

The art of money management

INTRODUCTION

In this seminar, we will look at money management. This is the nub of your trading system, and is one of the most important skills that you will learn from this book.

THE BASICS

Money management is about how much of your capital you should speculate on a given trade, and when.

When US trader Larry Williams in 1987 turned US$10,000 into US$1.1 million within 12 months, he attributed his success to money management. Williams bought more contracts when he had plenty of cash and less when he did not.

Rules

This leads us to the first rule of money management, which takes place even before you start trading. You must decide how much capital you will commit to trading, subdividing into each individual trade.

If you are on the cautious side, you could start with 10 per cent of your savings as trading capital. This should amount to at least £10,000, and preferably more. Make preserving this sum your priority.

When you make an individual trade, use only a percentage of this capital. If your trading capital is small, say £10,000–£20,000, you will need to commit as much as 5–10 per cent of this to every trade to make the dealing size meaningful. In practice, serious traders often have a much larger capital base of £100,000 plus, and commit only 1–2 per cent of this to every individual trade. Some have £500,000 plus in trading capital, and commit only 0.25 per cent of this to a trade.

Do not make the mistake of risking too much of your capital on a single trade. I have known traders risk 25 per cent of it at a time, and when they have taken a few big hits in succession, they are wiped out.

Never trade a large sum with the aim of achieving the optimal return that is defined by a theoretical model. The losses en route may be more than you can stand.

Trade positions where the potential rewards are high in relation to the risks. This can be hard to assess but, as a rule of thumb, the potential profit of a given situation should be 3× the potential loss. Some traders include a probability factor in the calculation.

Margin

Margin is the cash that you deposit with your broker as a proportion of the full sum that you are trading. In the UK, this is most relevant on derivatives, as on shares you will normally have to put up the full amount that you trade rather than margin.

I know of two UK brokers, however, that will trade shares on margin, like some of their US counterparts, and this is likely to become the way of the future.

If you are trading on margin, gains or losses on your margin will be geared, as they are directly proportionate to your full position. The margin set is typically 10–25 per cent of the whole, and will vary according to your broker's requirements, which are often set at least partly according to your own trading experience.

How much margin you put up has little to do with money management. If, for instance, the margin requirement on a stock position was halved, this should not trigger you to double your holding.

If your position moves against you, your broker will require you to add to your margin. If you want to be cautious, close out a declining position *before* the need for such a margin top-up arises.

Large and small companies

As a novice stock market speculator, you should favour larger companies, as their stocks are more liquid and may be traded at a narrow spread. In recent years, such stocks have become volatile, which has created huge profit opportunities for traders.

The shares of small companies are comparatively illiquid and, if you buy and the price plunges against you, you may find yourself as good as locked in. This is because you can often sell or buy these shares only in small quantities. If trading demand becomes significant, the market maker may shift the price sharply.

Terrible? Not really. It's all part of the game. Small companies can be fantastic for speculators if you get it right. This is because the share price can jump 30 per cent, 50 per cent or more within weeks, days or hours, entirely on sentiment. But wait until you are experienced before you trade such stocks.

Think like a speculator

If you buy shares directly, even for a short period, you will technically have a stake in the underlying company. As a speculator, do not make the mistake of becoming emotionally attached to any stock. It should mean nothing to you except as an instrument for trading.

Forget dividends unless these are part of a deliberate speculating strategy (see below). Growth companies often do not pay these as they put their earnings into developing the business rather than compensating shareholders. Instead, concentrate on stocks that are likely to show a capital gain quickly.

DIVIDEND SPECULATING STRATEGIES

If dividends are intrinsic to your speculating strategy, then you must of course pay attention to them. Although their main importance is to medium- to long-term investors, you can exploit them as a speculator.

Benjamin Graham, the father of value investing, said that dividends are responsible for nearly all gains realized by investors. This is because shareholders can make their gains only through dividends, or through capital gain, which has normally depended on the dividend rate.

It is precisely because dividends matter so much to investors that they also provide opportunities to speculators. In the present era, dividend yields (dividend divided by share price) are considerably down on earlier levels, which is partly why the focus of valuation has moved to earnings, a less reliable means of assessing value.

The O'Higgins method

A way of buying high-dividend shares that can bring you rewards as a speculator is through buying out-of-favour blue chips. As the share price for these companies will be deflated, the dividend yield may be large. If you buy such shares and hold for a while, precedent suggests that you will on balance outperform the market.

I have outlined the strategy, and precedent, exhaustively in my earlier book *How to Win in a Volatile Stock Market*, to which I would refer you if you want to pursue this strategy in detail.

At this point, I will explain the theory only briefly. Michael O'Higgins, a fund manager in Albany, New York, first popularized the technique of investing in high-dividend blue chip companies in his book *Beating the Dow*.

To implement the O'Higgins method in the UK, you will apply mechanical rules. You will invest in the 10 highest-yielding stocks in a major index (O'Higgins used the Dow Jones Industrial Average in the USA) or, as a further refinement, the five of these that have the lowest closing share price. The second-lowest priced of the 10 highest yielders is a likely good investment in itself. Change stocks annually and reinvest all dividends. The overall return beat the Dow Jones for 15 out of a sample 19 years.

Other US researchers have found that blue chips with high yields are out-performers. These include James O'Shaughnessy and David Dreman. In the UK, on various tests conducted by the *Financial Times*, *Investors Chronicle* and private client investment guru Jim Slater in conjunction with fund manager Charles Fry, the O'Higgins method, or a variation on the theme, when applied to the UK, has been found to produce a market-beating performance.

When the stock market plunged from March 2000, the strategy, like so many others, stopped working on either side of the Atlantic. Blue chip stocks have proved not so resilient in a bear market as the size and strength of the underlying company would suggest.

Having said that, if you buy blue chips with high dividends, you can still make good returns that beat the market, although this is for the medium to long term. Select carefully and avoid the complete dogs. Apply a stop loss. This way you are getting away from the full mechanical nature of the system and the convenience of this, but it cannot be helped.

Take the dividend and run

Let me also mention the *take the dividend and run* strategy that some traders are following now with significant success.

To implement this strategy, look for companies about to release end of year results that will pay out a dividend of more than 5 per cent gross. There are a fair number of cases. You will trade the stock and receive the dividend without ever paying for your shares.

First, negotiate a 20-day trading period with your stockbroker. This is known as T+20 and is easier if you already have a reliable trading track record.

Look for companies that are about to announce a final dividend and when it will be paid, as well as the ex-dividend (xd) date. Buy your shares at latest on the announcement as the company's share price should then rise. The rise will probably cover your broker's fees and stamp duty on the shares that you bought.

The shares are likely to continue to rise on the strength of the large pending dividend, although less so as the xd date approaches. Because you bought the shares, you will be registered as a shareholder on the ex-dividend date, which means that you will receive the dividend.

Once the share price gain and the dividend have together surpassed the costs, creating a profit, it is your cue to sell. This may be on, or shortly before, the xd date.

In some cases, it is worth while paying for the shares in full so that you can hold them for a short period beyond the T+20 period.

You can have several of these positions at once.

Market and limit orders

When you buy shares, you can place a market order, which means that you will buy at the market price. Problem is, the share price can change rapidly, and you may find yourself paying too much.

Instead, control what you pay by setting a limit order, as professional traders do. This means that if the order is not fulfilled at the price that you have specified, it is cancelled. As I suggested in Seminar 2, you require a broker that offers this facility.

Among such firms, you want one that will accept your limit order and will cancel only if it is not fulfilled on the day. This is more flexible than the fill-or-kill strategy of some brokers, under which they will either execute your limit order immediately, at the price specified, or will cancel it.

If you have access to Level 11 data, you will be able to see orders ahead of yours in the queue with market makers, and so assess their impact on the share price before your deal is executed. Using this expensive service makes placing a limit order less imperative, but I would still advise it. Be warned, too, that some orders in the queue are placed to mislead, and are withdrawn before they actually take place.

Variations on the limit order

Let us now look at some variations on the simple limit order. It may be difficult to find a broker to implement these, but it can be worth it.

Stop limit order

The stop limit order combines a limit order on a purchase with a stop loss on a sale. The stop loss is the percentage level of decline in the share price at which you will automatically sell out. It is an important safety net that we shall be discussing further in this seminar.

If the share price declines by the stop loss percentage, your broker will automatically sell your shares. A limit order for the repurchase of the shares then becomes active. This will be at a lower price level than at which you had sold.

Market-if-touched order

The market-if-touched order is similar to a limit order but less demanding. It triggers a market order, only if the price limit is touched, even if this will not have been sustained by the time that you place the order.

Time stop

The time stop requires you to sell a stock if it fails to reach a price target by the date that you have specified.

Selling shares

When you sell shares, you could also place a limit order, so specifying the lowest price that you will accept for your shares.

I advise against this, particularly in a fast-moving market. I have known traders place one sell limit order after another, and none goes through because the share price keeps spiralling downwards.

Instead, place a market order to sell. This means that your share sale will be carried out faster, even if the market price is lower than you would like. You can use the proceeds for a more profitable trade.

Profit and loss control

As part of disciplined money management, you should cut your losses and run your profits.

On this basis, traders can make money even when most of the stocks in which they trade turn out to have been a wrong choice. On Pareto's principle, 80 per cent of their profits will have derived from 20 per cent of their trading.

Cut your losses

On balance, it is best to cut losses. This is because a losing share is likely to trend downwards. As speculator George Soros put it, it does not matter how often you are right when you trade, but only how much you lose when you are wrong.

Stop loss

Unless you have extraordinary self-discipline as a trader, you will find that the easiest way to cut your losses is by using a stop loss. As UK trader Mike Boydell suggested, not using a stop loss is like running across the M25 with your head in a bucket.

Put your stop loss in place *before* you enter your trade. If the stock declines below your cut-off point, sell automatically. Taking a small loss this way is not too painful provided that you do not reflect on the price level at which you bought the stock or to which it had risen since.

Also, trade on a normal three-day settlement basis. If you negotiated an extended settlement period, this will encourage you to stay in losing trades.

If you hold the stock without implementing a stop loss, and the value falls considerably further, as is likely, the pain can be severe. As US trading guru Victor Sperandeo puts it, if an alligator has your leg, sacrifice this, as, if you struggle, it will get more of your body.

Once you have decided to implement a stop loss, you need to decide what kind. If you use a *standard* stop loss, this is set at a percentage below the price that you paid for the stock. I recommend that you instead use a trailing stop loss, which is established against the previous day's closing price.

In setting the percentage for your stop loss, consider what US trader Marty Schwartz calls your uncle point. This is the point as in the children's game when you shout the word *uncle*, indicating that you give up.

I suggest that you set your stop loss percentage at 15 or 20 per cent. If it is less, it will require you to sell out on temporary dips. If you are trading shares in small companies, these tend to be volatile, and I favour a 30 or 40 per cent stop loss.

Some traders set two trailing stop losses. If the stock hits the lower stop, this serves as a warning. At this point, you may choose to sell half your shares. At the higher stop, it will require you to liquidate your holding.

Alternatively, set two stop losses to fit a short- and longer-term position that you are taking simultaneously on the same stock.

If you are finding that you are always using your stop losses, switch to buying Put options (see Seminar 17). I know of traders who have made this switch very profitably.

Pullbacks

Technical analysts have an alternative to the stop loss. They sell shares on the first technical pullback from a new low on the chart. This is when the share price rises again from the lowest-ever level.

The system has its drawbacks. You must watch the charts constantly. Even then, it is hard to detect the first pullback and, as always, to have the self-discipline to sell.

Run your profits

You should run your profits and so benefit from occasions when the share price soars beyond expectations. This makes up for previous losses.

Unfortunately, most traders cannot easily run profits. They have a set idea of what constitutes a normal profit and feel uncomfortable if their position overreaches this. You need to think flexibly.

Scalping

For those who hate running their profits too far, the technique of scalping often appeals and it can work well.

As a scalper, you will aim to snatch plenty of small profits rather than to ride a few large ones. You may be in and out of the same stock several times a day.

It is hard work, as you will need to do a lot of trades. You will be trading in small sums, which limits the size of your gains, but also of your losses.

Pyramiding

If you pyramid, you will keep buying more of a stock as it rises in value, although never as much as you did first time.

You will end up with a position that you have acquired at various stages and different prices. This is a risky strategy, but it can be immensely profitable in a bull market.

THE NEXT STEP

In Seminars 5 and 6, we start looking at how to profit from interpreting the company report and accounts. This is an essential skill if you are to win over the long term as a stock market speculator.

SEMINAR 4 GOLDEN RULES

▌ Use only a small part of your trading capital on every trade.

▌ Take positions where the potential rewards are high in relation to the risks.

▌ If you are trading cautiously, close out a declining position before you need a margin top-up.

▌ Favour stocks in large companies as these have narrow spreads and so are more liquid.

▌ Trade stocks in small companies, taking advantage of their volatility. But understand that wide spreads and lack of liquidity are part of the game.

▌ Do not seek shareholder perks as they are insignificant when you are trading for the short term.

▌ If you are speculating, dividends are insignificant. The exception is when they are part of your strategy. You may, for instance, be buying high-dividend, out-of-favour blue chip stocks, or trading shares short term shortly before the underlying company pays out its final dividend.

▌ Buy on a limit order, and sell on a market order.

▌ Set a stop loss and apply it rigidly, as this is the easiest way to cut your losses.

▌ Run your profits and so benefit from occasions when the share price soars beyond expectations.

▌ Scalping is a proven strategy if you do not want to run profits too far.

▌ In a bull market, pyramid your gains to increase your profits.

Part Two

Become your own analyst

Seminar 5

How to profit from the accounts – part 1

INTRODUCTION

Until you are able to interpret a company's accounts, you cannot always appreciate the significance of news items, company announcements, and analysts' valuations and forecasts.

In this seminar, we will examine how to read the first part of the company report and accounts, including the balance sheet and the profit and loss account. We will leave other parts, including the cash flow statement, until Seminar 6.

THE BASICS

The origins

The accounts are based on double-entry bookkeeping, which was first used in Italy at the end of the 15th century. Under this system, any amount entered on the right side of one account, known as a credit, must be balanced by the same amount entered on the left side of another account, known as a debit.

On this principle, the balance sheet has assets, or debit balances equal to liabilities, or credit balances. This is one of the key financial statements in the accounts.

A UK quoted company will issue accounts twice a year. It publishes an interim statement after the first six months, which is not necessarily a *pro rata* indication of the full year profits. Shortly after the full year, it will publish full year figures, known as preliminaries.

Next comes the full audited annual report and accounts, which provides a statement of the company's profits, its cash flow, and its financial position.

Principles

A company prepares its accounts according to principles.

The principle of *prudence* requires the company to report its numbers conservatively, taking likely losses but not likely gains into the profit and loss account, and writing off potential bad debts immediately. Stock should be valued at the lower of cost or market value.

The *accruals* principle requires revenue – even if it has not been paid yet – and costs to be matched on the profit and loss account at the time of the transaction. This sometimes conflicts with the prudence principle.

Under the principle of *consistency,* a company should account for items in a consistent way from one year to the next.

Under *substance over form,* the accounts should reflect the commercial reality – and not just the legal form – of what has happened.

The report and accounts are prepared according to the *going concern* principle, which assumes that the company will continue in business for the foreseeable future.

Under the principle of *materiality,* anything material, and so potentially affecting users' decisions, must be disclosed.

Obtain the accounts

We will now look at what constitutes the accounts. At this stage, it will be helpful, although not essential, to have a set in front of you.

To get hold of a report and accounts, telephone a company's registrar, and ask it to send you one.

Alternatively, obtain a copy of the *Financial Times,* and telephone its free service for ordering company reports and accounts.

As an alternative, you can download the accounts of some major companies from their own Web sites.

THE FINANCIAL STATEMENTS

The chairman's statement

The first item in the report and accounts is usually the chairman's statement. This is not subject to any accounting legislation or code of best practice.

SECRETS OF READING THE ACCOUNTS

To interpret a company report and accounts is a complex skill that you will not acquire overnight. Successful stock market speculators have found that the following three golden rules have helped them immensely.

1. **Focus on the numbers.** This means that you need to understand what the numbers mean, and how to calculate relevant ratios. We cover the basics in this Seminar and the next.

2. **Read different parts together.** You will only see a balanced picture if you look at the accounts as a whole. If, for instance, profits (as on the profit and loss account) are strong and cash flow (as on the cash flow statement) is weak, the discrepancy spells potential trouble.

    Scrutinize the notes to the accounts, where unflattering revelations are sometimes recorded. You will find the notes at the back, numbered against relevant parts of the financial statements.

3. **Compare with last year's accounts and peers.** This way, you can track the company's prowess. The latest figures are always presented with last year's. Compare also the accounts of comparable companies.

The chairman focuses, usually optimistically, on the company's trading performance, its strategy and its prospects. Read between the lines.

The directors' report

The directors' report typically comes next. This will help you to interpret the numbers in the accounts, and provides extra non-financial information.

You will find here details of the company's dividend policy, and a business review. Post-balance sheet events and any Research & Development (R&D) programme are covered.

Be alert for any mention of a reduction in R&D, which will bring short-term cash flow benefits at the expense of long-term development.

The directors' report also identifies major shareholders who hold 3 per cent or more of the company. Note when they trade their shares.

Find out here if the company has purchased its own shares. If so, this indicates that it could find no more profitable use for its spare cash. The transaction will have increased the earnings per share by redistributing earnings to fewer shareholders. The share price will normally have responded positively.

The operating and financial review

The operating and financial review is a voluntary statement that provides more about the company's operations and identifies key future trends.

The profit and loss account

The *profit and loss account* is one of the main financial statements, along with the balance sheet and the cash flow statement. Using figures contained in it, you will be able to calculate profit-related ratios, including earnings per share.

Here is a typical profit and loss account. Note that x stands for a positive amount and (x) for a negative amount.

The layout of a typical profit and loss account (usual style)

Turnover	x
Cost of sales	(x)
Gross profit	x
Administration costs	(x)
Distribution costs	(x)
Other operating income	x
Operating profit	x
Profit on sale of fixed assets	x
Net interest payable	(x)
Profit on ordinary activities before tax	x
Taxation on profit on ordinary activities	x
Profit on ordinary activities after taxation	x
Minority interests	(x)
Dividend	(x)
Retained profit for the financial year	x

Alternative layout

Here is a less common (alternative) layout for the top part of the profit and loss account:

Turnover	x
Raw materials	(x)
Staff costs	(x)

Change in stock and work-in-progress	(x)
Operating income	x
Operating profit	x

Let us now look at the profit and loss account (usual style) in more detail. I will include some items that may appear in the notes.

Turnover

Turnover, which is sales, comes first. In the notes, you will find a breakdown of turnover by each class of business and geographical segment. This reveals from where the company is generating its revenues.

Compare this year's turnover with last. If sales are up, it is a good sign, but it is not a firm buying signal. Also compare turnover with that of a similar company's, provided that it is calculated similarly.

Cost of sales

Cost of sales comes next. This includes production overheads, raw materials, employees, and product development. It also includes depreciation, and changes in stock level, which we will look at in more detail below.

As cost of sales is fixed, the lower the figure, the better. If it has risen by a higher percentage than sales, the profit margin will decline, which is a warning sign.

Depreciation

Depreciation is how far an asset's value is reduced due to wear and tear. An annual amount is deducted from the profit and loss account.

UK companies typically use the *straight-line* method of depreciation. On this basis, a company with £10,000 may depreciate £1,000 annually over 10 years, if we take this period to be its useful working life.

Under the *sum-of-the digits* depreciation method, the depreciation charge is higher. If an asset's useful working life is three years, add up the digits 1, 2, and 3 to make 6, and divide this into the number of years. On this basis, depreciation is, in the first year, 3/6 of asset value in the first year, and, in the second, 2/6.

The highest depreciation is to be found on application of the *reclining balance* method. This reduces the value of an asset by a fixed percentage annually.

The *usage-based* method of depreciation is based on how much the asset is used. This is used for machinery.

The *annuity* method of depreciation takes into account the cost of capital tied up in the asset.

Sometimes a company will change its method of depreciation to improve its profits. If so, it must reveal the change in the report and accounts.

Stock-level changes

Stock-level changes are calculated as opening stock + purchases – closing stock.

In the UK, stock is valued on the *First in first out* (FIFO) basis, which assumes that oldest items of stock held are used first.

In the USA, stock is often valued on a *Last in first out* basis (LIFO), which in inflationary times can create a smaller taxable profit than under FIFO.

Profit

Gross profit and operating costs

Sales less cost of sales is the gross profit. Deduct operating costs. These include administration, distribution, and marketing. They also include exceptional items, which are significant and unusual items.

Operating costs are not fixed. If they are growing faster than sales, this could be a cause for concern. Otherwise, this may be a useful investment.

Operating profit

Operating profit is profit before interest and tax, or PBIT. This is sales, less cost of sales and net operating costs.

Profit before tax

Profit before tax comes after the profit or loss (over book value) on any sales of fixed assets, and the payment of net interest.

Tax

On UK accounts, the tax charge is normally less than the pre-tax profit multiplied by the tax rate. It includes both corporation tax and deferred taxation.

Corporation tax

Corporation tax is paid on income and capital gains, usually nine months after the company's year-end.

The rate is 30 per cent, or 20 per cent for smaller companies with taxable profits of up to £300,000, with marginal relief for companies with profits between £300,000 and £1.5m.

Dividends received from UK companies are not subject to corporation tax as they have been paid from after-tax profits. This is known as franked income.

Deferred taxation

Deferred taxation adjusts the tax charge to reflect timing differences. These arise when items are charged to the profit and loss account in a different period for tax purposes than for accounting purposes.

As an example of a timing difference, interest payments may be charged to the profit and loss account on an accruals basis – not payable until later, but belonging to this time period. They are allowed for tax purposes only when actually paid.

Another example is the distinction between depreciation and capital allowances. Depreciation can vary between companies and so the Inland Revenue ignores it. Instead it gives every company a standard tax allowance known as a capital allowance, which allows writing down of 25 per cent per year on a reducing balance basis on plants and machinery.

There are also are permanent differences between the charge to the profit and loss account and the tax charge. An example of this is entertainment costs, which are not allowed for tax purposes.

Generally, the company provides for deferred taxation on the profit and loss account only 'to the extent that a liability or asset will crystallize'. In some circumstances, this is a matter of opinion, providing opportunities for creative accounting.

Net profit

After tax, the profit and loss account shows the net profit, which is attributable to shareholders. It will often distribute part of this as a dividend.

Final dividend

The proposed final (not interim) dividend must be approved by share-holders at the company's annual general meeting before it is distributed. It will be shown on the profit and loss account.

The unpaid amount appears as a current liability on the balance sheet, which we will be looking at shortly.

PROFIT AND SALES RATIOS

Price/sales

Divide the share price by sales, and express the result as a percentage. The lower the figure, the better value the shares are likely to be.

This ratio has been used to value young high-tech companies. It is less popular in bear markets, when investors are reminded that sales are no substitute for profits.

Profit margin

Divide the net or gross profit by turnover, and express the result as a percentage. The profit margin should be up on last year, and favourable against that of comparable companies.

Earnings per share

This is profit after tax, divided by the number of shares in issue. It should ideally be steadily rising every year.

The earnings per share can be calculated in various ways, including on a net basis, which is standard, or on a maximum distribution basis, which assumes that all earnings are distributed as dividends.

If the earnings per share are calculated on a nil distribution basis, the figure shows what earnings would have been without a dividend paid. If it is calculated on a fully diluted basis, it is assumed that all share options (giving an opportunity to buy shares) are exercised.

The financial press often uses the headline earnings, which exclude any profits or losses from the sale or termination of an operation, or from the sale or permanent diminution of fixed assets.

What matters most is that, when you are comparing the earnings per share of two companies, you are setting like against like.

The PE ratio

The PE ratio is the share price divided by earnings per share. The higher it is, the more highly the market rates the shares. A stock with a very low PE ratio may be an unrecognized bargain, or otherwise a dud.

The PE ratio can be based on last year's earnings, or on forecast earnings. Compare like with like, and within the same sector.

The PEG ratio

The PEG (price/earnings/growth) ratio is the company's PE ratio divided by the average annual growth rate of its earnings per share.

If the PEG is significantly below one, this indicates likely value in the company. The ratio works best for small growth companies.

Interest cover

Interest cover is operating profit divided by net interest payable. This tells you if the company can finance its net interest out of current profits.

Check in the notes how much interest, if any, has been capitalized, which means it will be included as an asset on the balance sheet. Add capitalized interest to the net interest figure.

Dividend yield

The dividend yield is the gross dividend per share, divided by the share price, expressed as a percentage. To calculate the gross dividend, find the net dividend – either on the profit and loss account or in the notes to the accounts – and gross it up.

Low growth companies, with low share prices, may have high yields because the dividend is a percentage of the low share price. This is useful from an income perspective, but can indicate a company in poor financial health.

The balance sheet

The balance sheet is a snapshot on a given day of the company's choice of how the business has used its money.

On a UK company balance sheet, assets are on the top half, and liabilities below. Assets are what the company has, and they are equal to its liabilities, which is what it owes. Here is the layout:

UK balance sheet
Fixed assets

Intangible assets	x
Tangible assets	x
Investments	x
Total fixed assets	x
Current assets	
Stocks	x
Debtors	x
Investments	x
Cash	x
Total current assets	x
Current Liabilities	
Creditors (short term)	(x)
Net current assets	x
Total assets less current liabilities	x
Creditors (over one year)	(x)
Provisions	(x)
Net assets	x
Capital and reserves	
Issued share capital	x
Share premium account	x

Revaluation reserve	x
Profit and loss account	x
	—
Shareholders' funds	x
Minority interests	x
	—
Total capital employed	x

Assets

Fixed assets are those that the company is not buying or selling as part of its business. They are subject to depreciation (see under Profit and loss account). Be warned that their value may not be as recorded on the balance sheet.

Intangible fixed assets include brand names, patents, licences, and development costs. They also include purchased goodwill, which is the difference between what one company paid for another and the target company's net asset value.

Most intangible fixed assets can be amortized over their economic life, which is up to 20 years (extendable if the assets retain value). The process is similar to depreciation. Note that brands are never amortized, partly because they have an indefinite life.

Some tangible assets, particularly brands, are notoriously hard to value, and the figure put on them is often subjective.

After fixed assets come current assets. These are assets that can be converted into cash within a year. They are cash or cash equivalents, debtors and stock.

The most reliable of these is cash. Debt will not all be repaid. Stock could fall in value. Some companies – particularly property developers – transfer some items from current to fixed assets.

Liabilities

Current liabilities are first. They include accrued expenses, such as salaries that have been earned but not yet paid, a bank overdraft, and trade creditors.

The more creditors there are, the better, as they enable the company to use cash free of interest charges. See the trade creditors' ratio in the box below.

Net current assets

Current assets deducted from current liabilities make net current assets, which are working capital. This is what you have available to pay bills now.

Net assets

Fixed assets plus net current assets are total assets less current liabilities.

We will next deduct medium- and long-term debts, and provisions, which represent assessable future costs to the company from past transactions or events. If an event is uncertain and the amount payable hard to assess, it is instead included in the notes under Contingent liabilities.

Total assets less total liabilities are net assets.

Issued share capital and reserves

Issued share capital and reserves make up shareholders' funds. These, coupled with minority interests (the proportion of a subsidiary owned by others than the parent company), are equal to total capital employed.

Capital employed is the total amount on the *bottom* half of the balance sheet. This is equal to net assets, which is the total amount of the *top* half.

The *issued* share capital consists only of shares that are issued to shareholders. The company may be able to issue more from its *authorized* share capital.

Issued shares are mostly *ordinary* shares, which entitle shareholders to all profits after tax and preference dividends have been paid, and to vote at annual general meetings.

Preference shares, which carry a fixed rate of dividend, may also be in issue. If the directors decide not to pay this dividend, preference shareholders have no legal redress, but, for so long as this lasts, no dividend is allowed to be paid on any other shares.

You may also find in issue non-voting shares, which have limited or no voting rights, and warrants, which are tradable securities giving holders the opportunity to buy new shares at a set price from the company (see Seminar 16, but do not confuse with covered warrants).

Reserves, like share capital, are part of shareholders' funds. They represent retained profit. The profit and loss account is the only reserve which may be distributed. The other reserves, being non-distributable, cannot be used to pay dividends. They can be used, for instance, in a scrip issue.

These reserves include the share premium account, which contains the premium to nominal value at which shares were issued. The revaluation reserve contains unrealized profits, and the capital revaluation reserve reflects changes in the valuation of fixed assets.

Capital employed

The total capital employed is shareholders' funds less minority interests.

BALANCE SHEET-RELATED RATIOS

Current ratio

The current ratio measures liquidity. It is current assets divided by current liabilities.

As a rule of thumb, it should be at least 2, which means that current liabilities are twice covered.

Quick ratio

The quick ratio (also known as the acid test) is current assets less stock, divided into current liabilities. Like the current ratio, it shows the company's liquidity, but it omits stock as this may not be quickly or easily convertible into cash.

As a rule of thumb, the quick ratio should be 1 or more.

Debtors ratio

The debtors ratio is trade debtors divided by turnover, all multiplied by 365.

This gives you the number of days that it takes the company to collect money from its customers.

If the figure is rising, the company is taking longer to collect its money, which is not good, although rising sales can compensate.

Trade creditors ratio

The trade creditors ratio is the number of trade creditors, divided by turnover, with the result multiplied by 365. It reveals how many days the company is taking to pay its trade creditors.

If creditor days are rising, this is a good sign as it leaves cash with the company.

Stock/turn ratio

The stock/turn ratio is turnover, or cost of sales, divided by stock. This reveals how many times a year a company is converting its stock into sales.

Ideally, the ratio will rise over the years, suggesting that the company is finding it easier to sell stock.

Gearing ratio

The gearing ratio consists of interest-bearing loans plus preference share capital, divided by ordinary shareholders' funds, and all expressed as a percentage. It represents the company's level of borrowings.

As a rule of thumb, if the gearing ratio is higher than 50 per cent, you should start asking questions.

Net asset value

The net asset value is the share price divided by net asset per share. To obtain the net asset per share, divide net assets by the number of shares in issue.

Net asset value is useful for valuing property companies and investment trusts. They should ideally be priced at a discount to net assets.

Return on capital employed

Return on capital employed is profit before interest and tax (taken from the profit and loss account), divided by year-end assets less liabilities, all expressed as a percentage. This measures management performance.

Ideally, this ratio will be rising, and higher than for rival companies.

THE NEXT STEP

In the next seminar, we will examine how to interpret the cash flow statement, which is the third main financial statement alongside the profit and loss account and the balance sheet.

We will also look at some other areas of accounting, so rounding up our coverage of this important subject.

SEMINAR 5 GOLDEN RULES

▮ In a company report and accounts, focus on the numbers.

▮ Read different parts of the accounts in conjunction.

▮ Compare this year's figures with last.

▮ The Chairman's statement is not subject to accounting legislation or best practice, so read between the lines.

▮ If cost of sales rises more than sales, this is a warning sign.

▮ A company can change its method of depreciation to improve its profits, but must record the change in its accounts.

▌ In UK accounts, the tax charge is normally less than the pre-tax profit multiplied by the tax rate.

▌ When you compare the earnings per share of two companies, make sure that you are setting like against like.

▌ A stock with a low PE ratio may be a bargain or, alternatively, a dud.

▌ If the PEG in a small growth company is significantly below 1, this indicates likely value.

▌ When you calculate interest cover, include capitalized interest.

▌ Companies with high yields may be in poor financial health.

▌ Some intangible assets are hard to value, and the figure put on them is subjective.

▌ The most reliable of the current assets is cash.

▌ The more creditors a company has, the better, as they free up cash.

▌ The current ratio should be at least 2, and the quick ratio 1.

▌ Look for a rising creditors ratio and a falling debtors ratio, as these leave more cash with the company.

▌ If a company's gearing is above 50 per cent, start asking questions.

▌ Property companies and investment trusts should ideally be priced at a discount to net assets.

▌ Return on capital employed measures management performance and should ideally be rising year on year, as well as higher than for rival companies.

Seminar 6

How to profit from the accounts – part 2

INTRODUCTION

In this seminar, we will examine the cash flow statement, and some remaining parts of the accounts. We will take a critical look at discounted cash flow analysis.

We will also investigate such areas as group accounting, manipulation of financial statements and inflation-adjusted accounting.

THE FINANCIAL STATEMENTS

The cash flow statement

The cash flow statement shows only cash movements. Unlike profits, these cannot be fudged.

The total of cash flows represents the increase or decrease in cash for the year.

A basic cash flow statement

	£,000
(1) Cash flow from operating activities	x
(2) Return on investment and servicing of finance	(x)

(3) Taxation	(x)
(4) Capital expenditure and financial investment	(x)
(5) Acquisitions & disposals	(x)
(6) Equity dividends paid	(x)
	(x)
(7) Management of liquid resources	x
(8) Financing:	
Proceeds of share issue	x
Reduction in debt	(x)
Increase in cash for the period	x

Cash flow from operating activities

The statement presents *Cash flow from operating activities*. If the company uses the direct presentation, it will show cash received, less cash paid.

More usually, the statement will represent the figures indirectly. In this case, it will reconcile the operating profit to the operating cash flow. It starts with the operating profit, and adds back depreciation, as this is not a cash flow. The statement will subtract any increase in debtors, which mean less cash for the company. It will add back any decrease in stocks or increase in creditors as either of these means more cash.

Net cash from operating activities should be about the same as (or higher than) the operating profit. If it is much less, the accountants may have massaged the profit and loss account.

The rest

Return on investments and servicing of finance includes cash inflows and outflows related to payment of interest, and non-equity dividends.

Taxation is the cash actually paid in the year for tax (typically not the same as the tax figure on the profit and loss account). This incorporates any rebates from the tax authorities.

Capital expenditure and financial investment includes cash inflows and outflows arising from buying and selling fixed assets (typically vehicles or heavy machinery).

Acquisitions and disposals are cash movements from the acquisition or sale of any subsidiary, associate or joint venture.

Equity dividends paid consist of cash flow from payment of equity dividends.

Management of liquid resources is cash flow related to the company's current investments. These must be easily convertible to cash at about the value shown on the financial statements.

Financing consists of cash flow related to receipts from or payments to external moneylenders. The company may borrow money or issue shares. It can also buy back shares, or redeem bonds.

Reconciliation

In the notes, cash movements will be reconciled to net debt. If the reconciliation is positive, it will show a *net funds* figure.

CASH FLOW-RELATED RATIOS

Operating cash flow/operating profit

This ratio consists of operating cash flow, divided by operating profit. If the result is more than one, you have probably found value. If it is much less, creative accounting has probably been at work.

EV/EBITDA

Use EV/EBITDA to value companies in capital-intensive industries such as telecommunications, where interest payments on huge borrowings may have hit earnings hard. In such cases, the ratio arguably presents a more realistic valuation than earnings per share as it ignores interest payments.

To find the EV/EBITDA, take the enterprise value or EV. This is the market capitalization, which is defined as share price multiplied by number of shares in issue, plus total debt less total cash. Divide this figure by EBITDA, which is earnings before interest, tax, depreciation and amortization.

The accounting profession has never recognized EV/EBITDA. The Worldcom accounting fraud exposed in 2002 highlighted the deficiencies of this ratio. Since then, analysts have still been using it, but more in conjunction with other ratios.

Discounted cash flow analysis

See the next section.

Statement of recognized gains and losses

The statement of recognized gains and losses links the profit and loss account (ie the financial statement) to the balance sheet. It shows any profit or loss, regardless of whether it is included on the profit and loss account.

The auditor's report

The auditor's report must state if the accounts have been properly prepared, and if required information was made available. It must say if the audit was properly conducted, and if the accounts show a true and fair view.

In a qualified audit report, the auditor may state that the accounts do not give a true and fair view. Less damaging, but still serious, is when it says that it cannot form an opinion that the accounts are true and fair.

If a company has a qualified audit report, do not risk investing in it. If you already hold shares in such a company, sell immediately.

DISCOUNTED CASH FLOW ANALYSIS

Net present value

Discounted cash flow (DCF) analysis translates future cash flows into present value. Although this is not, strictly speaking, part of the accounts, it is a major part of the analyst's work, and it is extrapolated from the company's financial position today.

To calculate the DCF of your chosen company, first find the net operating cash flow (NOCF). You will do this by taking the underlying company's earnings before interest and tax (EBIT) on the profit and loss account. Deduct corporation tax paid and capital expenditure. Add depreciation and amortization, which do not represent a movement of cash. Add or subtract the change in working capital, including movements in stock, in debtors and creditors, and in cash or cash equivalents.

This is the year's NOCF. You can calculate it also for future years, reduced in value to present-day terms by a discount rate broadly representing inflation in reverse. Cash flow will continue infinitely beyond the period over which the future cash flows are spread. This is the terminal value.

Present and future cash flows, together with the terminal value, make up the net present value. Its accuracy depends partly on the future NOCF forecasts, and the number of years used. Also, the larger the discount rate used, the smaller is the net present value of future cash flows.

The discount rate used by analysts is normally the company's weighted average cost of capital. This represents the cost of capital to the company weighted by debt and equity. This is split into its two parts. The cost of debt is the yield to maturity on the company's bonds. The cost of equity is typically measured by the Capital Asset Pricing Model (CAPM).

The CAPM is widely used but controversial. It assumes that investors should be rewarded for acquiring investments, which carry a larger amount of 'market' risk, which cannot be diversified away.

Given the uncertainties, analysts may plot DCF models using different discount rates to present alternative valuations. Undeniably, bankers often abuse the method to paint an over-optimistic picture of a favoured company.

In their exposé book on the investment banking industry, *Monkey Business, Swinging Through the Wall Street Jungle*, authors John Rolfe and Peter Troobe say that the DCF analysis, based on their own experience, is

CAPITAL ASSET PRICING MODEL

The Capital Asset Pricing Model aims to find the required rate of return on equity by comparing a stock's performance with the market. It stipulates that the return on a stock (R) is equal to the risk-free rate of return (Rf) plus the equity market risk premium, multiplied by the stock's beta. This may be expressed as:

Rate of return R = Rf + (Rm–Rf) beta

Rf, as the risk-free rate of return, is the interest rate on long-term government bonds, as listed on the currency and money pages of the *Financial Times*. Rm is the average return for the market as a whole, which is higher than Rf. The difference between Rf and Rm is known as the equity market risk premium.

The beta measures the stock's volatility against the market. If a share has a beta of 1, it is fluctuating in line with the market. If it has a beta of 0.5, it is fluctuating at half the rate of the market, and at 2.0, twice the rate.

As a historical figure, the beta is unreliable. In practice, the beta works better over a long period (decades rather than years) or at times when the stock market is fluctuating more than usual.

the 'grand-daddy of all crocks of shit' and is especially useful for valuing companies with no real business.

'A comp analysis, at least, requires that the company being valued have some revenues, cash flow or earnings *today* in order to have any value. The DCF analysis does not. It finesses the problem by only attributing value on the basis of how the company is projected to do in the future,' the authors say.

This unfortunately tallies with my own experience as an insider in the investment banking industries. Nonetheless, DCF analysis remains the most useful valuation method available, provided that the figures are well founded. To ascertain its value, you must also examine the underlying assumptions.

ADVANCED ACCOUNTING

If you have read so far in this and the last seminar, you have covered basic investment analysis as based on scrutiny of the report and accounts.

You know enough to start puzzling your way through a set of accounts, or to understand the gist of an analyst's report. We will now touch on group accounting.

Group accounting

If a company owns less than 20 per cent of shares in another company, this is an investment. If it owns more than 20 per cent but less than 50 per cent, this a participating interest unless there is evidence against it.

If the participating interest, as is usual, exercises a significant influence on the operating and financial activities of the other, the latter is an *associate*.

If a company has more than 50 per cent of shares in another, it has a *subsidiary*. In this case, the group prepares consolidated accounts, which combine the subsidiary's accounts with its own. It also prepares accounts for the parent company.

A *joint venture* is an entity in which the reporting company holds a joint controlling interest on a long-term basis.

A company uses equity accounting to include associates and joint ventures in its financial statements. It includes its share only of the associate's net assets as one line in the accounts, and this share is adjusted annually for value. Goodwill from acquiring the asset is included with its value (not with other goodwill). The consolidated cash flow statement separates dividends from associates.

In the past, companies have used equity accounting to represent their accounts in a more flattering way. In the 1980s, the associate sometimes took out a loan for which the group was liable. This way, the loan could be shown under *Loans from associates* rather than under *Borrowing* or *Interest* in the group accounts, where it would be more conspicuous. Under *Contingent liabilities* (in the notes), the company would state that it had guaranteed an associate's debt.

The *gross equity* method of accounting is used for joint ventures. It is similar to equity accounting but more detailed. The profit and loss account shows the other company's share of turnover, profit, interest and tax, and the balance sheet its share of gross assets and liabilities as well as net investment.

Creative accounting

Today's situation

'Accounting serves the user,' says trader Simon Cawkwell, who is a qualified accountant. 'I take the view that all directors are liars until proved otherwise.'

If so, their job is not getting easier, at least from the accounting perspective. It is now much harder than it was some years ago to account for large losses as one-off payments, because extraordinary items are much rarer.

The recent accounting manipulations revealed as a result of the collapses of Worldcom and Enron served as a catalyst for a further tightening up of the rules.

Enron had been capitalized at US$78bn shortly before it went bankrupt in December 2001. It had seen its share price soar as a result of its late but fashionable involvement in the broadband business. Few analysts had queried Enron's business plan, although it was largely based on debt.

The warnings came when Enron's auditor Arthur Andersen reinstated the accounts in October and November 2001 respectively. The large rating agencies Standard & Poors and Moody's Investment Services downgraded Enron's debt to junk bond status and, shortly afterwards, the company filed for bankruptcy.

In reaction to the Enron excesses, the US Congress ushered in the Sarbanes–Oxley Act. This affects accountants with auditing business in the USA, as well as companies that list in the USA, even if they are UK based.

Under the Sarbanes–Oxley Act, accountants are forbidden to mix auditing with any of a range of other activities, including actuarial or legal services, and bookkeeping, although tax services are still allowed. This part of the Act hits some accountants hard as auditing is now a commoditized, low-margin business and they rely on the other activities to survive.

Apart from the restriction on their side-activities, auditors under Sarbanes–Oxley are supervised by a body that is answerable to the Securities & Exchange Commission, the US regulator. In its implementation of the Act, the SEC, unusually, does not have a free hand.

The companies that list in the USA are subject to stringent rules that similarly discourage any sleight of hand in presenting the accounts. The chief executive and chief financial officer must sign off statements to confirm that they have complied with the provisions of the Securities & Exchange Act, 1934. It is difficult to confirm this reliably, according to lawyers.

In practice, UK residents who are registered as US directors will not be in the first line of fire, lawyers say. To chase any miscreants in their number, the SEC will need the cooperation of The Financial Services Authority, the UK regulator. This may not immediately be forthcoming.

In this environment, many foreign companies are finding London more attractive than New York as a financial centre in which to list their shares. In time, the tightening up of standards in the USA is expected to have more of a knock-on effect in Western Europe, but at this stage creative accounting here continues.

In the UK, companies are still recording sales on their profit and loss account before the contracts have been signed, and profit, unlike cash, remains a matter of opinion.

Quick way

Is there a quick way to detect creative accounting, a rule of thumb that you can apply even if you have no background in or understanding of financial statements' interpretation whatsoever?

Yes, according to Benford's law, which physician Frank Benford discovered in 1938. He found that the digit 'one' occurs in numbers more frequently than any other, with the next most frequent being 'two', and then 'three'. On a similar basis, the larger the digit, the less frequently it appears.

In 1996, an accountant called Mark Nigrini suggested that Benford's law could be used to catch fraud on financial documents. If the usual order of priority in the numbers does not appear, maybe the books have been cooked, he suggested.

Tell-tale signs

Of course, this approach would need verification. It helps to keep an eye out for tell-tale signs of creative accounting, some of which are as follows

Capitalizing costs

In bullish markets, it is still possible for a property builder legitimately to capitalize interest payments on the balance sheet rather than charge them to the profit and loss account. The move will boost the year's profits, but can encourage the company to take on too much debt.

Similarly, a company may capitalize development costs instead of charging them conventionally to the profit and loss account. This is legitimate if the development is for a clearly defined, and ultimately profitable, project that the company has the resources to complete.

On this basis, costs of development are amortized, and hit the profit and loss account gradually over the period expected to benefit. The company's profits are artificially enhanced. So far so good, but problems may arise if the development asset is later written down in value.

Leasing

A company may have scope for manipulation in how it defines its leasing arrangements. The distinction between finance (long-term) and operating (short-term) leases is not always clear, but the two are represented very differently in the accounts.

An asset on a finance lease is included on the company's balance sheet. It will be depreciated over its life, which is the shorter of the lease term and its anticipated useful life. The lease rentals will be split between interest and capital. Interest is charged to the profit and loss account, and capital repayments reduce a total for the leasing company that is included under *Creditors* on the balance sheet.

An asset on an operating lease does not provide the benefits of ownership, and is not included on the balance sheet. Instead, this is off-balance-sheet financing, which is conveniently inconspicuous in accounting terms. The lease rentals are charged as an operating cost to the profit and loss account.

Currency mismatching

Some companies practise currency mismatching, which is also known as interest rate arbitrage. They borrow money in currencies where interest rates are low, and invest it in currencies where interest rates are high. This strategy can make a quick profit but, in the long term, can be risky. When a company gains on the interest rate differential, this may be at least counterbalanced by a loss on the currency exchange rate.

Pension schemes

A company and its employees often contribute to a pension fund invested on their behalf. There are risks. Shortly after newspaper magnate Robert Maxwell died in 1991, it was confirmed that he had raided the pension fund of his employees, partly in order to fund a lavish personal life.

Since then, the rules have tightened up and the funds in a company pension scheme must now be under the control of independent trustees. Even so, be vigilant.

THE CHANGING FACE OF ACCOUNTING

Inflation-adjusted accounting

In preparing financial statements, UK companies use historical cost accounting based on the costs that the company has incurred in the year. In the profit and loss account, revenues and costs relate to sales made at the time. On the balance sheet, assets are shown at the lower of cost or net realizable value.

This approach fails to take account of inflation. Accountants have duly found ways to adjust the accounts. In the accounts of utilities companies, for instance, items may be restated after an adjustment for changes in the Retail Price Index. This is Current purchase power accounting. In other sectors, this adjustment is not used much as the resulting version of the accounts might not represent the company's specific experience.

To adjust for cost inflation is considered more accurate than Purchase power accounting as it is on the basis of the specific price inflation experienced by the company. This approach will hit the cost of sales and the working capital. Also, assets will be revalued and so will require extra depreciation. As a result, the company will probably record lower profit figures.

International accounting

Outside Western Europe and the USA, company accounts can be opaque. The International Accounting Standards Committee, an independent body, aims to standardize accounting principles in major world countries. At the time of writing, it has 119 members in 88 countries.

Standardization has a long way to go. In Russia, for instance, it is still the large companies, or those with ambitions to raise money on international capital markets, that prepare their financial statements according to US GAAP or international accounting standards (see Seminar 13). Russian accounting remains the usual choice. It is surprisingly opaque, and cannot yet properly represent such Western aspects as takeovers and mergers.

The accounts are only part of the picture

The accounts will inform you about a company's past. For the future there are many variables. In the short term, the share price is rarely driven by fundamental factors alone.

THE NEXT STEP

In the next seminar, we will start looking at technical analysis. So many traders use this that you cannot ignore its existence, even if you are one of the many sceptics.

SEMINAR 6 GOLDEN RULES

- The cash flow shows only cash movements and, unlike earnings, these cannot be fudged.
- If a company has a qualified audit report, do not risk investing in it.
- Profit, unlike cash, is still a matter of opinion.
- DCF analysis is easily abused, but it remains the most effective valuation method available.
- If a company capitalizes interest payments or development costs on the balance sheet, investigate whether it may be overextending itself.
- An operating lease is accounted for as off-balance sheet financing, which is conveniently inconspicuous.
- Interest rate arbitrage between currencies is risky, as the exchange rate can turn against you.
- Accounts adjusted for cost inflation will show fewer profits.
- International accounting is still far from standardized.
- The accounts tell you about a company's past, but for the future, there are many variables.

Seminar 7

The basics of technical analysis

INTRODUCTION

In this short seminar, we will look at technical analysis, and how it works. We will examine the arguments for and against. We will explore Dow theory in detail, and then look at trend theory.

THE BASICS

The scope of technical analysis

Technical analysis is the art of using charts and other technical indicators to assess and to interpret market movements and trends. Analysts focus not just on price, but also on volume of transactions. They are concerned with supply and demand. The charts are believed to reveal short-, medium- and long-term trends.

Analysts can advise on *timing* of stock purchases and sales, on the basis that the past repeats itself. A study of past price movements in the charts is crucial. Analysts also rely on knowledge of individual psychology – for example, an individual's unwillingness to sell out of a losing position – and of crowd psychology, which shows how investors *en masse* are prone to overreact to good or bad news.

To back up their reading of the charts, analysts use oscillators that focus on, among other things, whether the market is overbought or oversold, its relative performance and its rate of change.

Analysts can apply their analysis to other markets besides equities, including foreign exchange, interest rates and commodities, and in any country, developed or otherwise.

In its strongest form, technical analysis rejects fundamental analysis, which is assessing the likely movement of a stock according to the state of the underlying company in accounting and qualitative terms.

Otherwise, technical analysis rejects the conventional view of economists that distinguishable elements are disassociated unless proven otherwise. Technical analysts believe in harmonious cycles, in share price movements as in nature, and that higher cycles relate to lower. We will be examining these areas in Seminar 19 in relation to Fibonacci numbers and Elliott Wave theory.

Academics have mostly dismissed technical analysis as inconsistent with financial theory. They take insufficient account of the non-linear process that financial markets follow, according to Dr Ronald Giles, South Bank University Business school. In a paper commissioned by the Society of Technical Analysts, he suggested that irregular signals based on technical analysis rules cannot be accommodated by the linear process, and so technical trading has an important role in future models.

Researchers have found that share prices do not always adjust to information shocks for a period. This can offer technical trading opportunities, according to Giles.

Efficacy

Others disagree. The issue is whether technical analysis works at all. Can it tip the balance when predicting share price and broader market movements? Or is all this a false craft, akin to reading the future in the tea leaves?

The promoters of 'black box' trading systems do the reputation of technical analysis no favours. The computerized systems rely on a secret method of generating the buy, sell and hold signals. In fact they are often extremely simple, based on moving averages crossing or some other basic tenet of technical analysis, and the invariably high cost is unjustified.

Cynics suggest that technical analysis has always had a following because the charts – whether representing markets, individual companies, or the economy as a whole – create patterns.

As fund manager Ralph Wanger has pointed out, the human mind sees patterns, even in the clouds. Some, like Wanger, feel that these patterns are completely random, but others do not, and many take a position somewhere in between. The position varies even among technical analysts.

Wall Street trader Jim Rogers once said that he had never seen a rich technician except those who sell their services. US fund manager John Train regards all technical analysis as fakery, and told me that he has seen Wall

Street firms spend millions of dollars on installing technical analysis systems and then quietly dumping them.

Others take a more positive view. As a trader Marty Schwartz had only lost money in a full 10 years of trading on the basis of fundamental analysis. When he switched to technical analysis, he became rich, making a 25 per cent a month profit as a trader over the subsequent 10 years.

Great US trader Larry Williams is another fan. So is fund manager William O'Neil. 'Just as a doctor would be foolish not to use X-rays and ECGs, investors would be foolish not to use charts,' he says.

The gurus who instruct on technical analysis command enormous followings. Sometimes, they get their timing wrong. How far this detracts from the thrust of their analysis is open to debate, and is not normally subjected to vigorous tests.

A compromise

Technical analysis seems to be less accepted for the stock market than for currencies and commodities markets, and less for long-term investors than for traders.

Even for sceptics, the chart has value in that it provides a snapshot picture of past market performance. It is a fast means of assimilating information.

When interviewed by Andrew Leeming in *The Super Analysts* (John Wiley, 2000), Dr Mark Mobius, managing director of the Templeton Emerging Markets Fund, put it like this:

> Charts are a road map, and anything that is graphic is very useful because you can get a good picture of what has been happening relatively quickly and efficiently. But they are only one part of the equation, and I wouldn't want to give the impression that I'm a closet technician, because at the end of the day you have to look at a lot more than that.

Technical analysts agree on the basics, although they dispute the detail. They are unanimous that the share price or index moves in trends.

How do we detect a trend, and when is it breached? Dow theory offers one of the oldest answers.

In their classic textbook *Technical Analysis of Stock Trends*, Robert Edwards and John Magee describe Dow theory as the 'granddaddy of all technical market studies.'

DOW THEORY

The history

It all started with the researches of Charles Dow, a financial journalist of the Victorian era. To gauge business conditions, he developed two stock market indices in 1897.

The first index was the Industrial Average, which consisted of 12 blue chip companies (increased to 20 in 1916 and 30 in 1928). The second was the Rail Average, which included 20 railroad companies (the most important industry of the period).

Conveniently, Dow was editor of the *Wall Street Journal* and he used its pages to promote ideas that gave rise to Dow theory.

Dow died in 1902. William Hamilton succeeded him as editor, and developed his findings into an early version of Dow theory.

Another significant contributor to the development of Dow theory is Robert Rhea. He redefined its principles from the 1920s, developing related charts.

In his earlier writings, Rhea stressed that the Dow theory was designed as an instrument to enhance the speculator's knowledge. It was not an infallible theory that worked independently of knowledge of the economy or of fundamental market conditions.

The practice

The averages discount everything

Under the Dow theory, the averages discount everything that is known or knowable about the shares. Share price movements arise from the transactions of so many investors, some of whom know as much about the shares as is humanly possible.

Three trends

Under Dow theory, there are three trends in the market. To trace these, ignore intra-day volatility, and focus only on the closing prices. Let us look at each trend in turn.

The primary trend lasts for between a year and several years, and represents the market's broad direction. In a primary bull market, each rally in the market reaches a higher level, and each secondary fall-back is progressively less powerful. In a primary bear market, shares suffer a prolonged fall, punctuated by rallies.

As a speculator, it is not enough to pay attention to the primary market alone. Also watch for the secondary reaction. This is against the primary trend, and it lasts between three weeks and three months. The price will retrace between a third and two-thirds of prior movement, but then the primary trend will continue in its course.

There is also the minor trend. This typically lasts a few days, although it can be a few weeks, or hours. It often arises from trading activity that is aimed to drive the share price up or down.

Lines

When the share price moves sideways for at least two weeks, fluctuating within an approximate 5 per cent range, this creates a line. If this happens during a primary trend, it is a form of the secondary reaction.

The longer and narrower is this line, the more powerful is the eventual breakout when the price rises or falls outside the range, signifying a new trend.

Volume

Under Dow theory, trading volumes have a meaning that is second in importance only to price changes.

As shares rise or fall sharply, trading volume typically *rises* in coordination. On this basis, the rule is that the greater the volume, the more weight there is behind the price trend. If volume is declining, this indicates a pending share price reversal.

As we see elsewhere in this book, the same theory of volume is prevalent in other areas of technical analysis, although there are dissenters who think it is light volume that puts weight behind a market trend.

Trends

To be valid under Dow theory, a trend should be confirmed by the two indices. The underlying principle is that goods manufactured by companies in the Industrial Average are transported to distributors in the Rail Average. To make the chain effect work, both sides need to be in good shape.

The trend will continue until there is a firm reverse signal. The earlier the reversal is, the more long-lived it is likely to be.

When a new trend is confirmed, it is your cue to *buy* the shares, if the direction is now up, or to *sell* if it is down.

Criticisms

1. **Late signals.** As you will buy or sell *after* the trend reversal has happened, rather than anticipating it, you may miss up to 25 per cent or so of a profitable move.

   This is so, but the same criticism can be made of any cautious trend-following methods. By waiting, you will at least have seen that the trend reversal is genuine.

2. **A person cannot buy and sell the averages.** This is no longer true. Spread betting and other futures trading, for instance, have made it possible to trade the index.

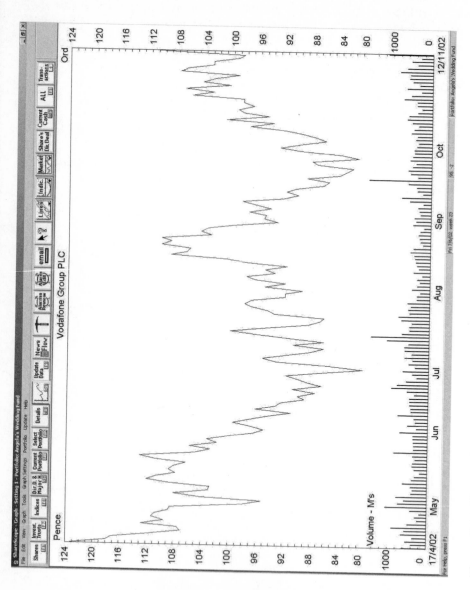

Figure 7.1 Share price vs. volume

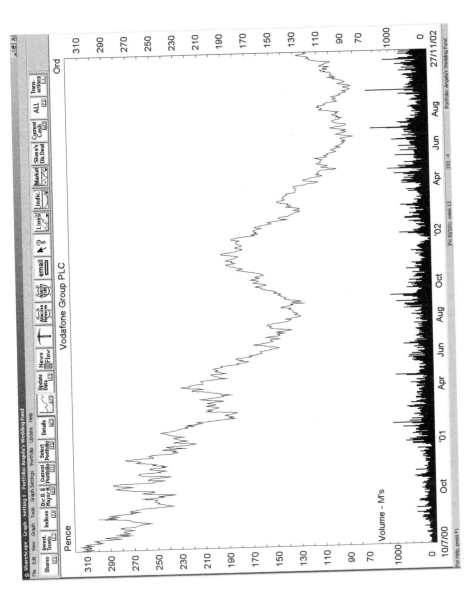

Figure 7.2 Volume bars

3. **Dow theory is not infallible.** This is true, but no form of analysis is infallible.

4. **Inapplicable today.** Some say that Dow theory is inapplicable today because it was applied to indices that do not now have substitutes.

   Against this, supporters of Dow theory argue that the theory remains applicable to at least two US indices. First, today's Dow Jones Industrial Average, which consists of 30 stocks, and, second, the Transportation Index, which is a broader version of the original Rail Average.

THE BROADER PICTURE

Now that you have got to grips with the Dow theory, you will find that it has enormous influence on trend theory.

Trend theory

Technical analysts broadly agree that if the trend line on the chart of an individual stock or market is up, you should buy. If it is down, you should sell.

As in Dow theory, the longer is the trend, the more reliable it is considered, particularly if it is backed by rising volume. When the trend breaks, it is time to take reverse action, buying if you were a seller, or selling if you were a buyer.

There are cynics. One of the best informed is Victor Niederhoffer, a great US speculator and former hedge fund manager who has experienced heights of success and failure alike in the stock market.

He has conducted tests on trend theory and scrutinized the results of others, and concludes that the entire concept is false. In his view, the stock market does not move in trends, which undermines the roots of technical analysis in its entirety. For details of his recent book, which is a must-read, see Seminar 21.

FURTHER RESEARCH

We will be exploring technical analysis in a lot more detail later in this book. At this stage, however, I would like to alert you to some valuable extra reading into which you could plunge if the bug is already starting to bite.

For valuable definitions and explanations visit the Web site of Technical Analysis from A to Z (www.equis.com/free/taaz).

For some intelligent and readable analysis of what works and what does not, check out some of the articles of Colin Nicholson, an Australian

STOCK MARKET SPECULATORS' HALL OF FAME

Member No 1 – Joseph Granville

US technical analyst and guru Joseph Granville reached a pinnacle of fame in the 1970s and early 1980s. He argued that trading volume drives share price movement. The theory came to him when he was relaxing in his bathroom at home, and gazing at the patterns on his tiles.

His canny self-publicity, coupled with some accurate forecasting, made him famous. But his fortunes were to prove as volatile as the stock market itself.

'Everyone I touch I make rich,' said Granville at his peak. At his packed-out investment seminars across the USA, he put in a virtuoso performance, singing and playing the piano. When asked how he kept in touch with the market while travelling, Granville dropped his trousers and revealed stock quotes written on his underpants.

Granville attracted many followers. Markets started to hang on his every word. In this way, his advice sometimes became a self-fulfilling prophecy. But no guru is right forever.

At one point, when markets soared, Granville warned his subscribers that a crash was about to happen, and that they should sell stocks and go short. But stocks continued to rise. At a low point, Granville lost all his money, and ended up sleeping rough.

Like any self-respecting guru, Granville always had a good answer. When once asked why some of his recommendations were wrong, he said that he had been on drugs – referring to his passion for golf – and so had not fully attended to the charts.

technician. Visit his Web site at www.bwts.com.au. Make this a priority as his stuff is really good. He offers a question and answer session, and he also sends out a free newsletter.

You will find a good rundown on the basics of charting at www.stock charts.com. Go to the Chart School section. Another useful site is Incredible Charts (www.incrediblecharts.com). This was set up by an accountant turned trader based in Australia, and explains technical analysis clearly and simply.

To pull up specific charts, and compare the share price performance of a company with the market's, use the charting facility at FTMarketWatch (www.ftmarket-watch.com). The facility also offers moving averages.

If it helps you to get a feel for them, draw some charts by hand. If you want to draw your own trend lines, use the AIQ charts in the mytrack program (www.mytrack.com). A particularly convenient way to gain access to comprehensive charting facilities is through dedicated technical software. In Seminar 12, I recommend ShareScope.

If you become committed, consider joining the Society of Technical Analysts (www.sta-uk.org). This organization has 600 members, mostly professionals. It offers expensive classes for an examination that leads to a recognized diploma. Members can also attend the Society's monthly talks, and have free access to a lending library.

THE NEXT STEP

In this seminar, we have defined technical analysis, and looked briefly at its origins. In Seminar 8, we will look at the choice of charts at your disposal, and how to use them.

SEMINAR 7 GOLDEN RULES

▌ Do not rely on technical analysis exclusively.

▌ The longer a trend, the more reliable it is, particularly when it is backed by rising volume.

▌ If you are following a trend and this breaks, it is time to take reverse action.

▌ No guru is right forever.

▌ If you become seriously interested in technical analysis, consider joining the Society of Technical Analysts.

Seminar 8

Your choice of charts

INTRODUCTION

In this section, we will look at the types of chart available to you as a technical analyst, how to select from these, and how to use them to the best advantage.

THE CHARTS

The broad view

As a speculator, you will be most interested in charts that focus on short-term price movements. The daily bar chart will typically cover a period of six to nine months. You should also have some longer-term charts, which will have less detail but will provide a broader perspective. This can be incredibly useful to put the daily charts in context. Long-term trends often persist, which makes the charts that show them of value to you even as a short-term speculator.

A professional technical analyst of my acquaintance looks at daily, weekly and monthly charts for every stock that interests him. This way, he often picks up signs that he would have missed from only one chart. I would advise you to follow suit.

Scale

Charts can be plotted on a semi-logarithmic scale. This shows share price or index movements in percentage terms, which puts them in perspective.

As an alternative, charts may be plotted on an arithmetic, or linear, scale. This emphasizes absolute share price movements, and so presents a more sensitive picture. It is suitable if the price range moves only slightly.

The difference between the two is best illustrated by a brief example. On the semi-logarithmic scale, the distance between points 2 and 4 is the same as between 10 and 20, because in both cases it represents a 100 per cent rise. On the arithmetic scale, the latter rise is five times larger than the former because it is measured in absolute terms.

In general, commercial stock chart services use the semi-logarithmic scale. Technical analysis technical packages will allow you to switch from one to another.

Types

You can select between types of chart. The main categories are the line chart, the bar chart, the point and figure chart, equivolume, and Japanese candlesticks. At the bottom of some charts, you will find trading volume represented by vertical bars.

Line chart

The line chart is the simplest kind. As in Figure 8.1, the chart plots the price on the Y-axis, which is vertical, against time on the X-axis, which is horizontal.

The line plots only the closing mid-price of a share, which aficionados feel is the most significant price information. As it does not record the opening stock price or its high and low, it cuts out the noise of intra-day changes. As a result, the chart is short on detail, but it has the advantage of never appearing cluttered.

Some stock market speculators insist on using a line chart, as its very simplicity makes it easy to detect a trend. But none rely on it completely, as they require more information than it provides. A bar chart can be a better bet.

Bar chart

The bar chart is the most popular form of chart. It sometimes has a cluttered appearance, although investment software (see Seminar 12) enables you to zoom in on part of the chart. The scale is more often arithmetic than semi-logarithmic, which is good for focusing on intra-day detail.

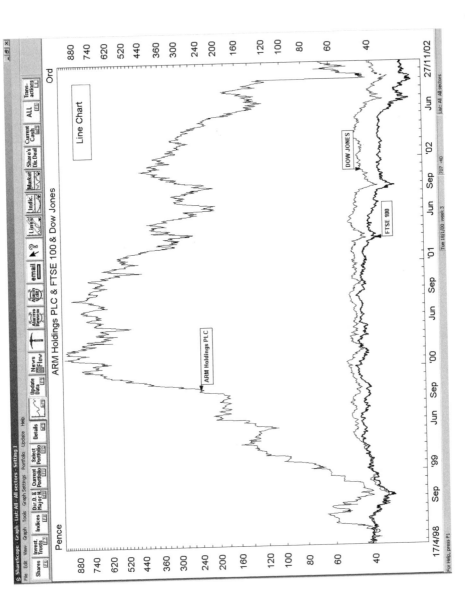

Figure 8.1 Line chart

As in a line chart, the share price is plotted against time. See Figure 8.2 for an example. For each time period, a bar is drawn. The top of the bar represents the high over the period, and the bottom the low. On the left of the bar, a tick shows the opening price. On the right, another tick shows the closing price.

The bar chart often focuses on *daily* price action, within a five-day week, although intra-day bar charts, showing price changes at short intervals throughout the day, and, at the other extreme, longer-term bar charts covering weekly or monthly time periods, are not uncommon. The bar chart typically has volume of trading activity shown underneath in the form of a vertical bar.

These days, users of bar charts focus a lot on the opening price, and this is because of the influence of candlesticks (see below).

Point and figure chart

Introduction

The point and figure chart shows price action in a more concentrated framework than the other types of chart because it ignores the passage of time and records only significant movements. As a result, it is demonstrably easier to detect trend changes, and because you can vary the extent of price movements recorded, the chart has enormous flexibility.

There are drawbacks. Unlike, for instance, the bar chart, the point and figure chart does not record volume separately, although aficionados argue that this is largely reflected in the price changes. It misses out on significant intra-day detail that could have its own message.

A small band of technical analysts use only the point and figure chart. In his book *Point & Figure: Commodity & Stock Trading Techniques* (Traders Press), Kermit C Zieg has said that the average investor can become skilled in the use of this stock market tool in a few minutes. No maths skills, no prior market knowledge or special tools are required.

Many do not share Zieg's optimism. For the uninitiated, the point and figure chart can seem almost incomprehensible compared with, for example, the line chart. Once you are used to it, the going is much easier.

The point and figure chart is based on the premise that the price of a security is governed only by supply and demand. It shows the struggle between the two, and nothing more. If supply is dominant, the share price falls. If demand takes over, the share price rises. If the two are equal, the share price makes sideways movements. The buy and sell signals, unlike on bar charts for instance, are unequivocal, and you are also shown where to place a stop loss.

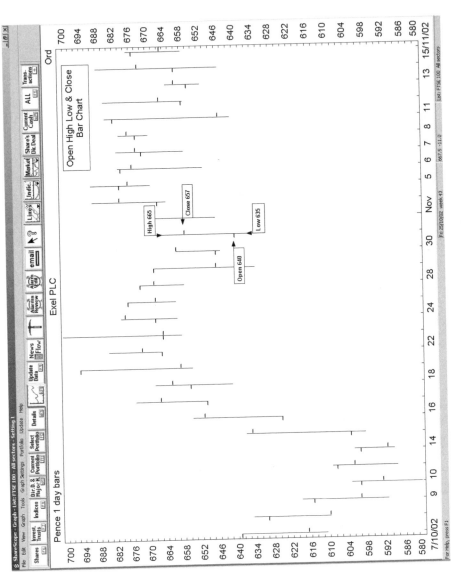

Figure 8.2 Bar chart

Manual maintenance is realistic

Get yourself some graph paper, a pencil, and a copy of a daily newspaper that contains the highs and lows for the previous day, and you can manually maintain your own point and figure charts easily and quickly. The entry and exit points for a stock are clear. By manual charting, you will get a better feel for point and figure than if you use software, although it will take more of your time. It is essential to keep up your charts daily or they become useless.

Incidentally, if you do use software to compose relevant charts (see Seminar 12), as you will eventually if the point and figure bug bites, be wary. Point and figure is a rather weak link in some charting software.

Although this type of chart has existed since the end of the Victorian era, it only came into wider use as a result of the publication in 1958 of *A W Cohen's* book *The Three Box Reversal Method of Point and Figure Stock Market Trading* (Chartcraft, Inc). In the past few years there has been something of a revival in it, and, if used correctly, it can help in your trading. For some traders who stumble upon it late in life, it proves the missing link, the method that they were looking for, albeit not the holy grail.

The three box reversal method is the most popular version of point and figure charting today. It uses the day's high and low prices only, rather than intra-day movements. It has simplified, and, as a result, popularized, the entire process. Investment banks such as Salomon Smith Barney have used the original intra-day method, and both techniques are in operation today. Zieg recommends the three-box reversal method.

As you will see in Figure 8.3, this type of chart resembles a spot-the-ball competition entry, in the words of technical analyst David Charters. The vertical line on the chart represents the share price.

How it works

The noughts and crosses that you will see on the chart are organized logically. If the share price has been trending up, it will need to move by a given measure before an X is recorded. If it has been trending down, it will need to achieve the same measure of movement, although in the other direction, before an O is registered. If the share price changes direction sufficiently, you will start a new column with an X if your previous column was down, or an O if your previous column was up. You will never see an X and an O in the same column.

The measure used to trigger the chart changes is known as the box. The higher the share price of the company on which the chart focuses, the bigger the box will be. For UK shares, the box is typically between 1 and 4 times the share price. In the USA, Dorsey & Associates, a specialist point and figure advisory service, includes on its Web site a table setting the box at 0.25 times any share price up to US\$5.00, and 0.50 times the share price between US\$5.00 and US\$20.00. The box size is 1.00 times the share price between US\$21.00 and US\$100, and 2.00 times that of US\$102 or more.

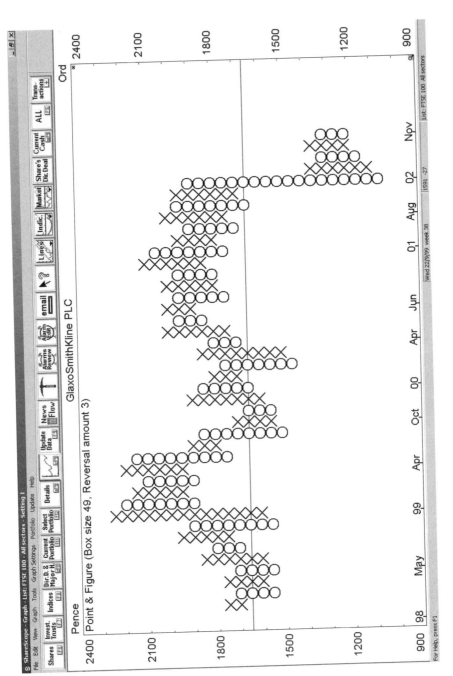

Figure 8.3 Point and figure chart

To provide a time perspective, the chart may have numbers 1–9 that appear instead of X or O to denote the first day of a month in chronological order. For example, on 1 June, the number '6' may appear instead of an 'X' or 'O'. On 1 August, the number '8' may appear. The months of October, November and December are denoted by 'A', 'B' and 'C' respectively as there is not room to have a double-digit number in the box on the chart.

For technical analysts who want to conduct a thorough analysis, it is desirable to have several charts of a single share. Each of these will have a different fraction of the box size normally applied to the stock, which itself becomes larger in accordance with the share price. For long-term observation, you could have a 50 per cent box size, and, for the medium term, as little as 25 per cent.

On computer-generated charts, upward-pointing chevrons indicate price rises, and downward-pointing chevrons the reverse.

Reversal

If the share price breaks the trend and changes direction, it will need to register a reversal before this appears on the chart.

The reversal is often larger than the box size. The most usual type is the three-box reversal, in which case it must be three times the box size.

If there is an upward reversal, an X will be marked, changing from an O. If the reversal is down, an O will be marked, against an X. In either case, a new column will be opened up, which will start one square across.

In the case of both the box and – to a greater extent – the reversal, sideways trading with insignificant share price changes is ignored.

In a book *Point and Figure Trading, A Computer Evaluation* (Dunn & Hargitt), Charles C Thiel and Robert E Davis concluded from lengthy research that the results from the three-box reversal method of point and figure charting could be enhanced by optimization of the box size and the reversal length.

Some technical analysts use a method known as the Count to forecast share price movements. This is an alternative to trend analysis or, for an especially thorough approach, can be used in conjunction with it. The Count is either vertical or horizontal (see box below).

Chart concentration

The sizes of the box and reversal respectively dictate how concentrated the chart will be. If the box and reversal are small, the number of X and O columns tends to be large. Such a chart may cover a day's trading. If the box and reversal are bigger, the columns will be fewer and the chart may cover several weeks or even months.

THE COUNT

The Count gives you a price objective, either vertical or horizontal. You will use the Vertical Count more often, although the Horizontal Count is preferable if you are projecting a breakout from a wide horizontal base on your chart. In the following examples, I will assume that you are using three-box reversal point and figure charting.

The Vertical Count can be bullish or bearish. For the bullish version, count the Xs in the column that has the first buy signal up from the bottom. You will multiply the result by 3 (based on the three-box reversal method), and multiply this by the box value. You will add the resulting figure to the value of the lowest X.

If, for instance, there are five Xs and the box value is 1, and the lowest X is at 20, your formula for the Vertical Count is calculated as follows: $(5 \times 3) \times 1 + 20 = 35$. Therefore, your price objective is 35, although you should take this as very approximate.

The bearish Vertical Count is a similar – not identical – process in reverse. You will count the Os from the first sell signal down from the top, and multiply the figure by 2 (rather than 3 in the bullish equivalent), and multiply this by the value of the box. Subtract the result from the value of the highest O.

The bullish Horizontal Price Objective involves measuring the number of columns in the broadest horizontal line of the base that is complete, ie without gaps. You will multiply this figure by 3, and the result by the value of the box, and then add this to the value of the lowest line in the base.

Here is your price objective. The bearish version involves multiplying the columns across the base by 2, and this result by the box's value, and then subtracting the overall result from the value at the top of the base.

Your calculation becomes slightly more complicated when the box size changes on the chart as the share price shifts. If you are measuring a price objective, you will, as we have seen, use the value of the box in your calculation. For some of your calculation, the box may, for example, be 0.5, and for the rest of it – based on a share price that has risen – 1. In such a case, you will have to calculate each part separately and add them together.

Patterns and trend lines

On intra-day point and figure charts, patterns are similar to those on bar charts. They often include a congestion area, which is known as a fulcrum. Trend analysis is also as applied to bar charts.

On three-box reversal point and figure charts, the trend line (see Seminar 9) is always drawn at 45 degrees. There are four main types. There is the bullish support line and the bullish resistance line, which create their own trading channel. The bearish support line and the bearish resistance line do similar. You can redraw new trend lines as price action develops, so redefining boundaries for your own trading action. For example, if the share price in a bull market declines to the bullish support line, you may expect it to bounce up, and may buy on weakness. If it breaks the support line, this is bearish. We will look at support and resistance lines, and the trading channels sandwiched between them, in more detail elsewhere in the book.

The verdict

The point and figure chart is ridiculed and misunderstood, ignored and hated. By a vociferous and expert minority, it is loved and cherished. The side of the camp where *you* end up will depend on how much you find out about this time-tested method, and whether you acknowledge that supply and demand are everything in assessing securities for likely future performance. Remember, you can use point and figure in conjunction with other charting techniques, although you must avoid an overkill.

Jeremy du Plessis, dubbed the UK's most qualified technical analyst, favours the point and figure chart as, in his own words, he finds he can become intimately engaged with it, although he has other strings to his bow. David Fuller, another well-known technical analyst, focuses on this type of chart, but again has a much broader expertise. Not everybody is so convinced (see box opposite).

If you want to explore point and figure charting further, an excellent place to start is the Web site of Dorsey Wright Associates (www.dorsey wright.com), a US stockbroking advisory service that specializes in this type of charting. You will find here a free course at its online Point and Figure University. All you need to do is to register to get started. I have in my time been a student on this course and let me tell you that it is absolutely excellent.

Equivolume chart

On an equivolume chart, price changes are correlated with volume but not with time. The chart takes the form of a box whose width is determined by volume. The top line shows the highest price reached, and the bottom line the lowest.

Candlesticks

Basics

Japanese traders have been using candlesticks since the Japanese stock market started in the 1870s. It is only recently that the method became

CONFESSIONS OF A POINT AND FIGURE EXPERT

Here is a letter I received via my Web site advisory service (I have changed the writer's name). I think it is self-explanatory and I applaud the writer for his honesty.

Dear Mr Davidson,
I borrowed a copy of your book *How to Win in a Volatile Stock Market* from the local library. May I congratulate on the content that hopefully will enable me to be a little more successful than relying on the art, if one may call it that, of interpreting charts.

Back in the early 1970s I ran an investment advisory service for private investors using point and figure charts as the basis for my forecasts. I correctly called the impending bear market in early 1974, advising clients to sell in advance.

Then I started finding that technical analysis alone did not work. My approach was proving too narrow, and it was missing the mark. Fundamentals – what were they? The way that I worked, you did not even have to know what the company did. I was worried by the prospect of my clients going to ground.

The upshot was that I decided to close the business, offering clients a refund or transferring their subscription to my service elsewhere. I then followed an entirely different business career until selling out in the 1980s, reinvesting in the stock market and getting caught for some £20,000 with my so-called expert knowledge of Point & Figure. This seems to bear out some of your criticisms of technical analysis.

Now being a little older and wiser, I intend to invest £40,000 to £45,000 selecting stocks on fundamentals using the Bargain Hunters Investment Flexi-System explained in your book. As a gesture to technical analysis, I will, however, endeavour to use Overbought/Oversold and Relative Strength to assist timing.

Regards
Francis Evans

popular in the West. Like any form of technical analysis, candlesticks retain an element of subjectivity – tipping the balance of probability perhaps, but never more.

Candlesticks make a memorable form of chart, due partly to their contrasting blacks and whites (originally green and red), as shown in Figure 8.5. Many individual candlestick patterns are easily remembered from their graphic names such as Hammer or Morning Star. Others such as the Yoriki

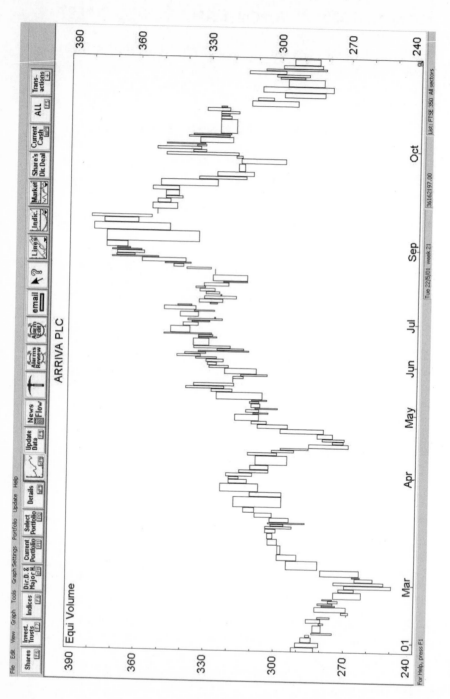

Figure 8.4 Equivolume

STOCK MARKET SPECULATORS' HALL OF FAME

Member No 2 – Steve Nison

Steven Nison is considered on an only half tongue-in-cheek basis as the father of Japanese candlesticks. He has written the definitive books on the subject, *Japanese Candlestick Charting Techniques* and *Beyond Candlesticks*, which have together sold over 75,000 copies.

In the 1980s, Nison was working in the futures research department of broker Shearson Lehman Hutton. He was providing trade recommendations to futures traders which were, unknown to them, based on candlestick charts, a concept then largely unknown in the West.

Subsequently, Nison moved to broker Merrill Lynch as a senior technical analyst, where he wrote a 15-page booklet on candle charts. The bank received 10,000 requests for it.

Nison recommends that investors should use candlesticks as a tool and not a system. He mixes candlestick usage with various traditional Western methods of technical analysis.

Today, Nison runs seminars on candlestick analysis around the world, including, recently, in the UK. He advises that you should never place a trade as a result of candle signals until you have considered its risk/reward potential.

To find out more about Steve Nison and his life work, visit his informative Web site at www.candlecharts.com.

---

are blatantly Japanese. As the Japanese say, no two persons' faces are the same, and this principle applies to candle patterns.

Steven Nison has done more than anybody else to popularize candlesticks (see box above).

As Nison has made clear, candlesticks have their limitations. They can only be created when the opening share price is available, as they focus on its relationship with the closing price.

This can create a vivid and useful picture of share price movements. It can play havoc with the portrayal of major index movements due to the extreme volatility that can take place at the start of the day, setting the technical opening level for an index at a premature and so unrealistic level.

Bar charts, in contrast, treat all share price information equally, although record opening and closing prices as ticks, so giving them less emphasis. Differences in emphasis apart, bar charts and candlesticks provide broadly the same information.

Candlesticks give more priority to *reversal* than *continuation* signals. This way, a reversal is signalled quickly, whereas if you use Western techniques

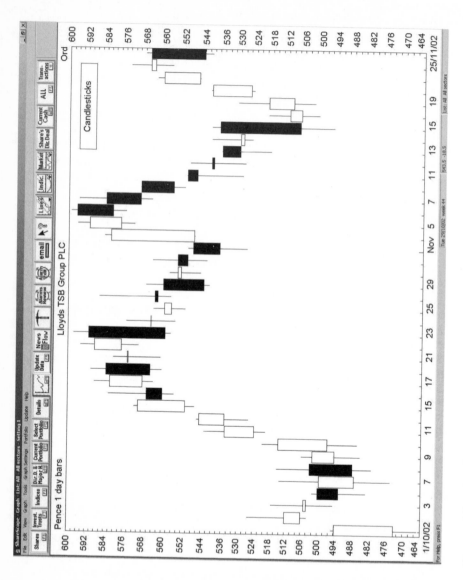

Figure 8.5 Candlesticks

such as trends or moving averages with a different type of chart, it can take much longer. Candlesticks traditionally ignore volume and trend lines, although the software is now incorporating these as innovations.

Given this profile, candlesticks are best used for examining share price movements over a short period, which is useful for traders but not so much for medium- to long-term investors. As candles need a closing as well as opening price, you must either wait until the end of your time frame, or you can cut it short and take an instant check.

As in any technical analysis, candlesticks are considered more reliable if more than one pattern is confirming the signal or trend.

Formation

The candle is based initially on a vertical line that extends from the high to the low of the share price over the given period (often a day). A horizontal line crosses this vertical line at the stock's opening price, and another crosses it at the closing price. The two horizontal lines are joined up on either side, creating a vertical rectangle known as a *real body*.

If the price became lower at close than it had been at opening, the real body is black (bearish). If the price became higher, the real body is white (bullish). This represents a market struggle between bulls and bears in a vivid, immediately accessible form.

The *shadows* on the candlestick represent the high and low prices where these have extended beyond the range between the opening and closing price. The straight line above the rectangle is the *upper* shadow, and the straight line below the rectangle is the *lower* shadow.

The taller the candle, the stronger the signal. It shows, if white, that the bulls have triumphed in an extended range or, if black, that the bears have won.

A tall, white candle opening at or near a trading session's low and closing at or near its high is a strong bullish sign. A long black candle that opens at or near the high of a session is bearish.

Pay attention to the shadows, however. These show where the market has accepted or rejected prices that are outside the open and close. For instance, a tall, white candle is less bullish if it has a tall, upper shadow as this shows that buyers have declined to sustain a higher intra-session price by close. A black candle is similarly less bearish if it has a long lower shadow, so showing that the market has rejected by close an intra-session decline to new lows.

Add volume analysis and this will give a further dimension to a candlestick's likely significance. If a move is backed by high volume, it will be much stronger than if the volume is low.

If the price of the real body is the same at close as it was at opening, the candle is called a doji. You will find the doji in markets that are either trendless or about to become so, representing investor indecisiveness. The doji warns you that a decisive trend shift may be about to occur.

Figure 8.6   Real body (black)

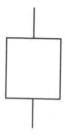

Figure 8.7   Real body (white)

Should it arise after a share price rally, the doji is a strong signal that you should get out of the shares as the bull trend is tired and may be on the verge of lapsing. The doji does not so easily signify a market bottom.

Figure 8.8   Doji

Advantages

The advantage of candlesticks over other charts is the sheer amount of extra information that they provide. The key to this is the shadows, as well as how these combine with the real bodies to provide, on balance, more information than any other type of chart, and clearly.

Candlesticks are not enough on their own and should be only one technical method that you use. As when used with volume, candlesticks are compatible with Western charting techniques, either alongside each other or, to some extent, merged.

For instance, candles will indicate likely reversals, but not the extent of the likely turn. To set price targets, you will also need a Western type of chart.

Candlesticks indicate points of support and resistance, one of the most basic techniques in Western technical analysis. If, for example, a market is trading sideways for a period, this is, in candlesticks terminology, within a box range. The Western equivalent is consolidation.

If the share price breaks below the box range, it is breaching the support line that forms the range's lower boundary, demonstrating that buyers were not prepared to support the price. It is a bearish signal. If, however, the price breaks above the range, so passing the resistance line that forms the range's upper boundary, it is bullish sign.

We will look at support and resistance again in Seminar 9. We will also then look at trend lines, which are drawn against a session's high and low. In candles, these are represented by the tips of the upper and lower shadows.

Western attitudes

Candlesticks have an eastern aura about them. They are said to offer an intuitive element to advanced users.

UK technical analysts seem to be increasingly impressed with candlesticks. The Society of Technical Analysts once invited me to a lecture by leading technical analyst Tom Pelc. He had a dual message. First, technical analysts should persist against cynicism. Second, candlesticks were the way forward. Not all are so enthusiastic.

We will take a further look at candlestick patterns in Seminar 10.

THE NEXT STEP

Once you have selected your charts, how will you use them? We shall turn our attention to this in the next seminar.

SEMINAR 8 GOLDEN RULES

▌ Use more than one chart for stocks in which you are interested.

▌ The chart plotted on an arithmetic scale shows absolute price movements, which is suitable if these are small. If it is plotted on a semi-logarithmic scale, it shows percentage movements, which provides a sense of perspective.

▌ The line chart offers uncluttered information, making it easy to spot a trend, but it is otherwise not very informative.

❚ The bar chart is the most popular kind. It offers similar information to candlesticks but with different emphasis.

❚ The point and figure chart does not show time or volume. It cuts out distracting noise, and gives very definite buy and sell signals.

❚ Equivolume charts show price changes correlated with volume but not with time.

❚ Candlesticks focus on the relationship between opening and closing prices, and so are valuable for traders and short-term investors. They can and should be used in conjunction with Western methods of technical analysis.

❚ The taller the candle, the stronger its signal.

Seminar 9

More secrets of technical analysis

INTRODUCTION

In this section, we will look at trend theory. As part of this we will scrutinize some of the well-known patterns in technical analysis.

TREND ANALYSIS

The basics

As a trader, you should follow the trend, according to every creed of technical analysis. To make serious money, it is best to get in near the start, which means that you need to detect a trend change early. You should first identify the original trend, and then the crucial reversal signal. If this signal is confirmed, you should act.

To detect a change in trend in this way is one of the hardest skills of technical analysis. It is also one of the most important. You must aim for probabilities, not certainties, and to be right more often than you are wrong.

Even if the majority of your trades lose money, you can still make money on the winners if you cut your losses and run your profits, as I demonstrated in Seminar 4.

The nature of trends

A trend can be long-, medium-, or short-term, and we can be following any one or more of these. A long-term trend is made up of shorter ones, and these can be split further.

If you are watching the market as a whole, you will be concerned with the primary trend, as explained by Dow theory (see Seminar 7). This could be as short as five months, but usually lasts at least a year or two, perhaps longer.

If the primary trend is up, this represents a bull market, and, if down, a bear market. As a rule of thumb, you should trade with the primary trend.

A good tactic is to wait until the primary trend reverses into what Dow Theory has termed a secondary reaction. This is a retracement of between one and two-thirds of the previous gain.

The market will then rally in a medium-term trend that lasts typically between one and eight months. This may take longer than the previous market reaction.

Catch this medium-term trend early, and you will make money as a speculator. Note that you will be trading in the direction of the primary as well as the medium-term trend.

You will find it more difficult to catch short-term trends as these last for only three to seven weeks. These are the equivalent to the minor trend in Dow theory, and similarly often arise from market manipulation.

Trend lines

To detect a trend on your charts, draw a trend line. You will have this if you can draw a straight line between any two or, preferably, three tops on your chart that are rising or falling in one direction, and a similar line in the same direction for any two or three bottoms.

The straight line through the tops is termed the trend line and the straight line through the bottoms is the return line.

So long as tops and bottoms keep rising, an up trend continues. Conversely, while they fall, there is a down trend. As a speculator you should be watching for a reversal, at which point, perhaps before further price movement confirms it, you should take action.

Fan lines

A trend is not always confirmed. Sometimes, the market starts to show a trend, then this breaks, and a separate trend is initiated, and then this is broken again to give way to another. These trend lines, all drawn from the same starting point, are called fan lines.

Support and resistance

On the chart, the share price typically rises within limits defined by previous investor action.

The resistance level is the highest point that a share or index will reach. It is here that past investors have declined to buy further and so the price has stopped rising, with sellers moving in. History often repeats itself, and this establishes a firm resistance level.

On the same principle, the support level is where investors have stopped selling and so the price has stopped falling, and buyers move in. Again, past investor action is likely to have established this.

As a rule of thumb, the longer a support or resistance line lasts, or the more it is tested, the more effective it will be.

Support and resistance often occur at round numbers. For the FTSE 100, for instance, the 4,000 level has proved significant. In the case of stocks, 90p, 100p or 200p have proved watersheds.

Stock market trader David Jones, who operates training courses in London, bases many of his own trading decisions on support and resistance. 'If a share price rises through the resistance line, you buy,' he has said. 'If it goes through the support line, you sell. This works for any market.'

In Jones's view, the best traders are those who can reverse their trade from long to short in an instant.

The trend channel

Now that we are familiar with the concepts of support and resistance, we can construct a trend channel on our imaginary chart.

First, let us recall the imaginary trend line that we have drawn, defined as touching three tops. For the purpose of our trend channel, it indicates resistance. The return line that we have drawn, which touches three bottoms, indicates support.

Between the trend line and the return line runs the trend channel. For a volatile stock, its trend channel will be large. In this case, you will be able to buy and sell profitably on price fluctuations within the channel.

Let us be more specific and divide the trend channel along the middle with a horizontal line. When the share price is below this line, it is your cue to buy the shares. When it rises above it, you should sell.

Trend penetration

The big moment for a trader is when the share price falls below the support level or rises above the resistance level. In such cases, it _penetrates_ the trend.

If the share price falls below the support level, this becomes the new resistance line. The change is logical due to shareholder action. Some

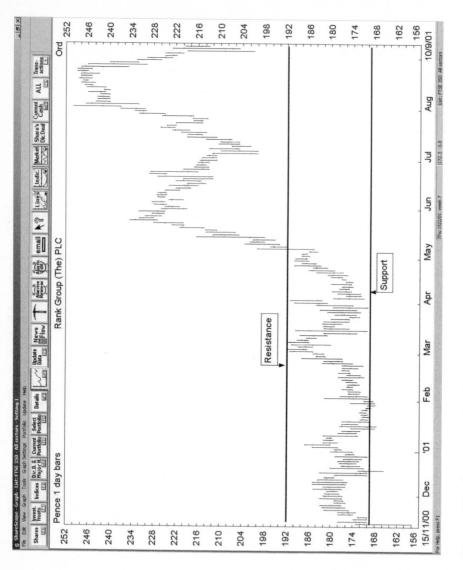

Figure 9.1 Support and resistance

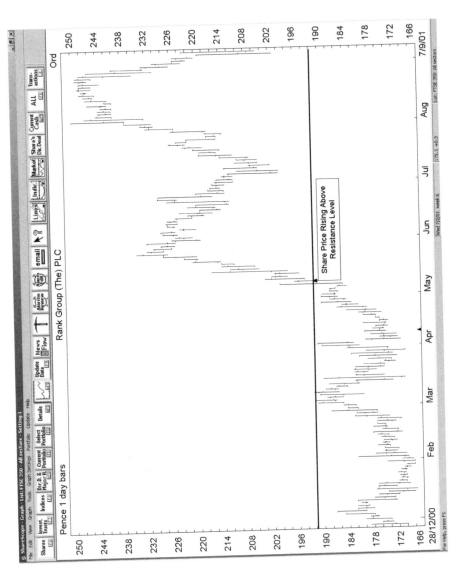

Figure 9.2 Share prices rises above resistance line

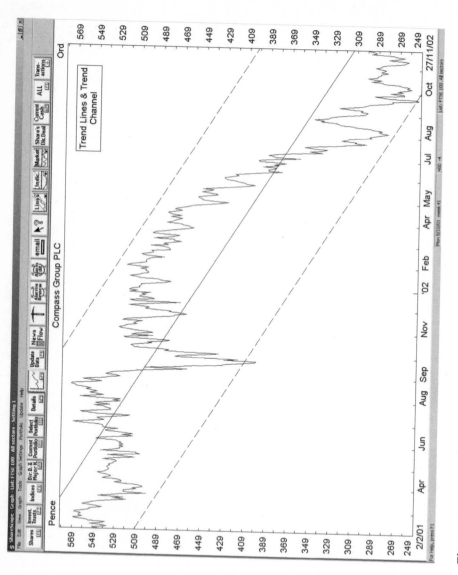

Figure 9.3 Trend lines and trend channel

shareholders will have failed to sell out before the price plummeted. If it rises back to the old support line they will seize this second opportunity and sell, so establishing this as a resistance level.

On the same principle, the resistance level after the share price has risen above it becomes the new support level.

To speculate at less risk, buy or sell as soon as possible after penetration of the trend.

To reduce the risk of acting on a share price movement that turns out false, make sure that the penetration is significant and is accompanied by heavy trading volume. If it was instigated by important news such as takeover interest, this also increases the odds of a genuine penetration.

In the next few pages, we will look at patterns that help you to detect a change in trend.

PATTERNS

Introduction

A line that is in fluctuation over a period will represent a struggle between buyers and sellers. The result is a pattern that, in its completed form, can resemble recognized shapes such as a triangle or rectangle. On this basis, it is named and categorized.

Eventually, one side of the fluctuating pattern on the chart gets the upper hand, and breaks out. If it does so decisively, this forms the tail out of the pattern. It indicates not that more buyers or sellers have arrived, but simply that more of the existing players have decided, on balance, to make the decisive move.

The move could be either up or down, and this is theoretically dictated by the type of pattern formed. Continuation patterns *confirm* the trend by indicating that the share price will continue in the direction that it had been taking before the pattern started. Reversal patterns indicate that the trend is *changing*. For these patterns to have validity, there will obviously need to have been a preceding trend.

If a pattern is the means by which a share price that has risen reverses and falls, this is a distribution top. If the pattern enables a share price that has fallen to rise again, this is an accumulation bottom.

No patterns are completely reliable, and some technical analysts such as David Fuller will not give them much credibility. Others are selective in their faith. Many consider that the head and shoulders, for instance, is quite reliable, but are more sceptical about the triangle. We will be looking at these and other patterns later in this seminar.

The believers agree that the larger and the longer lasting is the pattern, the more impact it will have on the share price. They reason that if the battle between buyers and sellers is prolonged, this will weaken the losing side and strengthen the winning side.

Trading volume will usually rise with the breakout, and it has more significance on an upside than on a downside movement. At the point of breakout, the losers will need time to re-gather strength.

Following the breakout, there is often a temporary retracement. This is likely to extend back to the original pattern, or nearly so. This is not in itself significant, but you should beware of false breakouts. When assessing long-term trends, you could use a filter, and consider a move to be a breakout only if it achieves 5 per cent or more of the share price. If a high volume of trading accompanies the breakout in either direction, this is a corroborating force.

How long will the breakout last? The rule is that you measure the full depth of the pattern, and project this as a minimum target from the point of breakout. In the examples that follow, I will sometimes apply this to specific patterns, but the rule works generally. As a maximum, the pattern following breakout could last as long as the previous market movement.

Continuation patterns

Continuation patterns tend to last for a shorter time than reversal patterns. Here are some of the main types.

The rectangle

The rectangle consists of two lines on the chart. The top one indicates resistance, the lower one support. The share price will reach peaks and troughs within these boundaries as it fluctuates. In this way, it will create a rectangular trend channel. Traders can profit on the small price swings within the rectangle that represent a conflict between buyers and sellers. This market will remain trendless until a breakout, which will typically take months.

Most often, the breakout will continue the trend that prevailed before the rectangle arose. This is most likely to be so if, as the share price fluctuates, the volume is heavier on the up movements than on the down. If the volume does the reverse, the rectangle is more likely to lead to a breakout in the opposite direction from the trend that prevailed before the pattern commenced.

Once you have a breakout, the target minimum price movement should be the width of the preceding rectangle. If the breakout is up, the former resistance line, which is the top one on the rectangle, will become a support line. If the breakout is down, the former support line, which is the bottom line of the rectangle, will become a resistance line.

The triangle

The triangle is so named because the share price movement on the chart is shaped in this form. As the share price zigzags across the chart, at least

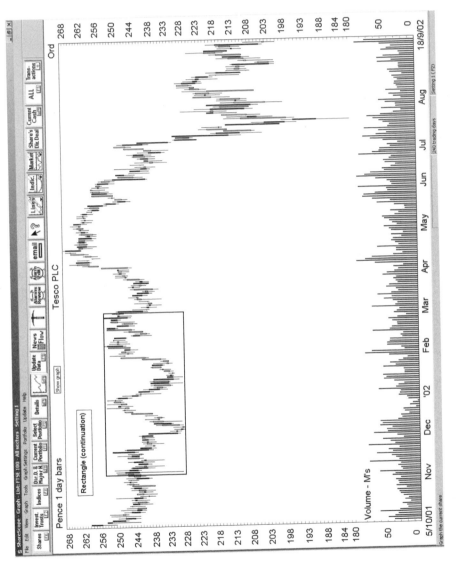

Figure 9.4 Rectangle

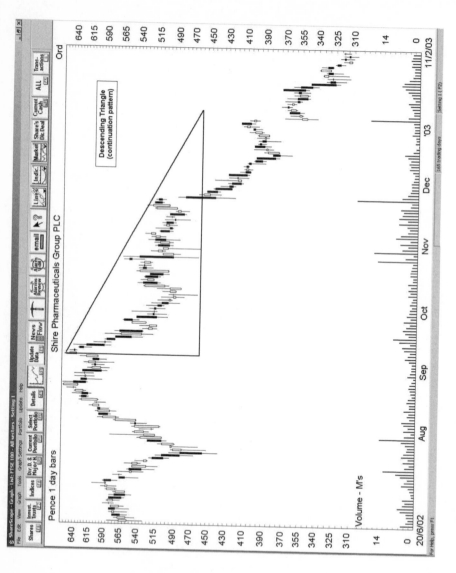

Figure 9.5 Descending triangle

two trend tops are required, which means that the share price must have dipped significantly in the periods between their occurrence.

Like the rectangle, the triangle is mostly a continuation pattern, but it is considered less trustworthy and sometimes instead signals a reversal. It may turn into a rectangle, or a breakout may occur in the opposite direction to that expected. Sometimes the triangle needs redrawing altogether.

The triangle may be symmetrical, which means that its upper trend line descends, and its lower one ascends, and the two converge. It may alternatively be an ascending type, which has a flat upper trend line, and a rising lower one, or a descending type, which has a rising upper trend line and a flat lower one.

The descending and ascending types of triangle are also known as the right-angled triangle. Many believe that this is the most reliable type. In addition, it is a sign of reliability for any triangle when the price frequently touches its sides.

Another name for the triangle is the coil, as this is how it looks after price fluctuations have narrowed. This also describes the breakout action, which is as if from a spring wound ever more tightly that has suddenly been freed.

If the breakout arises after half but before three-quarters of the length of the triangle (between its start and its point), it is said to be more trustworthy. If it lingers further into the apex (the technical word for its point), it loses its force.

Following the breakout, expect the initial rise or fall of the share price to correspond with the depth of the triangle.

Generally, volume of trading should decline as the pattern proceeds, but should rise sharply on breakout, indicating buying strength behind the move. As generally in patterns, it is more significant when the share price is rising than when it is falling.

The flag

The flag is a fairly common continuation pattern, and is considered highly reliable. This is a brief consolidation in the share price in about the middle of a move in the market, and is effectively a bent rectangle, with the two trend lines typically slanted in the opposite direction of the trend. In an up trend, the flag forms after a steep and almost straight upturn in the share price. Trading volume will have risen, driven largely by profit takers.

Eventually, the share price stagnates, and a rally comes that fails to regain previous heights or trading volume. The share price will then fluctuate. Tops and bottoms are likely to sink, on declining trading volume. In a down trend, the flag does the same in reverse.

You will find flags mainly on short-term charts, as the pattern is typically completed in less than three weeks. In a down trend, it tends to be faster.

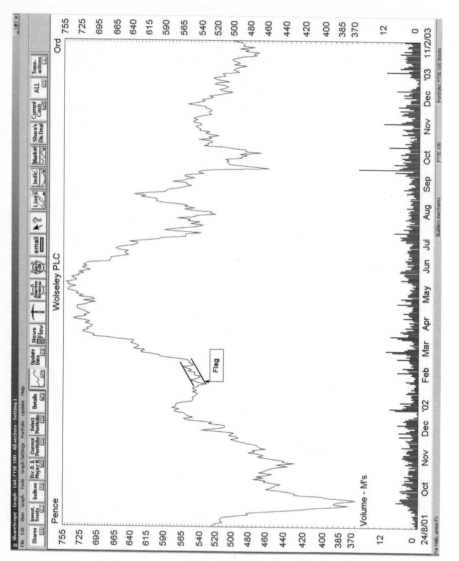

Figure 9.6 Flag

The pennant

A pennant is similar to a flag, with the difference that its boundary lines converge rather than run parallel. It is similarly formed on declining volume after the share price has moved up or down fast in the middle of a market move. See Fig 9.7 for an example.

Another way to view a pennant is as a triangle that slopes *down* during an upturn, and *up* in a downturn. It is also a version of the wedge, which we will examine shortly.

As with the flag, the pennant is usually completed in less than three weeks, with greater speed in a down trend.

The wedge

The wedge has boundary lines that slope together either up or down into an apex. It is similar to a symmetrical triangle. The difference is that the symmetrical triangle has the top line slanting down and the bottom one up. By way of further comparison, the right-angled triangle has the top line either up or down, and the bottom one horizontal.

The wedge is slanted against the prevailing trend, and you must view it accordingly. If the wedge is falling, this is a bullish sign, and if it is rising, this is bearish.

The wedge takes more than three weeks to finish, failing which it is better classified as a pennant, and typically less than three months. See the example in Fig 9.8.

As a rising pattern, the wedge is common in bear market rallies. The two lines progress up from left to right, with the lower one naturally steeper. As prices advance towards a point, trading volume typically declines. A breakout follows on the downside, and the share price declines sharply. Pundits see this as evidence that a bear market is continuing during depressed market conditions.

In a falling wedge, the lines progress down from left to right. Following a breakout, the share price is likely to drift but then to start rising.

Reversal patterns

The head and shoulders

The head and shoulders is usually a reversal pattern, although it occasionally indicates continuation. This pattern is said to demonstrate the Dow Theory working for an individual share in a down trend.

Many technicians see the head and shoulders as an unmistakable sign of a downturn in the share price or index, as comes at the end of a bull market, although tests suggest that it is unreliable.

The head and shoulders develops as the share price on the chart moves up and back forming the left shoulder, to the accompaniment of a higher

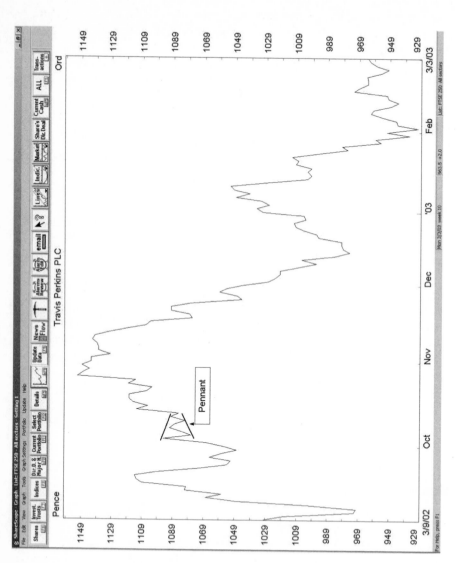

Figure 9.7 Pennant

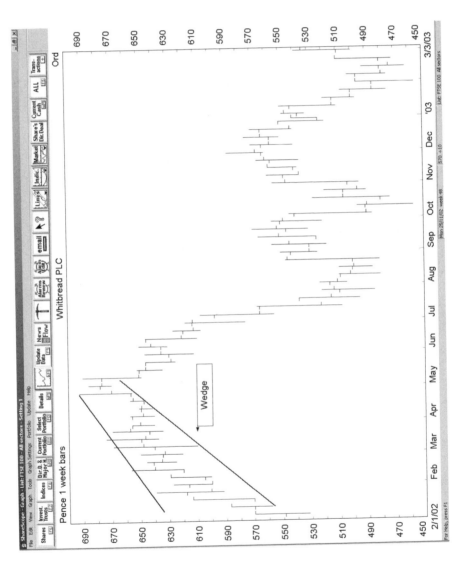

Figure 9.8 Wedge

level of trading volume than usual. The price then rises to a new high, again on substantial volume, and drops back again on lower volume. This creates the head. The level to which it has dropped back in forming the pattern is known as the neckline. This is basically a support level across the bottoms of the left shoulder and neck.

Next, the share price again rises, this time to form the right shoulder, which is lower than the head. The move is on lower volume than when either the left shoulder or the head were formed. The share price will then drop back to break the neckline by at least 3 per cent.

Once the breakout has occurred, pundits expect the share price to fall by at least an amount equivalent to the measurable distance between the top of the head and the neckline. It could move as much as the entire previous trend.

Given the variables, how can you detect a *bona fide* head and shoulders in its early stages? As we have seen, trading volume should decline as the right shoulder rises. This corroborates that the right shoulder represents an initial rally in a downward trend.

There is also a reverse head and shoulders, with a similar measuring technique. Here is a bullish reversal signal that technical analysts look for at the end of a bear market. In this case volume should increase from a low level on the right shoulder rally, and particularly from the point of upward breakout.

Technicians make the head and shoulders sound precise, but, in practice, it is anything but. The pattern can slope in any direction, and no formation of the head and shoulders is exactly like another.

Sometimes the head and shoulders form, and the unexpected happens. The price may move only slightly below the neckline or not as far as that. Next thing, buyers may pile in, encouraged by the temporary weakness in the share price, and short sellers may rush to cover their position. As a result, the share price may soar, with trading volume also up enormously.

The broadening formation

The broadening formation, also known as megaphone, is rare, and happens when a market is at its peak and out of control, with investors reacting to wild rumours.

In this pattern, the price fluctuations become broader on rising volume, forming a pattern that is the reverse to the triangle, in which volume declines. You should join the pattern's tops, of which there should be at least three, with one trend line. You should similarly join the bottoms, of which there should be at least two, with another trend line. The two trend lines will diverge.

A sharp decline often follows the broadening formation, with a temporary retracement. This pattern is bearish and is likely to arise in the final stages of a tired bull market. It can resemble the head and shoulders, only without the right side shoulder.

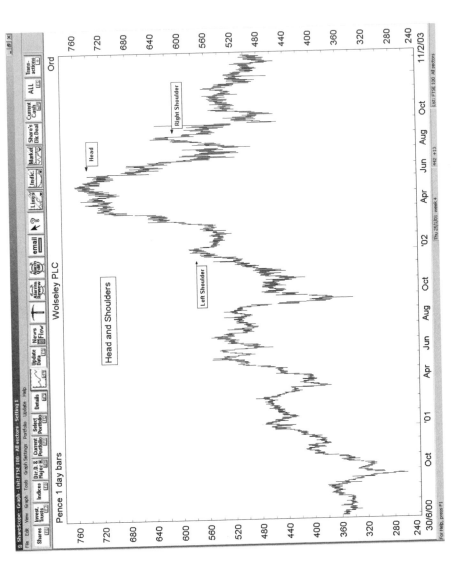

Figure 9.9 Head and shoulders

THE FLIP TEST

Think you have spotted a pattern in the charts? Does it stand the flip test? Jeremy du Plessis, a seasoned technical analyst, introduced this technique to me.

If a chart seems to show a buy signal the right side up, flip it. Now that it is upside down, does it seem to show a sell signal? If this corroborating factor is there, the pattern is more likely to be *bona fide*.

You can also use the method in reverse. A chart showing a sell signal, when reversed, should seem to show a buy signal.

The double top

The double top, also known as the M pattern, arises quite frequently, although is rarely perfectly formed. It is said to be quite reliable, but it is hard to detect until it has actually happened.

The pattern is formed from a share price that rises to a new high typically on higher volume, then declines on lower volume and rises again, but on less trading volume, which is itself a bearish indicator. It is likely to reach the previous peak but will not succeed in going higher.

At a breakout downward, trading volume may increase, and the minimum target price should be a length that corresponds with that of the height of the pattern, on the same principle as with the head and shoulders.

The double bottom

The double bottom, also known as the W pattern, is a double top in reverse, and is a bullish sign. This pattern is only reliable if the second bottom is accompanied by overall rising volume. If the price level during the second bottom declines a little, this is not significant.

In late 2002, a double bottom had arisen in the two main US stock market indices, the Dow Jones Industrial Average, and, more strongly, in the S&P 500. But trading volume had not increased. This suggested that investors were not rushing to buy, and that the bullish chart signals were weak. Time proved the diagnosis right.

Triple or quadruple tops

Double tops can become triple or quadruple tops, leading to a likely stronger downward trend.

These rare reversal patterns are formed in various ways. If they are genuine, they are prolonged versions of the double top, with the tops often spaced more closely and less evenly. The pattern resembles a head and shoulders with a low head.

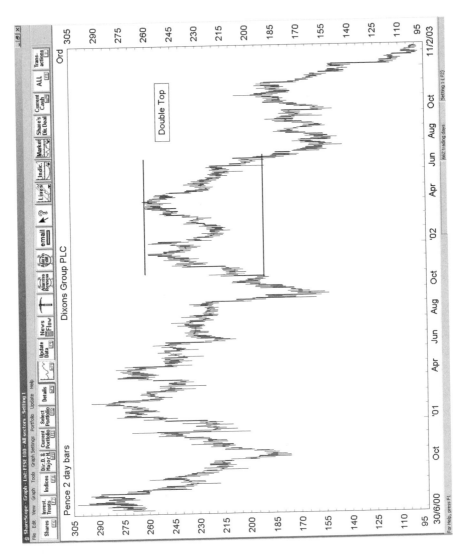

Figure 9.10 Double top

In all cases, trading volume should decline with each top. Following the third or fourth top, the share price should fall below the level of the valley floor.

Triple or quadruple bottoms

These rare bullish reversal patterns are triple or quadruple tops in reverse.

The diamond

The diamond is a rare bearish reversal pattern that can arise in highly active markets. It is a broadening formation that converts into a symmetrical triangle. In appearance, it is a form of head and shoulders with a V-shaped neckline. See below.

The one-day reversal

The one-day reversal comes after the share price has been rising or falling for a long time. In this pattern, the share price may open higher than the previous night's close, so leaving a gap on the chart (see Seminar 10).

The share price will rise sharply and continually during the day, accompanied by very high trading volume. At some point before close, the price will reverse, falling back to the level at which it had started in the morning. Subsequently, the price will consolidate for a while.

The two-day reversal

The two-day reversal is an extended version of the above. On the first day, the share price moves to a new high, and closes at or near this level. On the second day, it opens at a similar level, but, by close, it will have retraced the entire first day's advance.

Saucers

Also known as rounded tops or rounded bottoms, saucers occur only infrequently. They represent a gradual reversal, and are typically on longer-term charts. The longer they last, the more likely they are to lead to reversal, but it is notoriously hard to detect the breakout point.

Sometimes, you have one saucer following another very quickly. In this sequence, which may develop when a stock with a large market float is rising in value from a low point, they indicate continuation. Several saucers may occur in three weeks or more on rising trading volume.

Spikes

These are shaped like a V, arise very quickly, and create an abrupt reversal on substantial volume.

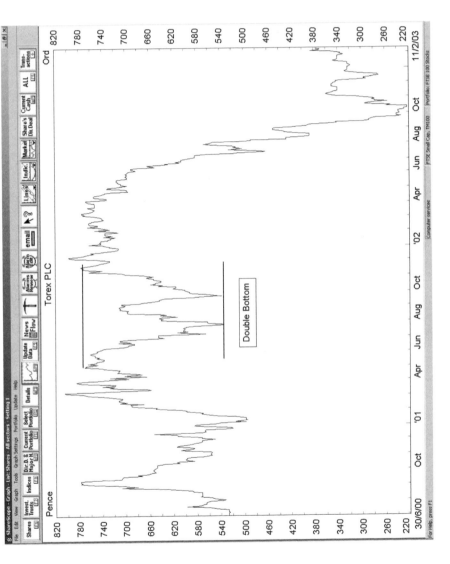

Figure 9.11 Double bottom

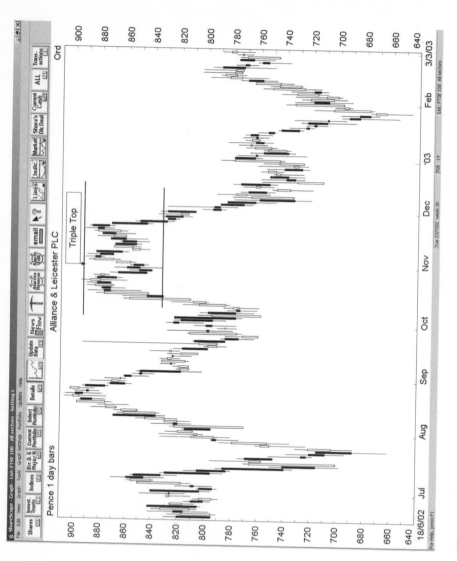

Figure 9.12 Triple top

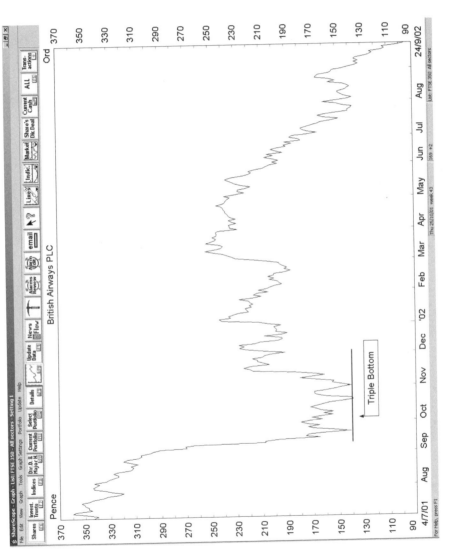

Figure 9.13 Triple bottom

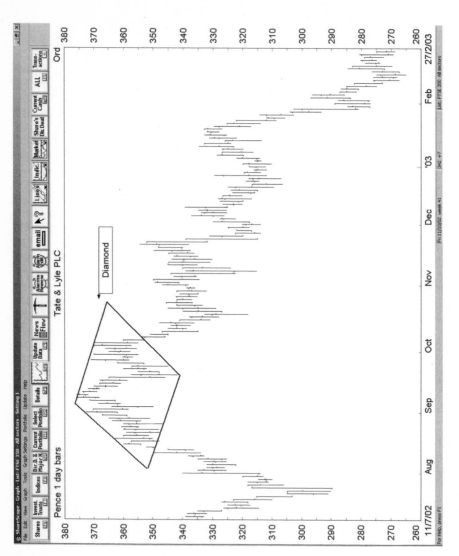

Figure 9.14 Diamond

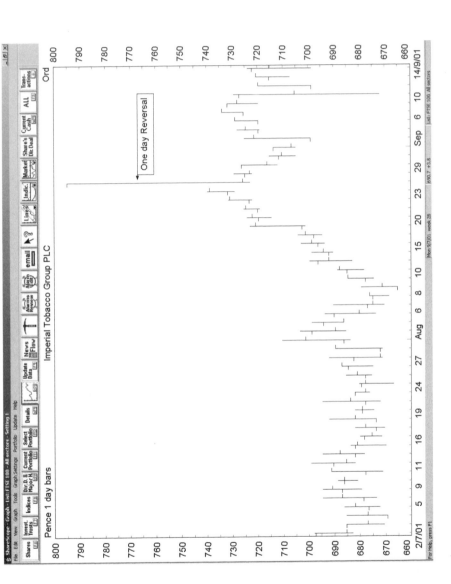

Figure 9.15 One-day reversal

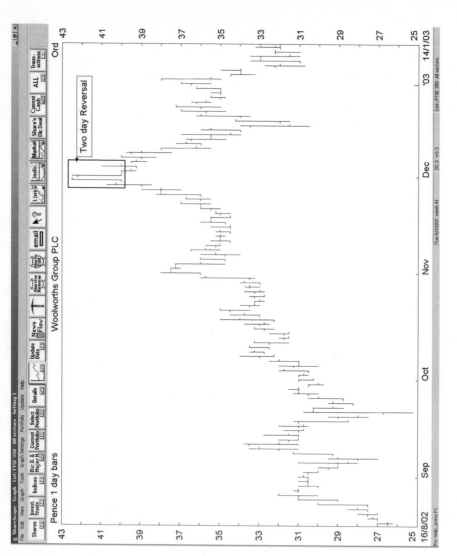

Figure 9.16 Two-day reversal

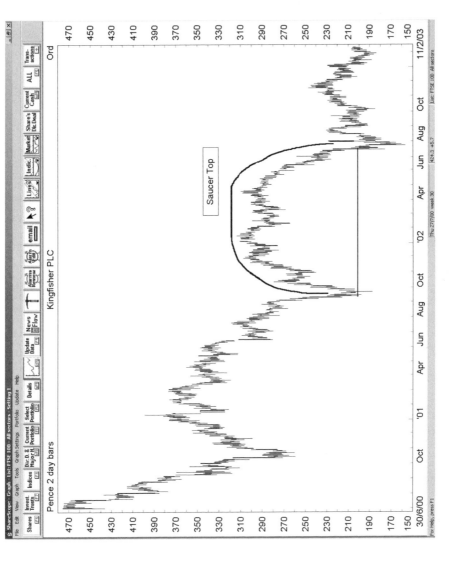

Figure 9.17 Saucer top

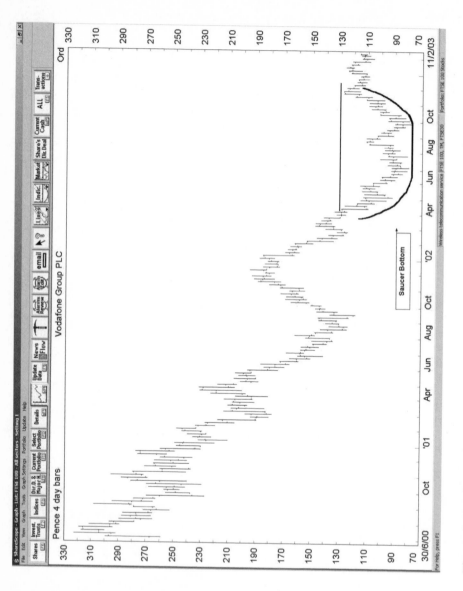

Figure 9.18 Saucer bottom

THE NEXT STEP

In the next seminar, we will look at some further important price patterns.

SEMINAR 9 GOLDEN RULES

▌ Follow the trend in your trading, and get in early.

▌ Catch a medium trend early in the direction of the primary trend, and you can make money.

▌ Watch for a reversal in an up or down trend. This is your signal to take action.

▌ The longer a support or resistance line lasts, the more effective it will be. It often occurs at round numbers.

▌ Patterns are never reliable. But some such as the head and shoulders are trusted more than others.

▌ Technical analysts expect a breakout to be at least the length of a preceding pattern.

▌ The rectangle is usually a continuation pattern, but can instead indicate reversal.

▌ The triangle is seen as more reliable if it is right-angled, if the price frequently touches the sides and if the breakout arises after half but before three-quarters of the pattern's length.

▌ On saucers and rounding tops, it is difficult to establish the breaking point.

▌ The double top is considered a reliable bearish reversal sign, but it is initially hard to detect.

▌ The triple or quadruple top is seen as likely to lead to a stronger downward trend than the double top.

▌ Confirm a chart pattern by flipping it. If it shows the reverse, this confirms that the pattern exists.

Seminar 10

Further chart patterns

INTRODUCTION

In this seminar, we will look at some more price patterns, including gaps. We will examine in more detail how candlesticks are formed.

GAPS

Basics

We say that there is a gap on the chart when a zone appears in which there is no trading, and so no prices are recorded. Instead, the price will have jumped from one price to another, leaving a gap. The gap, like other patterns, is more significant if accompanied by a rise in volume. It is more often than not a continuation pattern.

An example of a gap is when the share price opens above the highest level that it had reached on the previous trading session. You can detect such an up gap immediately as it creates a physical gap on the chart, and it is a bullish sign. Contrary to popular fallacy, this gap does not have to close again before the share price rises.

On the same principle, a down gap arises when the share price opens below the level of its previous trading. It is a bearish sign.

Less significant are _intra-day_ gaps, which arise when the share price jumps more than one point during the day's trading. This can happen frequently.

If, for instance, a gap arises on the chart of a stock that is going ex-dividend, this has no meaning in terms of trend analysis. Similarly, a gap that arises quite frequently in a relatively illiquid stock has no deep message.

It is the infrequent gaps in the share price of heavily traded stocks that have the greatest significance in technical analysis.

Types

There are four types of gap. These are the common gap, the breakaway gap, the runaway gap and the exhaustion gap. They will often indicate continuation. Sometimes, the gap is not sustained to its initial level, and this can give rise to a risky short selling opportunity (see Seminar 13). Let us take a look at each kind.

The common gap

The common gap arises when trading volume is low, and buying and selling become congested. It is a deviation from the rule that does not particularly signify continuation or reversal.

The breakaway gap

The breakaway gap can be bullish or bearish. If bullish, it can arise after a long downturn – which will perhaps have been expressed in the form of a pattern such as the head and shoulders – or a consolidation.

If a bullish breakaway gap appears, expect a breakout. The shares may quickly soar, and trading volume with it. If so, the gap will probably not close until trading volume slows.

A bearish breakaway gap can follow a rally or consolidation, and operates on the principle of its bullish counterpart but in reverse.

The runaway gap

The runaway – also known as continuation – gap appears less often than the common or breakaway kind, and it indicates a continuing trend. It may push forward a share price that is rising sharply, or, conversely, push back one that is declining.

The gap is likely to arise halfway between the breakout that started the share price push, and the reversal that will end it. On this basis, you can forecast that the share price will continue beyond the gap about as far as it went from the breakout to that point.

Occasionally, two or three runaway gaps will appear in succession. This is most likely when a thinly traded stock is running hard. With two gaps,

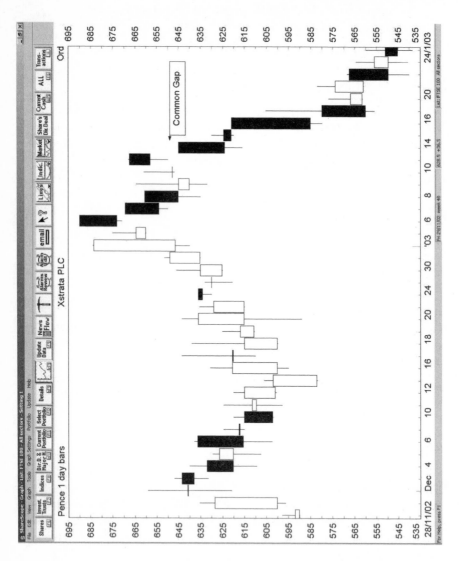

Figure 10.1 Common gap

the halfway point between the breakout and the reversal is likely to be midway between them. A third gap is likely only to bring the share price much closer to the point where it runs out of steam

The exhaustion gap

The exhaustion gap, as its name implies, arises when a fast move in the share price – either up or down – is almost at an end. If the gap arises and, on the following day, trading volume intensifies but the share price slows, this is likely to be an exhaustion gap. It can lead to a reversal – closing the gap – or, just as often, a continuation.

The island reversal

The island reversal is, as the name implies, a reversal pattern. It arises when a fast-moving share price is followed by an exhaustion gap, and then, after a speedy reversal, a breakaway gap, which may close quickly. The sequence can take place in one day or more, and is accompanied by high volume.

On the chart will appear a first gap when the price has gapped up or down, some trading at the new level, and then a gap reversing the original rise or fall so that the share price passes the original gap. The effect is that of an island with gaps on either side.

For the benefit of pattern-spotters, this can create a hat for the head in the head and shoulders pattern (see Seminar 9).

The island reversal is made easier when the share price is moving through a range that has lacked buyers or sellers. Otherwise, such parties would be protecting their own interests, and making the pattern harder to happen.

OUTSIDE AND INSIDE DAYS

The outside – also known as key reversal – day is where a share price reaches a new high in a rally but slips back to close below the previous day's closing price. The signal is bearish and is stronger if backed by high volume.

The inside day is the reverse, arising when the day's trading stays within the previous day's range.

These two patterns have their Eastern counterparts in the bullish and bearish engulfing patterns that we shall discuss in the next session under Candlesticks.

MORE ABOUT CANDLESTICKS

As we discussed in Seminar 8, candlesticks are an Eastern version of technical analysis that has gained popularity in the West. We have seen

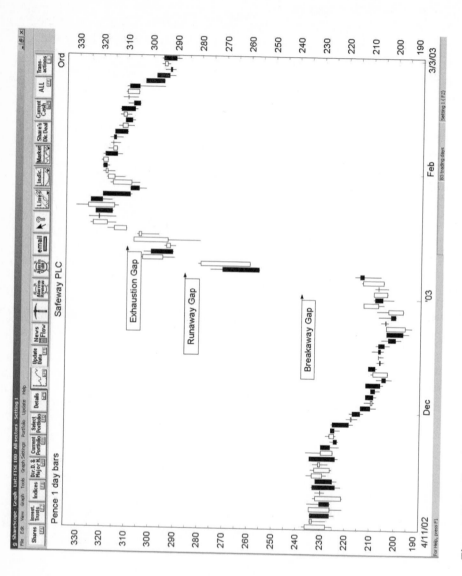

Figure 10.2 Breakaway, runaway and exhaustion gaps

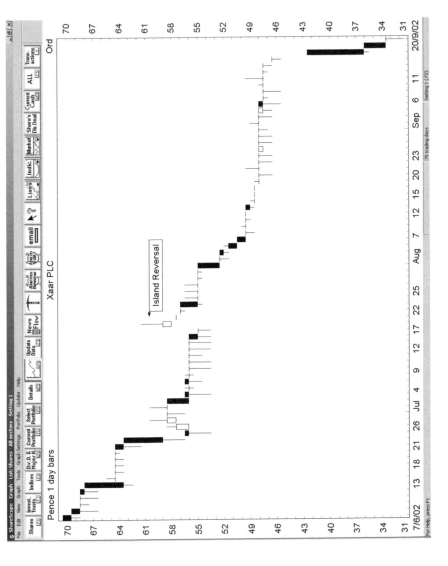

Figure 10.3 Island reversal

how candlesticks are formed out of a real body, black or white, and, where they exist, an upper and lower shadow.

Engulfing

If a white real body comes after a black real body and proves longer than it at both ends, it is said to wrap round it. This is a bullish engulfing pattern, and shows that the bears are losing the struggle against the bulls. In this case, the low of the white candle can represent a support level on the chart, meaning that the share price should not easily sink lower and, if it should, this would be significant.

As the reverse of a bullish engulfing pattern, a white real body is followed by a black real body that is longer at both ends. This is a bearish engulfing pattern, and indicates that the bears have seized the upper hand from the bulls.

Piercing and dark cloud cover

The piercing pattern sends out a bullish signal after a market decline. It is particularly significant if the decline has been substantial. The pattern starts with a tall, black real body that was created in the decline. A white real body follows that opens lower than its predecessor but closes ideally above its centre. In this way it pierces the black candle, and so by proxy the downtrend.

Figure 10.4   Piercing pattern

The opposite pattern is dark cloud cover, which is a bearish signal that follows a rally. It consists of a tall, white real body, followed by a black one that opens above the high of its predecessor and closes ideally below its centre. This can indicate a short selling opportunity.

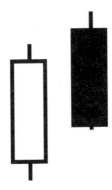

Figure 10.5   Dark cloud cover

Counterattack lines

Counterattack lines are slightly weaker alternatives to the piercing pattern and dark cloud cover respectively. In a bullish counterattack line, a black candle is followed by a white one that closes where its predecessor did, although, unlike in a piercing pattern, it does not rise above this level. In a bearish counterattack line, a black candle follows a white, and closes at the same level.

Indecisiveness in trends

Doji

Candles are particularly useful for denoting hesitation in a trend. One of the most useful signals for this is the doji. This pattern arises where the price of the real body is the same at close as at opening, or almost so, therefore indicating that supply is in equilibrium with demand.

The doji consists of a horizontal line, rather than a black or white candle, which is crossing a shadow. It looks like a crucifix. If it appears, the doji warns you of a potential trend shift.

The shift is more likely to happen if the doji arises after a share price rally, in which case it signifies a tired bull trend. The doji is far less reliable in signifying a market bottom as the indecision that it represents may simply be a respite in a continued downward trend.

The less frequently the doji arises, the more significant it is. For the doji watcher, there are types, depending on where the open–close price line occurs along the shadow line. If, for example, the upper and lower shadow are both long, you have a long-legged doji, which sounds like some kind of spider.

Figure 10.6   Doji

Otherwise, a dragonfly doji has the open close line at the top of the shadow, or nearly so, indicating that buyers kept the price at close to the session's high. The opposite to this, with the open–close line at the bottom of the shadow, is the graveyard doji.

Spinning top

The spinning top is a half-sister to the doji, and similarly an indicator of indecision, although to a lesser extent.

Unlike the doji, the spinning top indicates that there has been a discernible change during the trading session, although not a large one. On this basis, the spinning top has only a small real body, which can be either black or white, and represents a close range between the opening and closing price. It may or may not have shadows.

The spinning top shows that the bulls, if the real body is white, or the bears, if it is black, are taking only limited control and that the battle between supply and demand of shares is not yet properly decided.

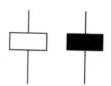

Figure 10.7   Spinning tops

High wave candle

If a small real body – black or white – has very long upper and lower shadows, it constitutes a high wave candle. This pattern indicates greater indecision than the spinning top, or doji, which is understandable given that the opening and closing prices are barely changed over the session despite price movements between a widely separated high and low.

In a bull trend, beware of spinning tops or high wave candles, whether black or white, as they suggest that the bulls may not be winning decisively. When trading sideways, these candlestick patterns are insignificant.

Umbrella – hammer and hanging man

The umbrella consists of a spinning top that has little or no upper shadow, but a lower shadow that is at least twice as long as the real body.

If the umbrella appears at or close to the bottom of a share price downturn, it is known as a hammer. If it rose to a new high following an up trend, it is a hanging man. In either case, the appearance is the same and the pattern signifies a reversal.

Figure 10.8   Hammer

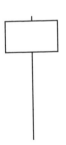

Figure 10.9   Hanging man

Harami

A spinning top is particularly significant if it occurs after a tall candle and is entirely smaller than it. This kind of pattern is known as a harami, based on the Japanese word for 'pregnant'. The tall candle is the symbolic mother and the small real body its baby.

If a doji rather than a spinning top follows the tall candle, this is known as a harami cross.

In either case, the pattern signals a possible trend change, regardless of the colours of the real bodies. A reversal is in practice more likely if it follows a rally rather than a downtrend.

Star

We will now look at the star, which is a small real body, ideally separated from a previous real body and a subsequent one by gaps (windows in Candlesticks terminology). It signals a reversal – with its own small real body representing indecision.

The shooting star is a bearish reversal signal that appears in an upturn, and it resembles an upside-down hammer. The longer upper shadow that is part of it indicates that the market cannot support the continued rising price.

The evening star is another bearish signal. It has a long white body, followed by a higher, shorter spinning top, and then a long but lower black real body that overlaps heavily with the original white one. All three candles are separated by gaps. If the middle candle is a doji rather than a spinning top, the pattern is called an evening doji.

Figure 10.10   Shooting star

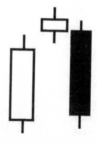

Figure 10.11   Evening star

As a counterpart to this, the morning star signals a likely bullish reversal following a downturn, and consists of a black candle followed by a spinning top of either colour. It is followed in its turn by a long white candle that overlaps heavily with the original black one. As we have seen is true of the star generally, the sequence is separated by gaps.

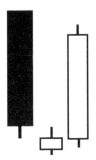

Figure 10.12   Morning star

The doji star is where a gap is followed by a doji. It comes after a long move, and may indicate a major watershed in the market.

Figure 10.13   Doji star

Continuation patterns

Earlier in this seminar, we took a look at gaps. As we have already briefly indicated, the candlesticks equivalent to these is windows, and they are similarly in the main a continuation signal.

A rising window – defined as a price gap between the last trading session's high (tip of upper shadow) and the present session's low (tip of lower shadow) – is bullish.

A falling window – a gap between the previous session's low and the present session's high – is bearish.

In accordance with this definition, if the real bodies have a distance between them, this does not in itself constitute a gap. It is the shadows that count. The window will form an area of support when it is rising, or of resistance when it is falling. For support or resistance to be breached, the entire window must be broken through.

Other patterns

We have barely scratched the surface of Japanese candlesticks, and in particular patterns that consist of several candles in succession.

There are, for instance, tweezers, which consist of candlesticks with matching highs or lows. In longer-term charts particularly, they are a sign of potential reversal.

The tower, which looks like it sounds on the candle chart, is a still stronger reversal sign.

If three long white candles show rising prices in succession, with each closing at or near its high, this is a bullish sign and is known as three white soldiers. The reverse pattern is three black crows.

Taking candles further

If you want to take candles further, there are a number of books available. See my recommendations in Seminar 21.

A word of warning before we move on. Candlesticks do not suit everybody. Renowned trader Jack Schwager conducted some computerized tests applying candlesticks to retrospective trades, and they proved a poor predictor. But the test was probably too simplified to do candlesticks justice.

Conduct your own tests, which will not be too hard as candlesticks are available on most investment software, including ShareScope's (see Seminar 12), and make up your own mind.

THE NEXT STEP

In the next seminar, we will focus on technical indicators, including moving averages.

SEMINAR 10 GOLDEN RULES

▌ Gaps are significant when they occur infrequently in heavily traded shares.

▌ The common gap does not particularly signify continuation or reversal.

▌ The breakaway gap can be bullish or bearish.

▌ The runaway gap indicates a continuing trend.

▌ The exhaustion gap leads equally either to a continuation or a reversal.

▌ An island reversal indicates a reversal. It is made easier when the share price is moving through a range that has lacked buyers or sellers.

▌ The outside day is bearish, and the inside day the reverse.

▌ The piercing pattern is bullish. The bearish opposite is dark cloud cover.

▌ The doji denotes hesitation in a trend. The less frequently it arises, the more significant it is.

▌ The spinning top is to a lesser extent an indicator of indecision.

▌ The high wave candle indicates significant indecision.

▌ The harami indicates a possible trend change, as does the harami cross.

▌ The shooting star and the evening star are bearish reversal signals.

▌ The morning star signals a bullish reversal.

Seminar 11

How to use technical indicators

INTRODUCTION

The range of technical indicators available is increasing as computer technology advances. The indicators offer a useful backup to analysis of share price trends, but never an alternative. You can often use them in combination.

We will be looking first at price-focused indicators. They tend to lag the market (MACD is a partial exception as it shows the difference between two moving averages, which is itself a leading indicator). They move after the trend has turned.

We will also be looking at volume indicators. Next, we will examine momentum indicators such as ROC, RSI and Stochastics. These will often change ahead of the market and are useful for trendless market conditions.

In this seminar, we will look at some of the more popular types in each of these categories, and how you can use them to your best advantage.

TECHNICAL INDICATORS

Basics

A technical indicator usually takes the form of a horizontal range on the lower part of a daily chart. In real time, it will register a level – either on a scale of perhaps 1–100, or in some cases without a scale.

If the price is very low, this is a backup buying signal and, if it is very high, the reverse. If the indicator sends out a message that contradicts the price charts, this is a warning sign.

In this section, we will look at technical indicators in three categories. These are price-focused, volume and momentum.

Price-focused indicators

Relative strength

If a stock has relative strength, this means that it has outperformed against its sector or the market. Do not confuse this with the Relative Strength Indicator, often abbreviated to RSI, which focuses on momentum. We will look at the RSI later in this seminar.

You can calculate relative strength manually, although software will produce a line for you. Take the share price, and divide it daily or weekly by the FT All-Share index. The result is the stock's relative strength. Plot this on your chart against price and volume.

If everything is right about the stock, good relative strength is a confirming signal that you should buy. On precedent, shares that have outperformed the market consistently over the last month and year often continue to outperform, and the reverse is also true. Even Jim Slater, a UK stock market guru (for private investors) who is cynical about technical analysis, has acknowledged this.

As a speculator, you should therefore keep an eye out for changes in relative strength, as this can lead to obvious trading opportunities, including taking a short position (see Seminar 13). If relative strength falters, the share price is likely to decline. This typically happens to shares in a weak company that have been carried higher in a bull market but can no longer sustain the pace. Another victim is the strong company that has just encountered problems.

Moving averages

The moving average is a popular indicator that represents changes in the *average* share price over a specified period. It lags rather than leads the action.

Technical analysts use the moving average to pinpoint the end of an old trend and the beginning of a new. More research has been done into its use than on any other technical indicator. One researcher found that crossover moving averages achieved better returns in his trading over a long time than a buy and hold strategy.

Types

The three main categories of moving average are simple, weighted and exponential.

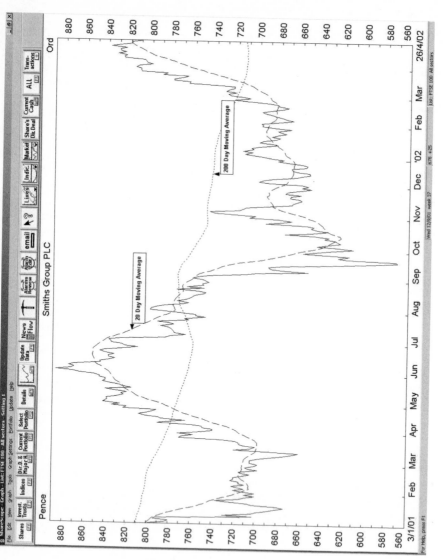

Figure 11.1 20- and 200-day moving average

The simple moving average is the most popular kind and is accessible through any technical software (see Seminar 12). It is calculated as the sum of closing prices (ie the total added together) for a given stock over a selected period, divided by the number of days included.

This version of the moving average has the advantage of not responding too quickly to signals that may turn out false. But if they turn out real, the indicator may have worked too slowly, causing you to miss out on profits from the early part of the trend change.

The weighted moving average gives more weight to recent share prices, and so is linearly weighted. To calculate, for instance, a 20-day moving average, the price on the 15th day is multiplied by 15 and on the 20th day by 20, and so on. The sum of the prices over the period of the moving average is then divided by the sum of the multiples.

The exponential moving average similarly attributes more significance to recent prices, but it includes additional price information outside the period of the moving average.

Time spans

The length of a moving average is linked to cycles, and is typically 5, 10, 20 or 40 days. Note that all of these numbers are fractions or multiples of a 20-day trading cycle.

If, for example, your moving average covers 10 consecutive days, it is a 10-day moving average. The shorter the period, the more sensitive the moving average is and the more suitable for short-term trading.

Short-term moving averages (for example, 10-day) are best when shares are moving sideways rather than in a trend. The risk is that they show false movements in the share price, which are known as whipsaws.

To avoid being caught by these, wait up to a few days before acting on a signal, or seek confirmation elsewhere on your charts. Otherwise, wait for the share to close a specified percentage beyond the moving average before you take action. This percentage may be marked by a line parallel to that of the moving average, creating an envelope (see later in this seminar).

If the share price is moving in a trend rather than sideways, a *long-term* moving average is most useful, as great sensitivity would serve only as a distraction. The 200-day moving average, for example, is much less volatile than the 10-day as the averages are taken over a longer period, and so you will receive the signals later.

This suits those who are investing for the medium to long term, and also provides an extra perspective for traders who are watching short-term moving averages. In this way, the trader may usefully keep track of two moving averages simultaneously.

More often, traders keep track of only one moving average against the share price on a daily chart. As a rule of thumb, you should buy shares when the price is below the moving average, but has started to rise.

Conversely, you should sell when the price is above the moving average, but has started to fall.

Moving average convergence/divergence indicator

One of the most popular oscillators is the moving average convergence/divergence indicator or MACD (pronounced MacD). It is constructed on the basis that as the market rises, a short moving average moves above the less sensitive longer one.

In this way, the MACD is constructed from two exponential moving averages. One of these is usually 12 days, and the other 26 days. The difference between them is the MACD line, which is plotted as a solid line on a chart. It measures how the two exponential moving averages converge and diverge.

If the MACD rises in a downward trending market, or falls in an upward trending market, this signals a change in trend. There is no set range, and the level of change that is significant will vary between markets.

The MACD line is subject to a 9-day (sometimes 10- or 15-day) exponential moving average itself, which is called the signal line and is dotted. If the signal line crosses *above* the MACD at a low level, this is a buy sign. If it crosses *below* the MACD at a high level, this is a sell sign.

The MACD may also be plotted on a histogram. Gerald Appel of Signalert, the MACD's founder, believes that 8-, 17- and 9-day moving averages should be used.

Golden and dead cross

The golden cross arises when two moving averages cross over on your chart as they move upwards. This is a bullish indicator. The dead cross arises when they cross as they move downwards, and it is bearish. In either case, the indicator is more reliable if increasing trading volume backs it.

The triple golden, or dead, cross involves three moving averages crossing (typically 5-, 10- and 20-day), and is considered less effective.

Commodity channel index

The Commodity Channel Index was developed by Donald Lambert. It operates on the theory that if there is heavy irrational buying in the market, this is likely to continue.

To calculate the Index, find the differential between the underlying share price and its moving average. Divide the result by the average differential between the two numbers over the period of the moving average.

When the line is above 100, the market is overbought, but is considered to be still rising until proved otherwise, and so you should continue to buy. Only if the line slips below 100 should you take a short position.

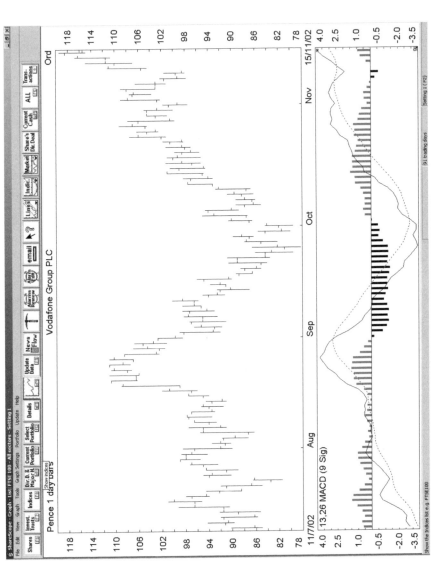

Figure 11.2   Moving average convergence/divergence indicator

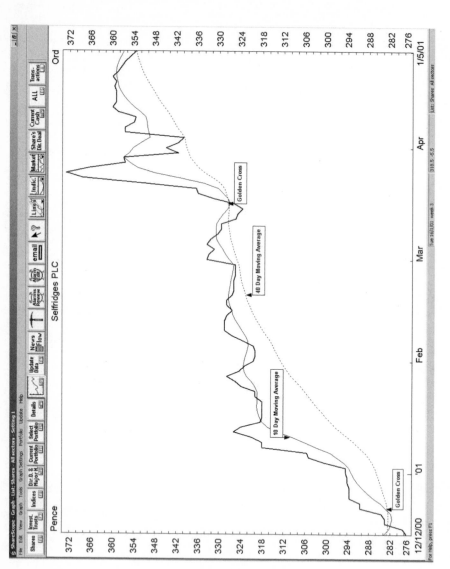

Figure 11.3 Golden cross

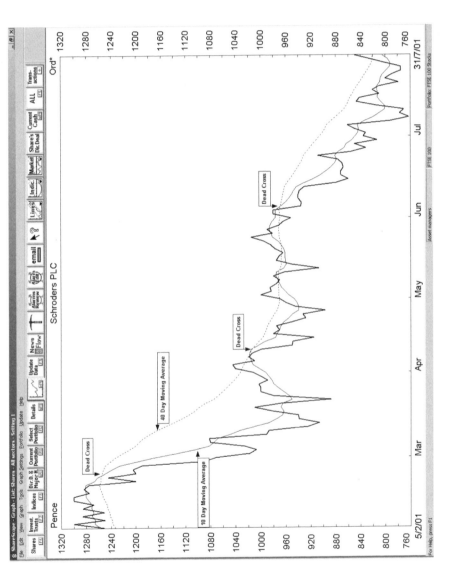

Figure 11.4 Dead cross

Envelopes

The envelope has two lines that are plotted a fixed amount (typically 3–4 per cent) both above and below a moving average. If the share price touches the upper band, this indicates that enthusiastic buyers have driven it relatively high. If the price touches the lower band, it is a sign that sellers have pushed it relatively low.

Of the envelope family, Bollinger bands are the best known, and, like moving averages, are available even on basic charting software. They are the brainchild of John Bollinger, who was a trader of options and warrants in the late 1970s when he became especially interested in volatility.

On this basis, Bollinger bands are plotted at standard deviation, a volatility measure, both above and below a simple moving average. The bands are based on the Intermediate trend, which makes a 20-day period most suitable, although you can vary this to suit market conditions.

The bands are normally constructed on closing prices, although there are variations such as the weighted closing price, or the typical closing price (high + low + closing price, divided by three). To find out more, visit Bollinger's excellent Web site at www.BollingerBands.com.

HOW TO CALCULATE STANDARD DEVIATION

1. Take a simple moving average of the closing share price or indicator. This will be within a given period unit such as a day.

2. Add up the squares of the difference between the share price and its moving average over the relevant number of units.

3. Divide this total by the given unit.

4. Take the result and calculate its square root.

When share prices are volatile, standard deviation becomes high and the Bollinger bands bulge. When prices are stable, the reverse is true and the bands tighten. If the share price moves outside the bands, the trend is said to be likely to continue.

Using the stop loss

If the share price trend turns against you, it is, as we have seen, a cardinal rule of all trading that you should cut your losses and sell early. There are indicators that help you.

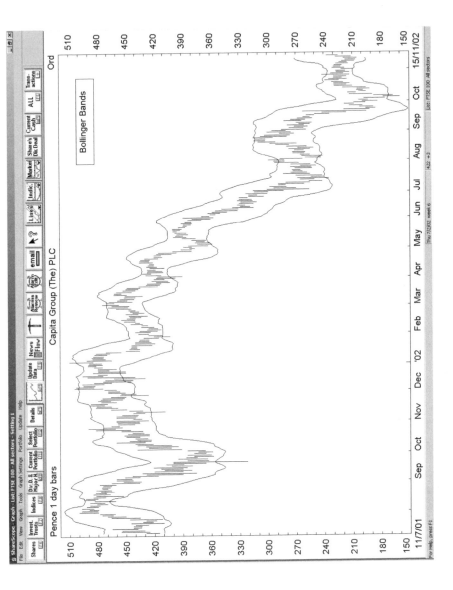

Figure 11.5 Bollinger bands

Stop and reverse points

Stop and reverse points, known as SARs, offer you a trading system that keeps you in the market. They are plotted as dotted lines that define a trend. SARs will stop you out of a long position and tell you to go short, or the reverse.

A popular version of SARs has been the Parabolic indicator, created by J Welles Wilder. It is so named from the parabola that the indicator forms in a fast upward move.

The Parabolic indicator is sensitive to time as well as price movements. It works best when the market is trading up or down, but not sideways.

The stop loss incorporated in the Parabolic indicator is ingenious. It follows the price trend, but accelerates should the price have reached a new extreme. If, at this point, the trade should falter even slightly, you will be stopped out.

How is the stop loss calculated? First, the present day's percentage stop loss is added to an acceleration factor, which is variable but is typically 2 per cent every day that a new high or low is reached. The result is multiplied by the highest share price reached since you bought the shares or the lowest price if you are shorting. Finally, the present day's stop loss is subtracted from the total.

The Volatility index

The Volatility index uses SARs that are calculated according to the volatility of the share price. If volatility increases, the stop loss widens proportionately. This way, the indicator helps you to ignore likely whipsaws.

Volume indicators

Trading volume

Trading volume shows how many shares are traded, with buyers balanced against sellers. The total may be represented on the lower part of your chart as vertical bars in a histogram. This way, trading volume is juxtaposed with the share price movement, and you can easily compare the two.

In general, trading volume leads the price. The higher the volume, the more weight there is behind a trend.

Pay attention if trading volume contradicts price movements. If a rally is accompanied by declining volume, or a price decline by rising volume, a trend reversal is likely.

In sideways trading, the market is indecisive and volumes are likely to be low.

Accumulation/Distribution line

The Accumulation/Distribution line, developed by Larry Williams, is a volume indicator that closely links share price and volume movements. Although it does not provide bought and sold perimeters, it enables you to monitor the trend.

The A/D line is positive if the price closes higher than at opening, and negative if the price closes lower.

On-balance volume

On-balance volume shows how far volume has risen or fallen on the day.

Momentum indicators

Scope

The momentum indictor measures the rate of change, or velocity of prices. It leads rather than lags the market. As with a moving average, the shorter the period that it covers, the more sensitive it is. If you can confirm the message of one momentum indicator with that of another, this makes the message more plausible.

Momentum oscillator

One of the most widely used momentum indicators is the Momentum oscillator, which plots today's closing price against the price a given number of days ago.

Let us take an example of a 15-day momentum. If the closing price is higher than 15 days ago, the momentum line will be above the zero line. If it is lower, the line will be below zero, and, if it is the same, the line will be flat. Every 15 days, the line will be reassessed.

If the line rises above zero, it is a signal to buy and, if below, to sell. The signal is stronger if the price movement breaches resistance levels, which you can draw in as horizontal lines. Alternatively, you can scale momentum lines between plus one and minus one.

You can draw trend lines in this oscillator, although you should give priority to analysing trends of the actual share price.

ROC

The rate of change indicator, known as ROC, is similar to the momentum indicator, but it plots today's price divided by the price a number of days ago. This is again against an equilibrium line.

The RSI

The Relative Strength Index, known as RSI, is the brainchild of J Welles Wilder Jr. It shows the rate of change in the share price, and should not be confused with relative strength as a measure of how well the price is performing against others (see under Price-focused indicators at the start of this seminar).

Some technical analysts describe the RSI as a less jerky version of the Momentum oscillator. It is sensitive and so best used in a trendless market.

The RSI is simple to calculate, and this is usually done over a 14-day period. First, focus on the RS, which is the average of the *up* closes over the period, divided by the average of the *down* closes. The RS should be added to 1 to create 1+RS. Divide the number into 100, and the resulting figure should be subtracted from 100. This gives you the RSI.

The index creates a constant range, which is between 0 and 100, by an indexing adjustment. Against this range, its overbought and oversold levels are predetermined, whereas, on the Momentum oscillator, you need to decide the range.

If the RSI is 50, this is neutral. Technical analysts normally consider the 70 level overbought, and the 30 level oversold, with such extremes or more creating what Wilder called failure swings.

If the RSI has breached 70 or 30 respectively in more than one move, and diverges from the price line, this suggests a future change in the current (probably strong) price trend. This change may not, however, happen yet. Wait for signs of a trend reversal on the price chart before you take action.

Technical analysts who use the RSI often calculate it over a 14-day period, as used by Wilder. Sometimes, they use it for shorter periods such as 9 days to give a more sensitive reading. In such cases, or if the shares are volatile, the analyst may extend the overbought–oversold perimeters to 80–20.

Opinions on the value of the RSI vary. William Eckhard, the partner of legendary trader Richard Dennis, considers the RSI almost worthless. Others are more positive. Investment Research of Cambridge, a former leading firm of technical analysts (now part of stockbroker Brown Shipley), has found the RSI useful and has renamed it ROC.

Stochastics

Stochastics, developed by Dr George Lane in the 1960s, is another popular oscillator that shows when the market is overbought or oversold. Its underlying principle is that, in an up trend, share prices close nearer the top of the price range and, in a down trend, nearer the bottom.

Stochastics shows the last closing price as a percentage of the price range over a chosen period. This is plotted as two lines. The first is the solid %K line, which represents the share price. The second is the dotted %D line,

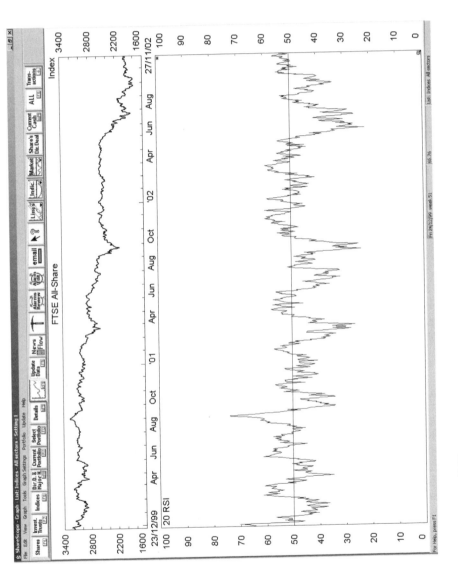

Figure 11.6 RSI

which is a three-day moving average of the first, and, although less sensitive, is considered the more important of the two.

The two lines oscillate between 1 and 100 on a scaled chart. As with the RSI, the overbought/oversold perimeters are usually 70–30.

When either line falls below 25 then rises above it, this is a *buy* signal. When the line overreaches 75, then slips back, this is a *sell* signal. If the moving average falls below the price line, this is often another *sell* signal.

Nowadays, the slow Stochastic is used more often than the original. This excludes the %K (solid) line on the grounds that it is too sensitive. The former %D (moving average) line becomes the slowed %K line. The slowed %D is a moving average of this.

US stock trader Harry Schultz is a fan of Stochastics and has used this oscillator to time his short sales in bear markets.

As a broad guide, Stochastics has much in common with the RSI, but provides much faster signals.

The Larry Williams %R

The Larry Williams %R, like Stochastics, measures the latest closing price against its price range over a set period, and is similarly calculated. The day's close is subtracted from the price high of a given range, and the result is divided by that range.

Unlike in Stochastics or the RSI, the Larry Williams %R is plotted in reverse. If the reading has moved from 20 to 0, the share is overbought. If the reading has moved from 80 to 100, the share is oversold.

The indicator lacks internal smoothing and so it tends to be volatile, which means that its signals can be false.

Meisels' Indicator

Meisels' Indicator, invented by Canadian broker Ron Meisels, is appealingly simple, and has worked well in the past. The indicator is calculated over a 10-day period. It rises one point every day that the index closes higher, and declines one point every day that it closes lower. If, for example, the market closes up for 7 days, and down for 3, the indicator will read +4.

On Meisels' criteria, the market is overbought if the indicator is +6 or higher, and oversold if it is –6 or lower.

The Coppock indicator

The Coppock indicator is a momentum indicator based on a moving average. Edward Coppock, a Texan who was less than five foot tall, invented it. The indicator started to achieve prominence in the 1960s.

Coppock noted that crowds overreact, as they are driven by emotions, not reason. The principle applies to buyers and sellers of shares. On this

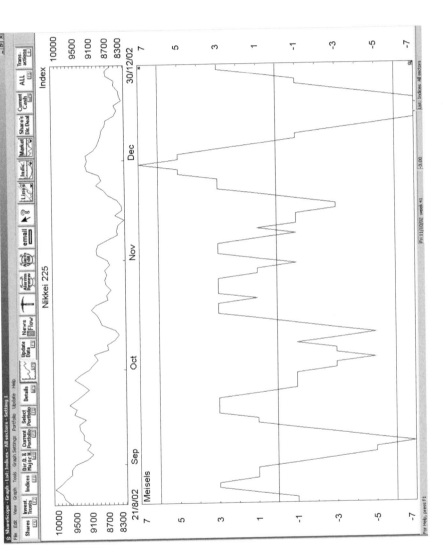

Figure 11.7 Meisels' Indicator applied to Japan's Nikkei 225 index

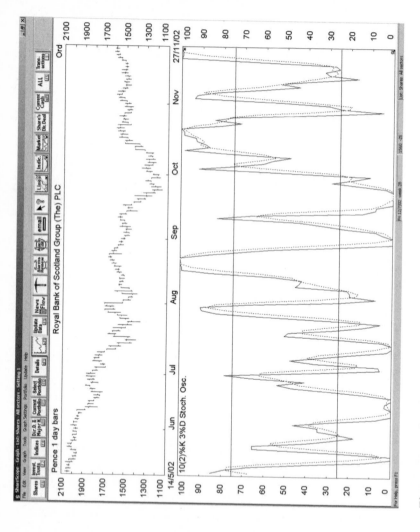

Figure 11.8 Stochastics

basis, Coppock asked local church officials how long the average person requires to grieve after bereavement. They told him that this was 11 to 14 months.

Coppock constructed his indicator accordingly. He calculated the percentage movement of the Dow Jones Industrial average over 11 and 14 months on a rolling basis. From the sum of these, he developed a 12-month weighted moving average for his oscillator.

The Coppock indicator oscillates around a zero or datum line. If it rises above this, it is a *buy* signal. There was never any sell signal, as Coppock did not foresee the need for US institutions to liquidate their portfolios.

The Coppock oscillator tends to catch the main moves but ignore the whipsaws.

On a retrospective application to the US market, it would have been highly effective in identifying incipient bull markets.

In 1963, *Investors Chronicle*, a UK investment magazine, applied a simplified version of the Coppock oscillator (with a rolling 12-month average) to the UK market as far back as 1940 and found it effective.

Since then, *Investors Chronicle* has published a modified version of the IC Coppock indicator every month for various markets. In the 1980s, the oscillator stopped working as well as it had previously, and it failed to call the bull market of the decade.

Since the 1990s, the Coppock indicator has had mixed results. It has at times worked well for the Australian All-Share index. But in November 2002, it was giving a buy signal on the S&P 500, a US -based stock market index, suggesting that a prolonged bear market was over.

At the time, the *Financial Times* warned its readers that Coppock was not to be relied on, and, sure enough, the bear market continued. Supporters said that Coppock was not meant to work under such conditions, but only for the Dow Jones Industrial average, which, unlike most indices, has only 30 constituent companies.

STOCK MARKET SPECULATORS' HALL OF FAME

Member No 3 – Bernice Cohen

Bernice Cohen (www.mrscohen.co.uk) is a private client stock market guru. A former dentist, she fell heavily into debt and climbed out of it by taking her finances in hand and learning to invest independently.

Cohen promotes herself as an ordinary housewife who by asking simple questions has found out what the stock market is all about. She attempts to demystify the investment world, and, this way, encourages beginners to dip their toe in the water.

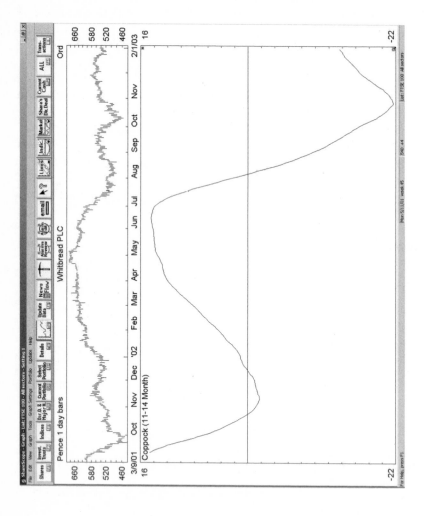

Figure 11.9 Coppock indicator

In a skilfully orchestrated publicity campaign, Cohen has written newspaper columns and several books on investment. She has presented her own show on Channel 4 television, *Mrs Cohen's Money*, in which she has challenged leading figures in the financial world.

Cohen provides a stock-picking formula that includes technical as well as fundamental analysis. She believes that the charts provide subtle clues about what is happening in the market. In her view, the more that this is reinforced by other clues, the more valuable is the insight.

THE NEXT STEP

In the next seminar, we will look at how to choose the right investment software for both technical and fundamental analysis. We will take a critical look at other information sources.

SEMINAR 11 GOLDEN RULES

▌ Technical indicators offer backup to analysis of share price trends, although not an alternative.

▌ If a technical indicator contradicts the price charts, this is a warning sign.

▌ Recent relative strength is a firm buying signal in a stock, and the reverse is also true.

▌ The moving average indicates the start or the end of a trend. Use a short-term version when the share price is moving sideways, and a long-term version when it moves in a trend. It can be useful to keep track of both.

▌ Use stop and reverse points as the basis of a trading system that keeps you in the market. It will indicate when you should go long or short.

▌ If trading volume contradicts price movements, the trend is likely to change.

▌ Corroborate the findings of one momentum indicator with those of another.

▌ Avoid relying too much on the forecasts of the Coppock indicator as this produces mixed results. It is designed only for the Dow Jones Industrial Average.

Part 3

Speculating secrets

Seminar 12

How to profit from the information age

INTRODUCTION

We are in the information age. There is a wide range of investment software providers. In addition, Web site and paper media alike are competing to provide increasingly more detailed and up-to-date stock market news, share prices, and related analysis.

You need only the best in each category. In this seminar, I will show you how to find this.

SOFTWARE

As a stock market speculator, you need access to share price information, news flow, detailed statistics on companies and relevant charts. These facilities are often available on the Internet, but not yet all on one site and with free access.

The most convenient way to obtain all that you need in one place is through investment software, and about 20,000 UK private investors take this route. Many of these are speculators. If you start using the right software for your own trading, you will wonder how you ever managed without it.

A basic software package can be had, at the time of writing, for under £200 a year. The level of information that it provides enables you to reduce expenditure on investment magazines, newspapers and Internet data provision. It has some level of filtering of information, and so also saves valuable time.

In this way, the deal can be cost-effective. But do not expect too much for such a modest outlay. If you require access to real-time prices, the costs will soar to not far short of £800 a year (at today's prices).

You can pay more. The more advanced the investment software, the greater the competition among producers. This is because the markup becomes higher.

Software that suits one trader may not suit another. Let the promoter send you sample software, or provide a live demo, and ask the right questions *before* you buy. Discover the strong and weak points of popular software from postings on the bulletin boards of financial Web sites. Here is a checklist that stock market speculators who have worked in the City have used.

Checklist

1. **Do you need investment software?** Too many investors have expensive investment software when they do not need it. If you trade only on a small scale, or do not select your own stocks, you could manage without this.

2. **Time investment.** If you are to use investment software effectively, you must take time to get to grips with its range of facilities. Are you prepared for this?

3. **Right facilities.** Even the most basic investment software has far more facilities than you will use. But you need to make sure it has those that are essential for *you*.

    If you are among the 50 per cent of investment software users who use technical analysis (see Seminar 7), you will need adequate charting facilities. If, for example, you use trend lines, make sure that your software will draw them for you.

    In any case, you will require access to company statistics, news flow and prices, including highs and lows. Good investment software should provide these facilities. It should also enable you to set stop losses, and alert you when these are reached. It should calculate your tax liability. You may also be able to create a number of portfolios simultaneously, and to liaise with other users.

    As an active trader, you will need real-time prices. Only the more expensive software provides these.

4. **Ease of use.** Some traders are not particularly technically minded, and so should opt for more user-friendly software. This should enable you, for instance, to enlarge a part of a graph by clicking on it. Fortunately, such software is readily available.

5. **Speed.** In stock market speculation, speed is everything. Choose software that works fast.

6. **Reliability.** Your investment software must be reliable. I know of claimed leading software promoted by a major UK manufacturer that constantly crashes. Most users seem to find this out only after they *have* started using it.

7. **Help facility.** Where the intuitive facilities of your software fail, you will need clear instructions for use. Less important, but still useful, are explanations of the more esoteric stock market trading terms.

    An instruction booklet will help you if it is clearly written, and organized for easy reference. This is not always the case. In addition, your software should offer a help facility. If, for example, you want to understand what Stochastics is, you should be able to click on a detailed definition.

8. **Technical support.** If you have limited time or technical knowledge, a good technical support service is crucial. Should something go wrong, whether it is the company's fault or not, you should have access to immediate help on the telephone. Check that there is a users' help line and that it is not constantly engaged. As calls can last a long time, you should be paying the cost of an ordinary call, and not a premium rate.

    Sometimes, if you have a complex problem, it can help to outline it by e-mail. You should have a facility for communicating this way with the customer help service and you should always receive a fast and satisfactory response.

9. **An all-inclusive price.** Check that the price for your software includes all that you need. A favourite trick of some promoters is to offer the basic product at a modest price, but with expensive add-ons.

10. **Free trial.** A free trial gives you a safety net, but make sure that this is *bona fide*. I know of one provider that offered investment software on the basis of money back if dissatisfied, no questions asked. Many were persuaded to buy. The product proved unreliable, and a high proportion of users claimed a refund.

    For some months, the company delayed returning their money, claiming that these users would continue to have the software on their computers. To avoid this kind of mishap, check out the company's track record *before* you buy.

My recommendation

Based on the above checklist, I favour software from ShareScope. This comes with a money-back guarantee. The firm's basic package gives only end-of-day prices, which is a limitation, but it is excellent value for money. At the time of writing, the cost is £11.95 a month (plus a £79.95 membership fee), inclusive of VAT.

As a user, I have found that the ShareScope product is simple to install and use, and works quickly, without crashing. There is a competent technical support service for the cost of a phone call. Software upgrades are free, and there is no minimum subscription period.

hemscott.net, the financial data provider, provides the statistics on the software. This will give you all the fundamental ratios that you need, so you will not have to calculate them yourself. This data is updated every Friday, which is perhaps a little slow. Analysts' forecasts and directors' dealings are included.

ShareScope's charting facilities are suitable for novice traders, and I have included examples in this book. You can instantly construct every main type of chart, including candlesticks, for the stock or index of your choice. The software also gives you access to many of the indicators described in this book, including the useful MACD (moving average convergence/divergence), RSI and Coppock. An intuitive help facility will explain any obscure terminology.

You can mix charts on this software. For example, you can construct a chart of share price movements in Vodafone, the UK mobile phone group, complete with volume, against the FTSE 100 and the Dow Jones.

Meanwhile, you can track your portfolio, or several, on ShareScope. Your capital gains tax will be calculated for you. News feeds into the software from AFX news agency, and, with share prices, is updated daily at 6.00 pm. This will serve your needs if you are able to check share prices only in the evenings.

If you are a more frequent trader, you will need ShareScope's real-time package. This has real-time prices that filter through to all the software's facilities, including charting and stop loss alerts. Split-level screens enable you to see plenty of data simultaneously, for which you will require at least a 17″ monitor.

This real-time software currently costs £84.95 a month (including VAT), plus the £79.95 membership fee. You will need to justify such a hefty financial outlay by the average profits that you make from speculating on the stock market. So do your sums before you buy.

So far so good but, if you trade on a significant scale, you will also need access to Level 11 information. This shows competing bids and offers on stocks that have not yet completed and so enables you better to anticipate price movements.

I know of some traders who use ShareScope Real Time and gain their Level 11 data from another source. Others instead go for a software system that incorporates Level 11 data.

The cost of Level 11 access varies, but so can the quality. One Internet-based Level 11 data provider at present offers access for a subscription of less than £60 a month. But it uses one licence for a number of subscribers, which means that in busy periods, some subscribers may have to queue for access.

Technical analysis

If you are mainly interested in technical analysis, you may prefer specialist software. Updata Technical Analyst offers useful technical features, including an eliminator of random noise from the chart. Metastock and Tradestation offer a facility for creating and testing your own trading system.

THE MEDIA

Newspapers

Your morning newspaper gives news that is already out of date. It also provides comment and perspectives, which may or may not have value. A lot depends on the quality of the journalist's contacts.

News apart, newspapers often carry share tips. The public relations agencies will often have fed these to the journalists, and this makes them suspect. As trader Simon Cawkwell has put it, the PR agent is like the good ambassador who is sent abroad to lie for his country.

The _Financial Times_ (FT) (articles also accessible through Web site www.ft.com) does not tip shares but it has good broad financial news coverage. The City takes this newspaper more seriously than the others, and its coverage has a noticeable influence on the market.

FT journalists are in the habit of quoting sources close to a deal or company, without naming them. This anonymity means that influential bankers and businessmen are prepared to speak quite openly to the FT journalists, and this gives the newspaper its authentic City flavour. You will also find here daily share prices, and brief fundamental data on quoted companies.

Specialist coverage in the FT is sometimes weak or late compared with the better trade press, but is usually better than in the financial pages of the other nationals. The _Lex_ column, on a back page, is particularly influential, and can move markets, but it is not always right.

The quality of _Lex_ comment depends largely on which analysts happen to feed the journalists with information on any given day. I once worked on the trading floor of a leading investment bank where our highly rated, senior banking analyst often dismissed comment in the _Lex_ column. Events tended to prove him right. It is, nonetheless, always worth at least checking what _Lex_ says, as most City professionals do.

Beyond the FT, _The Daily Telegraph_ is probably the most widely read newspaper in the City. Under the redoubtable editorship of Neil Collins, the paper's City pages – compiled and written at a separate office – offer comprehensive, if sometimes superficial reporting that has a reputation for reliability. Helen Dunne, who is well known for her humorous Trixie Trader column and the two novels to which this gave rise, is deputy City editor. The *Questor* column is the newspaper's nearest equivalent to *Lex*.

The Times is also a favourite in some City circles, and its own equivalent to *Lex* is the *Tempus* column, edited by Robert Cole, a journalist and writer with a formidable reputation.

It is a pity that the business pages of *The Independent* are not more read in the City. The newspaper tries hard to break new stories and offers some interesting critical perspectives.

The Guardian is similarly not read widely by City professionals, but you should not underestimate its financial coverage. Sometimes, this newspaper gets useful scoops.

The *Daily Mail* offers City pages with a gossipy flavour. The shorter words and sentences that you will find here are perhaps why market makers often favour the paper.

The Mirror, with its breezy guru *Suzy in the City*, and *The Sun* will give you an overview – sometimes a surprisingly good one – but not much more. Tabloid genius Kelvin McKenzie, when he was editor of *The Sun*, told me that his readers do not understand the stock market, although the newspaper's image has since developed.

Keep an eye on the financial pages of the Sunday national press. The business stories and comment and share tips both can be speculative, but they can move markets early the following week, so providing a trading opportunity. *The Sunday Times* has excellent broad business and personal finance coverage. *The Sunday Telegraph* breaks good stories. I personally like *The Business*, which takes an independent, critical approach for its small but sophisticated readership.

Do not confine your reading to the UK. Many experienced stock market speculators read the *Wall Street Journal*, where the US-biased coverage of world markets is comprehensive and internationally influential.

Magazines

The two most important magazines for private stock market traders and investors are *Investors Chronicle* and its newer rival *Shares* magazine. They are very different in their approach, but both are worth keeping an eye on. You may buy *Shares* on Thursday or *Investors Chronicle* on Friday at your newsagent. Otherwise, they are available on subscription.

Investors Chronicle updates its style every few years. Under the present editorship of Matthew Vincent, it is a fairly adventurous publication. True to the magazine's tradition, there are plenty of well-researched tips. The features have some depth and offer valuable instruction in the basics of stock market investment.

These days, the writers are not afraid to be controversial. I read a recent article that usefully challenged how useful it is to interpret financial statements before picking stocks. Unless you are *seriously* in the know, a subscription to *Investors Chronicle* amply repays the investment.

Shares magazine is a sparkier read, and is more geared towards the trader. You will find here good critical coverage of software systems. There is plenty on technical analysis, options, spread betting and similar. Specialist techniques such as short selling are well covered.

I tend to buy *Shares* magazine most weeks because it has articles that I cannot afford to miss. There is no greater compliment that I could pay a magazine. Although the writers sometimes have a commercial plug, they tend to be experts in their fields and not just hack journalists. Among these is David Linton on technical analysis, and Mike Boydell on trading. Philip Jenks, who jointly runs Global-investor.com, Britain's leading online seller of investment books, has sometimes contributed inspirational book reviews.

Shares sometimes make mistakes, as when it tipped too many high-tech stocks in the bubble up to March 2000. When the bubble burst, it was equally prompt in suggesting selling them. This magazine has enough muscle to make *Investors Chronicle* nervous. Following recent management changes, I am watching how this fabulous if flawed publishing enterprise develops.

In the area of personal finance, *Money Observer*, *Moneywise* and *Bloomberg Money* are all worth reading.

Tip sheets

The tips offered by newsletters can provide a useful starting point for your own research, but you should never follow them blindly. The writers tend to be journalists, in which case their skill is more in writing than analysis. They may well be regurgitating somebody else's ideas, which are only as good as their source. Occasionally, the writers have a City or accounting background, which may enable them to understand the company better. This does not always lead to an improvement in the tips.

If you are interested in penny shares (see Seminar 13), the newsletters can give you a useful steer. At the time of writing, some of these are merging due to fluctuations in demand, which is common in bear market conditions. Penny-share newsletters are still overwhelmingly the most popular kind.

If you are keen on technical analysis, but do not yet understand all the jargon, I recommend *Chart Profit* (published by Fleet Street Group) as the most accessible of the newsletters in the field. I just love the racy style, although the tipping record, as for all newsletters with any longevity, is varied.

The Internet

The Internet can give you hot financial news immediately, which is essential for trading. Some financial Web sites will send you news alerts by e-mail. Experienced stock market speculators tend to stick with a few tried and tested news sites.

Among these are Bloomberg (www.bloomberg.co.uk), which offers both useful news updates and incisive commentaries. Among its independent columnists is Matthew Lynn, whose comments are usually controversial and interesting. He also writes entertaining financial thrillers.

Ample (www.ample.co.uk) offers news, features, stock prices and analysis, online portfolio management and much more. Its roster of regular contributors includes Peter Temple, a former analyst, and Alpesh Patel, a trader. Both are also authors of best-selling investment books.

Motley Fool (UK) (www.fool.co.uk) offers an idiosyncratic, sometimes perceptive take on stock market news. Since one of its original founders, David Berger, has quit and returned to his original profession of doctor, I have not so much enjoyed the site, although it retains most of its original features.

Its writers can make the case for buying a share seem stronger than it is, as the dismal performance of some of the Motley Fool online share portfolios has proved. The site works best as a purveyor of stock market and other investment education for investors who are starting out or who have limited experience.

Analysts' research

Stockbrokers' research is often detailed, and may seem dull unless you have specialist knowledge of the industry. The stock recommendations are typically unreliable, and are aimed at institutions that know how to read between the lines. I still recommend that you get to see as much research as you can, for two reasons.

First, research reports educate you about a company, sector, or macro-economic overview. Second, the latest company report from a respected analyst will move the share price.

Occasionally, you will come across research output from an analyst who also happens to be a talented writer, and this makes it much easier to read. Readers of my various books will know that I am keen on the Russian stock market (see Seminar 13). My favourite research out of Russia is the strategic commentaries from Renaissance Capital, a Moscow-based investment bank.

The author of these articles is Roland Nash, the bank's head of research. He is an Englishman who also thoroughly understands Russia. He lives in Moscow, speaks the lingo, drives a Lada, and lives like one of the natives.

Russian banks, including Renaissance Capital (www.rencap.com), are good about distributing research free on the Internet, although this can be late. Western and US banks sometimes follow suit, but possibly for a limited period.

Otherwise, you can obtain analysts' research reports on a pay-as-you-go basis through specialist Web-based services. I advise you to avoid these. Only those brokers that choose to subscribe provide the research, and it is often out of date, which is annoying if you are paying highly for it.

There is a better way to obtain analysts' research, and it will cost you nothing more than a little legwork. Ring up analysts at broking houses and ask for a copy of their latest research. Analysts are at their most alert in the early morning. Contact them then with brief but pertinent questions and a request for their research.

You are most likely to receive cooperation if you can represent yourself as a journalist, researcher or similar. It helps too if you can pick up the research in person, which – as a bonus – may enable you to meet the analyst.

Consider any research report that you hold as only one of the information sources that you will use to help you make your trading decisions. Consider the following limitations.

Analysts can be biased

In the past 25 years, the role of the analyst has grown from that of a back-room researcher to a backup salesperson. As the expert that salespeople produce at client meetings, a good analyst can make the difference in obtaining a large order, which is why the top analysts earn millions of pounds a year.

Unfortunately, analysts are not always objective. If they are bullish about a company, this may be because the bank has a corporate relationship with it, which it declares, or it hopes to have this.

In the case of such a corporate relationship, the analyst will almost certainly have better access to the company, which should make its research more authoritative, despite the inevitable bias.

Following recent accounting scandals, and the decline of most Internet stocks, the issue of analysts' independence and integrity has come under the spotlight. A lot of analysts who made fortunes in the bull market up to March 2000 are now out of a job, and some are quite thankful about it.

Analysts often follow the herd

The company is seen to issue all analysts with the same information at the same time. Based on this, analysts will often produce similar earnings forecasts.

Overzealous analysts may swiftly find themselves *persona non grata* with the company. This could be suicide to their professional career.

Based on this situation, analysts are normally reluctant to offer a *Sell* recommendation on the company as it might then refuse to talk with them.

YOUR GUIDE TO ANALYST-SPEAK

Analysts write – and often speak – in a coded language that is aimed at institutional investors who understand how to read between the lines. The aim is to avoid being openly critical of the company. Here follows a guide to some of the most common terms used by analysts, followed by the hidden meaning. This is not a complete list, but will give you a feel for how the game works.

- *Reduce* – Sell shares urgently as something terrible may be about to happen

- *A hold* – The share price is unlikely to rise and it may go down.

- *A strong hold* – The company is unlikely to achieve much for a while, but the share price will probably not decline much either

- *A long-term hold* – This company is going nowhere and you should sell it.

- *The shares have attracted strong institutional interest* – Hedge funds and other short-term institutional shareholders have decided to buy and sell the shares and to make a quick buck on them. This will probably be extremely short-term, so trade quickly to make hay while the sun shines.

- *This company is run by colourful entrepreneur Jo Bloggs* – The top man is a crook, but we cannot say so for libel reasons. He has not yet been caught with his hand in the till, and so, at least in the short term, you may be able to make money trading his company's shares.

- *You can't argue with the sales figures. The company understands the concept of caveat emptor* – The company is a rogue operation selling a probably dubious product by hard-sell methods or chicanery but has, in the short term at least, got good sales results. For how long this will continue is anybody's guess.

If a favoured company issues an unexpected profit warning, the share price will plummet as institutional investors sell out.

Analysts who can flag problems in advance to institutional investors when their competitors fail to do so will develop a valued reputation for independent thinking. Their hardest task is to reconcile this with a tactful relationship with the underlying company.

Analysts with good information do not initially put it in their written research reports. They will instead pass it on through off-the-record telephone conversations with favoured clients.

All are scared to be seen to be offering insider information, which is against the law. One reputable analyst has confided in me: 'I break the law every day of my working life.'

Analysts are often outsiders

Analysts can write crisp, authoritative copy quickly about a company. In this respect, they are like journalists, although their information sources are better and their interpretive skills more honed.

Nonetheless, analysts may not know much about the companies that they cover. The forecast numbers that they use in their financial model may be little more than guesswork.

If an analyst is highly rated by independent surveys, this is for the quality of research but it does not mean that his or her recommendations are good. I know of one charming insurance companies analyst who had no credibility among his sales team because his tips were so terrible. This did not stop him from earning a six-figure income and winning an award for the quality of his research.

Analysts may not understand financial statements

As a bunch, analysts are of course numerate. However, only about 25 per cent of them are qualified accountants.

When they get drunk on Friday evenings in City bars, some analysts admit to me that they have limited understanding of creative accounting. They argue that to detect and expose this is not really what their job is about.

This is a severe limitation. In February 2003, Ample (www.ample.com) published online my article warning readers that creative accounting was still a major problem, and that traders should put a priority on detecting it. For more about interpreting financial statements, see Seminars 4 and 5.

Analysts change their minds quickly

Analysts are fickle. This can be appropriate in rapidly changing market conditions, or when the company's circumstances change. But it can also demonstrate how they do not know what they are saying and simply follow the fashion.

I have known analysts spout the bullish case for a stock when it is sharply rising, and become bearish on a sudden market reversal, although the company's fundamentals are unchanged. In the long run, such swaying with the wind can ruin their reputation.

STOCK MARKET SPECULATORS' HALL OF FAME

Member No 4 – Adventures of Sid

A great scientist once said that, in order to become a scientist, you do not need to have done well at science when at school. All that is required is a very strong interest in the subject. The same is arguably true of becoming a City analyst.

I know of one analyst who is still only in his mid-20s, but has climbed to great heights on false pretences. We shall call him Sid.

When Sid was at university, he achieved only a third-class degree (in a non-mathematical subject) and his only dream had been to work in the City.

After graduation, he claimed his degree was a 2.1, and, partly on this basis, he landed a job with a leading investment bank. He became apprenticed to an experienced analyst in one of the key sectors.

By moving from job to job, he came to earn a fantastic salary, and was producing astonishingly impressive sounding research reports that belied his fundamental ignorance.

Written research reports are often out of date

Institutional investors receive research reports immediately on publication. You may not see them until several days later. By then, they may be out of date. In any case, the share price will have already reacted, so greatly reducing or eliminating any trading opportunity that arose.

Your conclusions about analysts' research

The quality of analysts' research varies enormously, but in the final analysis, you must learn to treat it like the professionals do. Pay attention to the research itself which, in some cases, will be very high quality. Be wary, however, of the analyst's forecasts.

When an analyst mentions a certain number as, for instance, target earnings, his or her followers have a human tendency to become anchored to that number and so too easily attached to it. They then give credibility to what confirms the number and ignore what does not.

Avoid this and take into account in your assessment that investors become biased due to the anchoring effect. This is why, if a company produces results that are slightly below expectations, the market can react savagely.

THE NEXT STEP

In the next seminar, we shall look at special trading situations, including short selling.

SEMINAR 12 GOLDEN RULES

- Use investment software only if the profits justify the outlay.
- Make sure that any software that you buy is adequate for your level of trading.
- Your software should be fast, reliable and user-friendly.
- Look for a good help line from your software provider. A _bona fide_ money-back guarantee is a good sign.
- Keep an eye on newspapers, but be aware that they present out-of-date news.
- Use the Internet to gain up-to-date financial news as it happens.
- Use stock market tips only as a starting point for your own research.
- Obtain up-to-date stockbrokers' research directly from the analysts, and understand that it is often biased.

Seminar 13

Special trading situations

INTRODUCTION

In this seminar, we will look at some special trading techniques, which can help you to accelerate your profits once you have mastered the basics. One of the most useful but difficult is taking a short position, which enables you to benefit from falling markets.

We will also look at opportunities arising from merger and acquisition activity, and new equity issues. We will briefly examine rights and scrip issues, share splits, and an old favourite of mine, penny shares.

We will round off with a glance at investing in Russian equities, which is a particularly promising field right now.

TAKING A SHORT POSITION

The basics

In volatile or falling markets, take a short position and it can make you a fortune. You owe it to yourself to discover the secrets of the game. Even if you decide against it, remember others will play.

First, let us look at what short selling actually involves. If you were selling a stock short, you would be selling a stock that you do not own with the aim of buying it back at a lower price before you settled for the trade. Your aim would be to make a profit on the difference between the price at which you bought and sold (less dealing costs).

Such short selling of equities was popular before the London Stock Exchange introduced its electronic settlement system in 1987. Until this point, you could sell short and buy back during the standard 14-day accounting period. If you wished, you could then roll your position over to the next period.

Today, thanks to the nature of the new settlement system, selling equities short has become, for practical purposes, impossible.

There is a solution. When experienced stock market speculators take a short position, they trade contracts for difference (see Seminar 14) instead of shares directly. Legendary short seller Simon Cawkwell (see box below) has described these as opening up astonishing opportunities for short sellers. You can also take a short position through spread betting, although, as I make clear in Seminar 15, this can be a less transparent and more expensive route.

A controversial history

It is entirely legitimate to take a short position, but do not expect approval from the investment community if you get involved. Short selling has always aroused indignation in those who are jealous of the fast returns it can make.

This helps to explain its chequered history. In 1733, short selling became illegal in the UK, but the ban was revoked in 1860. It has been illegal at various times in France, Germany and the USA.

In 2002, short selling received a further battering in the USA and Europe. It was alleged that terrorist groups had raised vast funds by taking a short position on international stock markets before and shortly after the September 11 terrorist attacks on New York, of which they had enjoyed prior knowledge. This was never satisfactorily proven.

In its potential for abuse, short selling is like any form of trading. On a positive note, the practice provides much-needed liquidity to the market. In a recent investigation, the Financial Services Authority, the UK regulator, found short sells acceptable, although it called for more disclosure.

Rules of the game

In a bull market, you can use short selling to hedge a long position. In practice, stock market speculators have found that this is often a way to lose money. You are better off choosing your short trade as a worthwhile speculation in its own right.

If you are new to short selling, start by taking a single position, and use a stop loss. Small high-tech stocks can offer opportunities for making a huge profit fast. However, blue chips are a safer bet due to their greater liquidity and, these days, can often offer sufficient volatility to make you serious money from a well-timed short position.

Keep an eye on those stocks whose prices have soared on sentiment to a level unjustified on fundamentals. If trading volume has risen too, it means that there have been plenty of buyers.

Watch for signs of a bursting of the bubble. One golden rule is that you must never sell short until the shares have started to fall in value.

If, for instance, the shares should fall 10–20 per cent on sudden revelations of weakness in the company's accounts, this is your cue to take a short position. In such a case, get in early as some previous buyers will be rushing to sell and this will send the share price down faster.

A good way to find candidates for short selling is through the 'top movers' section on a financial Web site such as Ample.com (www.ample.com). Check short interest, which is how many shares have been sold short. Your broker should give you a figure on request. If short interest is more than 5–6 per cent of shares in issue, this is too high, and you should hold back as the stock may not have too much further down to go.

Also check days to cover, which tells you how long short sellers have before they have to buy back. This is the short interest divided by the average trading volume in a share (as published on financial Web sites). The shorter the days to cover, the better, as you can then complete your short trade quickly in line with others. Look for a figure under 15.

As a short seller, you need to achieve higher percentage moves than when you are in a long position to reap the same proportion of profit. If, for example, you are long in a stock that rises from 200p to 300p, you will have made a 50 per cent gain. If you are short on a stock that falls from 300p to 200p, you will have made only a 33 per cent gain.

It is often best to complete your trade in a day. If you wait overnight, the price may have moved against you owing to bargain hunters moving in.

Special short-selling situations

Lockup release

It is often advantageous to sell short shortly before venture capitalists and private equity firms are released from a lockup. This will have required them to hold shares in a company for a specific period following a share offering. The lockup is typically for six months or a year, but it could be for as long as three years. Also, watch for directors' selling.

Disaster situations

Disasters can produce opportunities for short sellers. Anybody who sold airlines or travel companies short after the September 11, 2001, terrorist attacks on New York made money, although at the time it would not have been political, or in good taste, to mention it.

STOCK MARKET SPECULATORS' HALL OF FAME

Member No 5 – Simon Cawkwell: King of short sellers

Simon Cawkwell is a trained accountant and intrepid short seller who is dubbed *Evil Knievel* in the national press. In the first nine months of 2002, he made £3 million from taking short positions on equities, and £500,000 from betting on horses. He has told me that he finds no difference between the two.

The son of a Classics don, Cawkwell lives with his family in Knightsbridge. As a speculator, he has about 60 positions open at any time. He makes mistakes, typically on small high-tech stocks, but is right more often than he is wrong. In Cawkwell's view, if you can't understand a business, it is, 9 times out of 10, the one that will give you a profitable short.

Cawkwell warns that short selling is *not a game for infants*, and that most traders will fail at it because they cannot take prompt decisions. In his view, timing is crucial. In early 2000, he noted that ARM Holdings, the semiconductor licensor, was overvalued, but he waited until the price started to fall. He then took a short position on the stock and made a killing.

In late 2002, Cawkwell forecast, as it turned out, accurately, that the bear market in European equities – led by the USA – was far from over. 'Failing to take short selling seriously over the next five years is shooting yourself in the foot,' he said.

Out-of-favour companies

Look for signs that a company is going out of favour with investors. Makers of obsolete products, who cannot adapt quickly, are potential candidates for short selling, as are companies whose directors have a bad reputation. If a company is about to release results and there are rumours that they will be bad, this could be another signal.

MERGERS AND ACQUISITIONS

Overview

Consider investing in companies that are subject to a takeover bid, or for which takeover rumours are circulating. This situation can give you the opportunity to make a fast profit.

Likely takeover targets are asset-rich companies, those with plenty of cash, or under-performers. When there is an obvious synergy between two companies, merger or takeover is possible. Sometimes companies have merged to rationalize their operations and compete more effectively against European rivals.

If you buy on rumours, these are likely to prove ill-founded. In this case, the tricky bit is to sell out when the bubble has almost reached a peak or started subsiding, but before the share price has fallen back dramatically as everyone realizes that the mooted deal will not happen.

The more solid are the rumours, the higher the share price may rise. Be wary of bid gossip in the Sunday newspapers as it is too often ill-founded, causing the share price to move only briefly.

When the shares are up, it is a tell-tale sign if one company is stake building, even if it denies any intention of bidding. Once the company holds nearly 30 per cent of the shares, this is typically the first step towards making a bid.

In most cases, takeover talk will come to nothing. The trick is to sell out after the bubble has almost reached a peak or has started subsiding but before the share price has fallen back dramatically as everybody realizes that the mooted deal will not happen.

If the takeover happens

To take control of a company, a predator must obtain over 50 per cent of its voting shares. Once its stake has reached 30 per cent, the predator must make a formal offer to all shareholders.

Under the Companies Act, 1989, anybody acquiring more than 3 per cent of a public company's share capital has to notify the company within five days. If this fails to happen the Takeover Panel, an independent body with no statutory powers but enormous influence, will intervene. It cooperates with the Financial Services Authority in a relationship that has not always been easy. The Panel enforces the Takeover Code.

Capitalize legally on suspected insider dealing

When a share price rises steadily over days in a company that is rumoured to be a takeover target, the deal may happen.

In such cases, there may be insider trading. Buyers of the shares may be working in concert in an illicit attempt to circumvent the rule that any owner of 3 per cent or more of the company must declare his or her interest.

If you suspect that this is happening, buy the shares early. You could make a 50 per cent plus gain.

In cases so far, any investigation by the FSA of potential market abuse has not affected the share price. In the past, it has been almost impossible to prove insider dealing 'beyond reasonable doubt', which is the standard required for a criminal prosecution. Now the FSA has the option of finding insider dealing 'on the balance of probability', which means treating it as a civil offence under the market abuse regime introduced in December 2001.

BASIC RULES OF THE TAKEOVER CODE

The bidding company sends shareholders an offer document within 28 days of its takeover announcement.

The target company has 14 days to reply with its defence. It may not put out defence material after day 39.

The bidder cannot increase the offer price after day 46.

The bidder has 60 days from the offer document's start to gain more than 50 per cent of voting stock required for control. If another bidder appears, the first day is reset to 0.

You have 42 days after the initial bid to change your mind about accepting any offer, provided that the bidder hasn't acquired control.

There are other potential obstacles to a takeover. Approval from the Department of Trade & Industry may be required. The DTI can refer a bid to the government-appointed UK Competition Commission or, in multinational takeovers, to the European Competition Commission, either of which can block a bid on competition grounds.

In July 2003, for instance, the UK Competition Commission was looking at the official £2.9 billion bid for supermarket Safeway by William Morrison, in the context of counter offers from J Sainsbury, Tesco, Asda parent Wal-Mart, and high street billionaire Philip Green.

The form of an offer

If you hold shares in a company and a bid proceeds, it will often be at a level above the market price. It may be in any combination of the bidder's shares, cash or loan stock.

If the offer is 'all cash', this is less risky than if it includes shares, and so its overall value may be lower.

After first news of an offer, the share price will typically soar because the market anticipates higher offers. If a counter bid is made, the takeover timetable starts again.

Accept or reject

When you receive an offer, ignore the representations of the bidder and target company. If the share price rises, the market is expecting a higher offer and you should wait to see what happens. If the shares stay at the offer price, the market is convinced that the deal will happen.

If you decline to take up an offer that proceeds, a buyer can acquire your shares compulsorily after holders of 90 per cent of the voting shares have accepted.

Trade predatory companies

You can make money out of trading predatory companies. Make sure that your chosen company has a broad acquisition strategy and does not focus only on a single deal. Its management should be experienced in merger and acquisition activity.

NEW EQUITY ISSUES

How the game works

If a company wants to issue new shares and to float on an exchange, it will hold a *beauty parade* in which banks compete for the role of book runner to the deal. This is a coveted job because it is lucrative. The competition is often stiff. For large deals, two book runners may be appointed. In the case of a flotation on the Alternative Investment Market (see later in this seminar under Penny shares), the procedure is slightly different, with one stock-broker usually acting as sponsor, broker and financial adviser to the issuing company.

For a conventional book build lasting several weeks, the book runner will appoint other issuing banks to a syndicate, giving them each a fancy name such as co-lead manager or joint lead manager. In smaller deals, perhaps raising only a few million pounds, a stockbroker is more likely to be book runner.

The book runner must then organize the sale of the shares and keep the books, so assessing how many shares have been distributed and to what extent subscription is full.

The first step is pre-marketing, in which the book runner informs institutions of the deal. Based on their reactions, it fixes a price range. Usually, the shares will be priced within this range, but not always.

The book runner will price the deal according to demand, and not fair value. It takes a percentage of all money raised from investors, so the higher the issue price, the more it stands to make. If there is insufficient demand, the deal will be priced below the price range, or cancelled altogether.

Institutional investors are usually given priority over their private counterparts, both in allocation and in ease of trading in the after market. This can be valuable when the issue is heavily subscribed.

If the issuing company is already listed on an exchange, but wants to issue new shares, or if a large seller wants to offload existing shares quickly, an accelerated book build is likely. This takes place typically in a day, although more time than this is allowed, and there is only one book runner.

The deal is sprung as a surprise so that opportunistic traders will not have already manipulated the share price. This avoids one of the main problems in a conventional book build, which is short selling by the hedge funds. The shares are sold to institutions at a maximum discount of 10 per cent to the existing share price.

Your trading strategy

You can make a good return on some new issues in a bull market. A popular deal is likely to be oversubscribed, although this to some extent describes a technical situation by which investors request more shares than they want in order to ensure adequate allocation.

Shares are typically issued at an inflated price, only to rise higher over the first days or weeks of secondary market trading as investors rush to buy. The momentum is there, particularly for small companies with a narrow free float (proportion of shares freely tradable).

Once the share price in early secondary market trading has risen above the issue price, you should not hesitate to snatch a profit by selling the shares quickly. This is usually the best way to make money from new issues.

Do not listen to the City's advice to hold for the long term. This serves the City well as it helps to support the share price. After a few weeks, the shares will lose their initial momentum and may sink below the offer price, turning what had been a potential profit into a loss.

In a bear market, you should avoid subscribing for new issues or secondary placings, unless under exceptional circumstances. These are, more often than not, a way to lose money.

RIGHTS ISSUES

How they work

If the company is issuing shares that are more than 5 per cent (often 10 per cent outside the UK) of its existing market capitalization (share price multiplied by the number of shares in issue), it is obliged to launch a rights issue.

In the process, existing shareholders are given an opportunity to subscribe to new shares pro rata to their holding. For example, in a 1 for 3 rights issue, shareholders can buy one new share for every three they hold.

The new shares are cheaper than the existing shares. In difficult markets, they might be as much as 40–50 per cent less, which is a deeply discounted rights issue, and more attractive to shareholders. This makes the deal more likely to succeed.

If, as a shareholder, you decline to get involved, you can sell what are known as your nil paid rights in the market. With the proceeds, you will be in a cash neutral position when, following the rights issue, the share price has adjusted downwards.

A rights issue typically runs for about three weeks, although it can do so for six weeks or more. The unsubscribed rights are known as the *rump*. Once the subscription period is over, the book runner will sell these to new investors in an accelerated book build.

Assess opportunities critically

If a company in which you invest invites you to subscribe to a rights issue, do so only if you are satisfied with how it plans to use the cash. If it intends to pay off debt, be wary as the cash raised may not be enough to get the company out of problems. If it is raising cash for an expansion programme, assess its potential.

Underwriting

Usually, major banks underwrite rights issues. This means that they will buy any shares not taken up by investors. This can prove very expensive for the issuing company, especially when it is in problems or when market conditions are terrible, but it guarantees full subscription to the deal.

In rare cases when a rights issue is not underwritten, the share price will tend to fluctuate violently during the subscription period. This happened in the case of the rights issue of Cookson, a UK-based mini-conglomerate, in 2002. In this case the deal was successful, much to the surprise of some bankers, as Cookson had plenty of support from share-holders.

A game for short sellers

In cases when the share price is volatile through the course of a rights issue subscription period, which is typically eight or nine weeks or longer, a trading opportunity arises. In a bear market, when the company is issuing rights to pay off debt, the shares are likely to fall more than they rise. This is your cue to emulate the mighty hedge funds and to take a short position.

SCRIP ISSUES

A psychological boost

A scrip, or capitalization, issue is when a company issues free shares to existing shareholders.

Following the scrip issue, the share price is reduced in proportion to the increase of shares in issue. As a result, every shareholder's overall holding is worth the same. In accounting terms, there has simply been a transfer within the company's reserves.

Under terms of a 3 for 1 scrip issue, for example, the shareholder who had one share priced at 60p will now have 3 at 20p each,

In practice, a company's share price typically rises on news of a planned scrip issue, as investors illogically favour lower priced shares (see Penny shares below).

SHARE SPLIT

Another psychological boost

Under a share split, the nominal value of a share is split, and the number of shares in issue proportionately increased. Unlike in a scrip issue, no new shares are issued.

For example, a company with a share price of 60p and a nominal value of 10p may split in two. The new share price will be 30p, and the nominal value 5p, while the number of shares in issue will have doubled.

The market tends to view share splits favourably. As in the case of a scrip issue, this can create an entrée for the speculator.

PENNY SHARES

A form of gambling

Penny shares can be former giants that have fallen on hard times, or shell situations where vigorous new management takes over. They can also be young growth companies. What they have in common is that they are cheap. There are no set price perimeters, but I personally think of penny shares as costing £1.00 or less.

If you get in early enough, you have a real chance of snapping up an undiscovered bargain. This is because the mainstream City does not bother much with penny stocks.

Small is beautiful, and the penny stock has greater percentage growth potential than its larger counterparts. If the market becomes interested, the share price may soar. If you buy early, you can reap any rewards forthcoming, but do not become blind to the risks.

Market-makers' tricks

There is often only one main market maker in a penny stock, although others may follow its lead. The spread will be wide and you will probably be able to deal only in limited sizes, perhaps 2,000 or 5,000 shares.

If, for example, the bid–offer spread on a share is 9–11, this is 2, which is 20 per cent of the mid-price of 10. This is a far larger spread than is typical on a blue chip company. If you try to sell more shares than the specified dealing size, the market maker will almost certainly drop his bid price further.

This way, a reasonable spread can rapidly become unacceptable. On a stock priced at less than 10p, an additional 1p on the spread has significant impact.

Avoid the specialist penny share dealers

In the penny share game, it can be fatal to rely on the advice of a specialist penny share dealer. The firm is likely to push on you stock that it has bought cheap. It is interested in a quick profit for itself, not for you. See the box below.

ONE DAY IN THE LIFE OF RIP-OFF JO, A PENNY SHARE DEALER

This fictionalized account may shock you, but any reader who has worked as a dealer in one of the penny-share-dealing firms will recognize its authenticity.

Rip-off Jo arrives at his office at 8.25 am, and sits at his desk where he is part of a team of six. The morning meeting kicks off. The firm's strategist pontificates into the microphone about the stock market's performance yesterday, and trade figures expected shortly. Like his colleagues, Jo listens hard and takes notes. He can use some of this stuff in his sales pitch.

Five minutes later, an analyst presents the latest penny stock that dealers must promote to clients for at least half the day. The underlying company has a promising Internet-based product, but, as yet, neither cash flow nor earnings. Its strategy is to increase market share in the hope that profits will follow.

Rip-off Jo grimaces as he hears this familiar story. It is hard to get rid of such stocks in present volatile markets. But he can do it, which is why he is so highly paid.

The selling starts, and a buzz fills the dealing floor. Jo telephones a carefully selected client, a self-employed businessman who is looking for a few speculative high fliers to boost his staid share portfolio. He persuades him to invest £10,000 in the new wonder stock. After concluding a deal before 9.00 am, he sits back in his chair and sighs with relief. But not for longer than a few minutes.

By midday, Jo has rung a dozen more clients, and has persuaded three of these to invest in the stock. His day's sales figure so far is £50,000. Not bad but, by his standards, nothing spectacular. He joins fellow dealers for lunch at a local pub. Unlike some of them, he avoids alcohol.

In the afternoon, Jo has to deal with a client who is complaining that his portfolio has declined 70 per cent. He had bought all the stocks on the recommendations of Jo's firm. The client wants to sell out, and it takes all Jo's skill to hold him in.

Jo presents all sorts of reasons – every one of them speculative – why the market should shortly be soaring, and why the stocks in the client's portfolio, despite heavy falls, should ultimately be winners. The client agrees to remain with his portfolio for another month.

At 5.30 pm, Rip-off Jo leaves work tired and uneasy. It has been a typical day. He pulls in an annual salary of at least £100,000, consisting of a small basic and commission, and he does not save much of it.

Jo knows that his life expectancy at the firm is not so long. Client complaints will eventually reach a higher level than he can tolerate. Faced with this pressure, dealers work here on average for only six months.

How to select penny stocks

In penny shares, the first rule is that you must select your own stocks. Take advice or follow tips if you must, but make your own buying and selling decisions. Be as informed as possible before you do so.

In these stocks, I prefer to see *earnings*, although I can make an exception if the growth story is strong. If the stock trades at a substantial discount to net asset value, this gives it a defensive backbone and makes the company an attractive takeover target. Corporate borrowings should ideally be low. See Seminars 5 and 6 for more on accounting ratios.

Regardless of fundamentals, a penny stock needs a trigger to set the share price moving. The turning point is often when new management moves in, and starts implementing changes.

Keep an eye on the trade press for this. If the management is youngish, but has a good track record, this is a better bet than if it consists of Internet entrepreneurs straight out of business school.

Do not necessarily expect a dividend. Any young company with fire in its belly will instead reinvest earnings in the company to fund growth. Instead, concentrate on stocks that are likely to achieve a good capital gain.

Buy promptly and diversify

Penny shares are speculative, and I advise you to invest only up to 15 per cent of your equity portfolio in them. Invest in several stocks rather than one, and you will not be hit so hard should one of the companies collapse.

When you spot a stock that you want, buy fast. The price can soar by 40 or 50 per cent within days.

In the penny share business, vested interests are at work. Watch for rigged promotions of dud stocks. The share price will soar, but only temporarily until the promoters see fit to sell out of their own large holdings acquired at a very low price.

Markets galore

It is safest to buy penny shares in companies listed on the London Stock Exchange (www.Londonstockexchange.com). Here, requirements for disclosure and track record are stringent, although they can be relaxed for high-tech stocks.

A riskier alternative is to buy shares quoted on the Alternative Investment Market (AIM) which was created and is regulated by the London Stock Exchange. This is a high-risk market in small companies, and its stocks can be volatile.

For still bigger risks, trade unquoted stocks on the OFEX market, which is run professionally by JP Jenkins, a market maker. The companies are less affected by broad market conditions than those with a Stock Exchange listing, and this can work in your favour in bearish conditions.

In researching OFEX companies, you will find that there is no substitute for talking to management. You will have your opportunity at the market's regular private client exhibitions, in London and sometimes in the provinces.

Some OFEX stocks have been trading for a few weeks, others for years. They may proceed to an AIM quotation or full listing, or they may go under. Be careful how large a holding you take as the OFEX market is not especially liquid. Also, avoid companies such as football clubs where the shares tend to be tightly held by family groups.

Avoid penny shares touted from abroad unless you really understand what you are buying. A listing on the US pink sheets market or the Vancouver exchange, for example, is no guarantee of respectability. Unproven high-tech or oil companies in particular can be suspect.

EMERGING MARKETS AND RUSSIA

General

Also on the wild side are emerging markets. If you buy and sell shares in countries such as China, Poland, Croatia, Turkey or Russia, the risks are high, but so are the potential rewards. Shares can rise or fall quickly, typically regardless of fundamentals. Often, corruption is either helping or hampering growth.

Readers of my books and journalism will know that I am keen on the Russian stock market. Anybody who invested in it sensibly over the past few years has seen high returns, and the market remains cheap.

Russia

The safest way to invest in Russian equities is to buy into the large oil companies. Oil is Russia's largest and most important industry, giving the country clout internationally, where it can negotiate how far it will cooperate with requests for price and quota restrictions.

When in 2002 and early 2003, the oil price had risen to US$30 a barrel, the Russian stock market was flourishing. When the US-led war against Iraq was over, the oil price slipped to US$25, but this remained high.

At the time of writing, Russian oil companies look cheap. The shares trade on a PE ratio (see Seminar 5) of about 8, which is less than half the sector average in the West. But there is little growth left in some of the companies, unless they merge.

Some analysts feel that there is better value elsewhere. Media, computer and food companies have growth potential. In mobile telecommunications, MTS and Vimpelcom are leaders, and their share prices on the New York Stock Exchange have held up better than those of their European peers.

Many companies in these and other sectors need to raise capital. At the time of writing, they find it cheap and easy to borrow through issuing ruble-denominated corporate bonds. The amount raised is often between US$10 million and US$20 million, which is diminutive by international standards. Some of the banks handling the deals are not checking the creditworthiness of the issuing companies. The bubble will at some point burst, according to MDM Bank.

Russian companies can also raise cash through an international public offering. If a company chooses to list locally, this is cheaper and less bureaucratic than the international alternative, but attracts fewer large investors.

If you plan to invest in Russian shares, it is safest to choose a company with a listing in New York or London. To achieve such a listing, the company will have needed to reach international standards of corporate governance, disclosure and accounting.

Many small companies still employ dubious managers who filter profits into private accounts, and award lucrative contracts to favoured candidates. Russians themselves are the most critical of this practice.

Companies in Russia that set up since the collapse of the old Soviet Union are often run on more Western lines, with managers who have been educated in the West. Be warned, however, that the business risks may be huge. Within Russia, it can be competitive to build a business in Moscow and St Petersburg and very expensive in the regions. But the opportunity is there.

Over the next five years, the Russian stock market may grow largely as a result of planned reforms of the pension and banking systems. The reforms may be delayed for political reasons but, when they happen, they will stimulate particularly local interest in investing in Russian shares.

How to invest

How can you yourself invest? Buy American depositary receipts (ADRs), which enable international investors to buy Russian (or other foreign) shares on US exchanges. Outside the USA, the equivalent is general depositary receipts.

To deal directly on the Russian stock market, including in companies that do not have ADRs, open an account with a Moscow-based stockbroker. Be warned that many smaller quoted companies have a liquidity problem.

If you want to invest in a wide spread of Russian shares, consider unit trusts. In *The Business* in August 2002, I recommended investing in the Baring Eastern European fund, which I feel is still a good bet.

THE NEXT STEP

In the next seminar, we will look at contracts for difference. These allow you to take a geared long or short position on stocks or indices.

SEMINAR 13 GOLDEN RULES

▮ If you take a short position, you can make a lot of money in volatile or falling markets.

▮ The best way to take a short position is to use contracts for difference.

▮ As a short seller, you will need higher percentage moves than in a long position in order to make the same level of profit.

▮ Using short selling simply to hedge a long position is a way to lose money. You should choose your short position entirely on its merits.

▌ Never sell short until the targeted stock has started falling in value.

▌ Sell short shortly before venture capitalists are released from a lockup period.

▌ Buy rumoured takeover targets early and sell before the bubble bursts.

▌ Subscribe to IPOs in a bull market, but sell out in early secondary market trading. Avoid them in a bear market.

▌ Consider taking a short position in companies that have launched a rights issue in a bear market to pay off debt.

▌ Scrip issues and share splits can cause the share price to rise for psychological reasons only.

▌ Penny shares have wide spreads and small dealing sizes. This can make them difficult to sell.

▌ Do not rely on advice from the specialist penny share dealers. They will act in their interests, not yours.

▌ A penny share should normally have earnings, and a trigger to make the share price move. This could be new management.

▌ Invest a maximum 15 per cent of your equity portfolio in penny shares, and diversify your risk by holding several companies.

▌ If you are buying penny shares, you are safest with those listed on the London Stock Exchange.

▌ Avoid buying OFEX shares that are tightly held by family groups as, for example, in the case of football clubs.

▌ Avoid penny shares touted from abroad unless you really understand what you are buying.

▌ Speculate on shares in the Russian market to benefit from pending pensions and banking reforms. These should give a boost to local shareholder ownership.

Seminar 14

How to trade contracts for difference

INTRODUCTION

In this seminar, we will take a look at contracts for difference, known as CFDs. This is a recommended way to place highly geared trades on equities and other financial instruments.

You can use CFDs either to speculate on financial instruments, or to hedge your portfolio.

THE BASICS

The marketplace

When stock markets are volatile, contracts for difference flourish as they enable you to make a geared profit from the fluctuations. They are available on the most liquid stocks in the UK, and on some in continental Europe and beyond, including Australia and Japan.

Institutional investors have been using CFDs since 1988. They do not pay stamp duty on purchases as they are not buying the underlying instrument, and this is a major attraction. Compared with equities, these save 0.5 per cent on every buy order.

Private investors did not become involved until 1998. To be suited, they should be intermediate customers (previously categorized as expert investors) under the rules of the UK regulator, the Financial Services Authority.

CFD providers accept your trades only on the basis that you understand the risks of this highly geared product.

The instrument

What form does a contract for difference take? The CFD is an agreement between two parties to exchange the difference between the opening and the closing price of a contract, multiplied by the specified number of shares, as calculated at the contract's close.

You can trade this instrument by telephone or via the Internet. As CFDs are an over-the-counter product, you are relying on the creditworthiness of your broker, although this has never yet in practice proved a problem.

As a CFD holder, you are not the registered owner of the underlying share, and so you will not have shareholders' voting rights or product discounts. However, the CFD's value will reflect dividend payments, special payouts and takeover activity.

You can trade CFDs when the underlying stock is tradable only on a *when issued* basis, and trading is conditional. Under these circumstances, you will have a time advantage over private investors who seek to trade the shares directly.

Settlement on CFDs is always in cash, based on the difference between the contract's opening and closing price. This is also so for short positions. The CFD has no expiry date and so there are no rollover charges.

Your CFD provider

Two types

In selecting your CFD provider, you must choose between a market maker and a broker. We will look at each type in turn.

The market maker does not charge commission, but instead includes its dealing charges in the spread (difference between the buying and selling price). In this way, these charges are concealed, and you cannot assess them.

You are better off using a broker as the transaction will then be transparent and, in many cases, more cost-effective. The firm will operate like a traditional stockbroker. You will pay the firm a fixed commission, which is typically as low as 0.25 per cent. You will trade on real market prices.

If you are trading the UK's 200 or so largest companies, some brokers will offer you the price set by SETS, which is the relevant electronic trading system. It is at this price that they hedge the position themselves. A few will offer you a better price.

Resources

In choosing your CFD provider, consider the quality of resources that it offers. Look for good research material, for earnings estimates, and live news flow. Buying and selling tips may also be on offer.

Some payment considerations

Margin

To trade CFDs, you are required to put up an initial deposit, known as margin. This is between 10 and 25 per cent of the full contract value (including charges) of any trade, depending on your trading experience and the underlying stock's size and volatility. You will effectively borrow the rest of the money required.

The practice of putting up only a proportion of the amount traded makes your position highly geared. The CFD need not move very much for you to see an extensive gain or loss.

If, for example, you buy a CFD of 20,000 shares at 50p each, this is worth £10,000, and you may have put up as your initial margin £2,000, representing 20 per cent of the position.

Should the price in this context rise by only 5p, you will make 20,000 × 5p, which is £1,000. This is only 10 per cent of the entire contract's value of £10,000. However, it is a full 50 per cent of the £2,000 that you have put up.

If you pulled out at this point, you would crystallize a 50 per cent return on cash invested (less dealing expenses) and your deposit would be returned to you.

If on the other hand the contract price should fall by the same 5p level, you will have *lost* 50 per cent of your cash put up, although only 10 per cent of the full contract. In this case, gearing will have intensified your percentage loss.

If you had instead bought the underlying shares, your potential gain would be more modest, although so would your potential losses. You would need to put up £10,000, which is more expensive than putting up £2,000 due to the greater lost opportunity cost.

If the share price rose by 5p, you would see your shares rise in value from £10,000 to £11,000, which is by just 10 per cent. This would be identical to your gain on cash invested since, in this case, there is no gearing. It would be a welcome result, but clearly not so spectacular as the 50 per cent cash gain on the CFDs for the same share price percentage rise.

Interest payments

When you purchase a CFD, the provider will charge interest on the proportion of your position above margin.

Check the interest rate payable by yourself *before* you open your account. It is likely to be three points over current base rate, which is more favourable than banks normally offer.

The interest payments work both ways. Your CFD provider will pay interest on money deposited, and also on a short position. In this case, the interest rate will be lower than from the bank, perhaps one point below base rate.

In all cases, interest payable is recalculated daily. If you buy and sell on the same day, you will not pay interest.

As with other derivatives, you will receive a margin call if your position starts losing money to a level that requires you to top up the amount deposited. The assessment, known as marking to market, takes place daily.

Cost-effectiveness

Because you do not pay stamp duty on your CFD purchases, the deals are cost-effective if you are a substantial trader. This only remains so, however, for perhaps 10 or 11 weeks.

The reason is that, when you are paying interest daily on your long position above margin, this eventually becomes more expensive than the stamp duty that you would have paid as a purchaser of the underlying shares. From this perspective, when interest rates rise, the period in which it is cost-effective to hold these CFDs declines. Despite this, some traders will hold if they have or foresee an overall gain.

Some of these traders do not have the capital to buy the underlying shares, which in the long term would be more cost-effective.

Hedging its position

When you buy a CFD, the provider will hedge its position with you in the stock market. If, for example, you buy a CFD on 5,000 shares in BT, the telecommunications group, the CFD provider will buy 5,000 shares directly in the company.

This way, if the BT share price rises sharply, and you cash in, the CFD provider will not have lost out overall. Its BT shares will have risen over the period to compensate for the loss on the CFD.

SPECULATING

Long positions

Index reviews

When a stock market index is reviewed and changes are made in its constituent companies, this can create an excellent trading opportunity for you. The price changes will usually come because the major institutional investors buy stocks that will move into the indices, and sell those that will leave it.

For funds that openly or otherwise track the major indices, there is little or no choice about the matter. They must have holdings in proportion to an index weighting so that their funds perform more or less in line with the market.

Let us take a look at how the FTSE-100 review works. Every quarter, the constituents of this index are reviewed. Companies in the FTSE 100 with a market capitalization below the 110th place are relegated, and, conversely, outsiders that meet these criteria are promoted.

You can often make money from trading CFDs in those stocks that are expected to enter the FTSE 100. Buy your CFDs a few days before the index entrants are formally announced, and you should catch the subsequent share price rise. Sell the CFD late in the day before the stock enters the FTSE 100 as, from this point, the share price often declines.

In parallel with this strategy you could take a short position on stocks likely to be relegated from the FTSE 100, and then reverse your position.

Besides this, watch when companies in the FTSE 100 or another major index plan a share issue. This may lead to a re-weighting in the index, the prospect of which creates another trading opportunity.

A key question is: how can you keep abreast of changes in the FTSE 100 and other indices? There are Web site services that track these. Start by visiting the Web site of FTSE International at www.ftse.com.

Also visit the Web site of GNI (www.gni.com) where you will find a table of the top 150 UK companies by market capitalization. You can use this list to forecast which companies will leave or join the FTSE 100.

Dual trading

Dual trading, also known as spread trading, is when you invest in the performance of one stock against another.

For instance, you will buy a CFD on a stock that seems a likely out-performer, and simultaneously sell a CFD on a stock that you consider undervalued. If you have judged rightly, you will profit from the future divergence.

For this strategy, traders often choose two stocks from the same sector, as these are directly comparable. The stocks will have historically reacted to the same industry issues and news.

As a variation, traders have been known to take a dual trading position in the same stock but listed in two different countries.

Auctions

In summer 2000, the London Stock Exchange introduced opening, intra-day and closing auctions applicable to the SETS order book. As we have seen, SETS includes the UK's 200 or so largest stocks.

These auctions see plenty of price volatility, which can give you substantial profit opportunities as a CFD trader.

The best trading opportunities arise in the post-market auction. This is between 4.30 pm and 4.35 pm immediately after ordinary trading has closed.

For this period, the auction suspends trading. Participants may submit limit orders. Alternatively, they may buy or sell *at market*, which can send the share price briefly soaring or plummeting from a liquidity imbalance. As a result, the share price often then reaches its day's high or low.

Over the five minutes of the auction, an *uncrossing* price is continuously calculated and displayed. Subsequently, all viable orders are matched and executed at the uncrossing price only.

Buybacks

When a company buys back its own shares, a trading opportunity – not confined to CFDs – can arise.

Any share buyback must be suspended for two months before the company issues results.

During this period, if the stock slips back, it can be a good opportunity to take a long position in CFDs.

When the results are out and the company starts buying its shares back again, the share price is likely to return to strength.

Short positions

Why use CFDS

If you think that the share price will fall, you can take a short position in CFDs. This way, you can profit from any decline. There is no expiry date. If things go too far wrong, you will need to top up your trade with extra margin to hold your position open.

Anecdotal evidence from CFD providers suggests that in a bear market, short selling accounts for 20–30 per cent of all CFD trades.

MONEY MANAGEMENT

Stop loss

Throughout this book, I have stressed the importance of the stop loss. When you apply it promptly to a losing position in highly geared derivatives such as CFDs, this can save you a much higher percentage loss than in equities.

Unfortunately, CFD providers will not implement stop losses strictly. This is because SETS does not accept them for CFDs.

But some CFD providers will carry non-held stop losses. On this basis, if your CFD falls below your stop loss, they will sell it at as close to this level as they can.

Otherwise, you can implement your own stop loss system and issue Sell orders directly, although this requires you to be watching your screens constantly.

Hedging

You can use CFDs to hedge your share portfolio or index tracker fund. To do this, take an equally sized but opposite position in CFDs on the same underlying shares or index.

If, for example, you have 1,000 shares in Marks & Spencer, you can sell a CFD of 1,000 shares in the company as a hedge. If the shares rise, as you hope, you can close your CFD position, as you will not need it. If the shares decline in value, the CFD will rise and so compensate for the loss, less dealing costs.

The danger with using CFDs for hedging is that you may evaluate a trade not for itself but merely in its technical capacity as a hedge. It may fulfil the hedging objective but lose you money.

If your main share portfolio is small and there are no capital gains tax implications in buying or selling shares, you may do better not to hedge it but instead to react to changing markets by trading the underlying shares directly.

RESOURCES

It is worth finding out more about CFDs *before* you commit your money. At the Web site of broker Sucden UK (www.igshares.com), you will find good explanations of how they work.

At the Web site of broker GNI (www.gni.com), you will find a daily market commentary, technical analysis, a Sunday newspaper roundup, and an archive of relevant articles

Although I do not normally favour brokers who offer commission-free CFD dealing, with charges built into the spread, CMC Group is one of the pioneers. Visit the company's Web site (www.deal4free.com) for a technical analysis commentary, and a calculator that enables you to compare the cost of trading CFDs with direct investment in shares.

Other prominent CFD providers include spread-betting firms such as IG Index, City Index and Deal4Free.

THE NEXT STEP

In the next seminar, we will look at spread betting, which offers a more expensive but highly accessible alternative to CFDs.

SEMINAR 14 GOLDEN RULES

▊ CFDs flourish in volatile markets as they offer the potential for making a geared profit from the fluctuations.

▊ You can trade CFDs when the underlying stock is tradable only on a *when issued* basis.

▊ Use a broker rather than a market maker to trade CFDs. The transaction will be more transparent, and often more cost-effective.

▊ Use a CFD provider that offers high quality research material and news flow.

▊ Before you open a position with a CFD provider, check the interest rate that it pays on your position above margin.

▊ As a substantial trader, you can trade CFDs comparatively cheaply because you do not pay stamp duty on purchases. But after 10–12 weeks, it may no longer be cost-effective due to interest payable on your long position.

▊ Buy FTSE-100 index entrants a few days before they are formally announced, and sell late in the day before entry.

▊ Trade CFDs in the post-market auctions applicable to the SETS order book.

▊ If a company suspends a buyback programme due to pending results, buy CFDs on temporary share price weakness.

▊ Use some sort of stop loss, although CFD providers will not implement this strictly.

▊ When you hedge with CFDs, you can lose money if the trade is not worthwhile in itself.

Seminar 15

How to make financial spread betting work for you

INTRODUCTION

Financial spread betting is a fast-growing method of taking a long or short position on a share, index or other financial instrument.

It is more accessible for new investors, and sometimes more user-friendly, than CFDs, but less cost-effective.

In this seminar, I will show you how to make the most of spread betting, and will explain the whole procedure in detail.

THE BASICS

The marketplace

The financial bookmakers are not advisory. They make their own markets and so you are dealing with the principals direct. There are about six major firms and it is easy to open an account.

You can bet on a wide range of instruments, including options and interest rates, as well as individual shares in the UK, continental Europe and the USA. You can also play the foreign exchange market.

You can punt on a variety of indices, most commonly the FTSE 100 or the Dow Jones Industrial Index but also the TechMARK 100 or a sectoral index.

As with CFDs, you can hedge your share portfolio by betting that a share price or index in which you are long will go down, or vice versa. This way, if your main investment goes awry, the gain on the bet will compensate.

Again as in CFDs, it is mostly speculators who use spread betting. In this case, about a third of the punters work in the City of London. These people understand financial markets and have money to burn.

Types of bets

If you want a punt on the FTSE-100 index, you can choose from all the main financial bookmakers. If you are placing specialized bets, your choice will be narrower. For example, Financial Spreads offers a service that is tailored to those who are placing a low size bet.

Bets fall into the following three categories: daily, futures-based and options based.

Daily

These are bets that last for only a day and are not necessarily based on a futures price. If you do not close your bet, the spread-betting firm will automatically do so at the end of the day.

To win on this type of bet, you will do best to watch your screens almost without a break.

Futures-based

Most financial spread bets are on futures, which, by *anticipating* movements, are likely to move faster than the underlying financial instrument.

More specifically, the bets are based on the price of future contracts that expire on or near the next quarter day or (if you think the price will move slowly) one subsequent to that. The quarter day is often the third Wednesday of March, June, September or December.

Options-based

You can also spread bet on options prices, but the spreads can be wide, and you will need to obtain prices by telephone rather than via the Internet.

This is a way of trading option prices without opening an account with a specialist broker, depositing funds with it, and signing the appropriate risk warning.

The practicalities

You will place your bet over the Internet or by e-mail, or by phone. If you think that the financial instrument will rise, you place an up bet, buying it. If you think it will go down, you will place a down bet, selling it. Remember that you are betting on the direction of the price movement, and do not own the underlying financial instrument.

You will nominate a unit stake, which on small transactions is typically £2–£5, per single point by which the price rises or falls.

Let us suppose that you stake £2 a point that a given index will fall from the level of 4,000. The more the index falls below this level, the more you gain. If you sell out when the index is at 3,960, your profit will be (4,000–3,960) = 40 × £2.00 = £80.

Conversely, the more the index rises above 4,000, the more you lose. If, for instance, you sell out when the index has risen to 4,030, you will lose 30 × £2.00 = £60.

The range of bets on offer is diverse. With some bookmakers, you can bet on company results, and on key City votes.

If the initial public offering (IPO) of a popular company is pending, you can sometimes place a grey market bet on the price at which you think that the shares will start trading in the secondary market. At most, only a few hundred people take bets in this specialist area, and the bookmakers have a very rough-and-ready way of forecasting the way the price will go. Nonetheless, the national press reports grey market price forecasts and sometimes uses them to back a bearish or bullish perspective on the IPO. Investors read the press, and the grey market price of a pending flotation can this way have significant and unwarranted impact on the book build.

If you are using only one bookmaker, you can bet simultaneously on more than one share index, although not on the same financial instrument with both *Buy* and *Sell* bets. There is, of course, nothing to stop you opening accounts with more than one firm.

Margin

The bookmaker will require you to have significantly more liquid funds than the account size that you require. You may need to provide evidence of your assets.

You will pay up-front only a proportion of the sum on which you are betting, which is useful if you are short of liquid funds.

This initial margin is based on the volatility of the underlying instrument and the size of your stake in it. It will probably be 10–15 per cent of the sum that you are betting, but this is not invariable. I have known it be as little as 3 per cent for index bets and 5 per cent on blue chip stocks, but as high as 30 per cent for small cap stocks.

The notional trading requirement (NTR), as this margin is known, should cover any initial loss, if the price were to move against you.

In this way, you are betting on margin, just as with CFDs. Spread betting is similarly geared as you will reap gains or losses based on the whole sum on which you bet.

Once you hold a credit account with a bookmaker, you may not be asked for initial margin, although you will of course be exposed to the same risk/reward ratio.

Later in this seminar, under the heading Account administration, we will look at how you may be required to top up your margin.

GETTING STARTED

Your plan of action

To get started, set aside some capital that you can afford to lose. Then decide on what stocks, indices or other financial instruments to place your bets.

Shop around for a bookmaker that suits your strategy. Some firms will invite you into their offices for coffee evenings. They will send representatives to speak at seminars.

As you will find out, the spread betting firms do not all offer the same bets, and where they do, the spreads (buying and selling price) may differ.

Once you have selected a bookmaker, start by making some small bets as you get used to the market. As a beginner, choose large popular financial instruments such as the FTSE-100 index where the spreads tend to be narrower.

Place your order

Place your bet only when you have reason to think that the underlying share price, index, interest rates or similar will move up or down sharply.

The dealer will quote you a spread, created by a person or team of people who work for the bookmaker.

Use a firm that quotes prices on a screen, available both to you and anybody else. If instead the dealer gives you his quote on the telephone, he may try to read your intentions and price the deal against you.

If you close the deal by telephone, rather than via the Internet, be careful to state your requirements clearly and accurately to your dealer, and don't expect advice. Make sure that the dealer understands what you have said. The firm will be taping the call in case of dispute.

The bookmaker will post you out a contract note on the day that you dealt. This has important details of the deal, including time and date, amount, description and similar. Check it carefully, and raise any discrepancies at once. Keep your contract note as evidence of the details of the deal.

As with CFDs, you will not be encumbered with the usual costs linked with buying shares. You will pay no stamp duty on purchase, and you will require neither a nominee account nor share certificates.

YOUR OPEN POSITION

The bookmaker lays off its position

Your bet will be valid only when your dealer has confirmed it. The bookmaker will then typically lay off the bet to protect its own position. This is normally by buying a CFD.

You will usually find it cheaper and more efficient if you buy the CFDs directly yourself (see Seminar 14) rather than place a spread bet. Most of the trading techniques that you will use in spread betting are also applicable to CFDs. These include short selling and pairs trading.

Occasionally the financial bookmaker keeps its own book and matches buy bets with sells. This way, a firm could give you prices out of synchronization with those of other bookmakers, and so create an arbitrage opportunity. We will be looking at arbitrage in more detail later in this seminar.

Account administration

Every day that your bet remains open, there is a settlement on your account. In this respect, spread betting is again like CFDs (or other derivatives). If the price goes against you beyond the NTR, your bookmaker will telephone or write to you with an instruction to provide further margin to maintain a valid deposit. This is a cash call, and you can arrange for the firm to make the required deduction by credit card.

Conversely, if the price moves enough in your favour to provide enough to meet the requirement for a new initial margin, you can ask your bookmaker to refund you the remaining amount credited to your account. Meanwhile, you should be receiving interest on all cash deposited.

If you fail to keep up any required addition to your deposit on an ongoing basis, the bookmaker will close out your bet. You will be liable to pay any debts.

MONEY MANAGEMENT

Stops and limits

You must manage your money, using stop losses and maybe limit orders. The bookmaker will, if you wish, set a stop loss for you when you place your bet.

The conventional stop loss is not always enough. If you are betting on a volatile share or other financial instrument, the price may fall so fast that the firm cannot effectively apply the stop.

As a more reliable alternative, use a *guaranteed* stop (unavailable on traded options), which the spread-betting firm automatically applies when losses reach a set percentage level. To pay for this facility, the spread on your bet will be slightly larger.

For when the deal is going well, consider also using a limit order. This will enable you to close a bet at a predetermined profit level. You will get out while the going is good.

Some traders place a stop loss and limit order simultaneously, so defining the perimeters within which they will make a profit and loss.

Making a profit

You will pay neither commission nor fees to your financial bookmaker. Instead, the spread on any transaction gives the firm its profit margin, as well as covering expenses and betting tax.

The difference between the price at which you placed your bet and that at which you close it out will be your profit or loss.

Your profits are free of capital gains tax, and you need not declare them to the Inland Revenue. The corollary is that you cannot offset your losses against capital gains elsewhere.

Closing your bet

Before expiry, you can close down your bet whenever you like. Bear in mind that you will also have to close a stop loss, if you have placed one.

Your position will be automatically closed out at expiry. If you then renew your bet, you will have to again pay through the spread.

ADVANCED FINANCIAL SPREAD BETTING

Arbitrage

Arbitrage is when you make a profit based on the difference in the spread on the same bet offered by two respective bookmakers.

The game works as follows. If the spread offered by one firm has an upper price that is less than the lower price of a rival firm, you can buy from one and sell to the other, making a guaranteed profit on the difference.

Some Web sites claim to offer you details of risk arbitrage opportunities – in financial and other spread betting – in return for a subscription fee. In practice, such opportunities disappear pretty quickly.

If you are going to make money from arbitrage in financial spread betting, you will need to have accounts with several bookmakers, and to be quick off the mark. It will also take a lot of your time.

The bookmakers, once they catch on, are likely to ban your trades, as has happened to arbitrageurs in the past.

Currency trading

Spread betting is a simple way to benefit from the highly geared foreign exchange (forex) market, which is the City's main business.

The forex market is highly liquid and so not easily manipulated. Its price movements are not subject to bull and bear markets.

It is open 24 hours a day – which the financial bookmaker may not be – with buyers and sellers operating by telephone worldwide. Settlement is in two days, or sometimes less.

The most popular trades are between the US dollar and either Sterling or the Euro. Your risk is that a currency bet could go the wrong way. To protect yourself, enter your trade with a target level and a stop loss.

If as you hope, the market goes in your favour, you can either close out the deal (and your stop loss) or roll on the contract.

The charts dominate currency trading. If you get involved, make sure you get to grips with the principles of technical analysis explained in this book.

Besides spread betting, options and futures offer a way to trade forex. See Seminars 17 and 18 respectively.

RISKS AND REASSURANCES

A losers' club

Spread betting is a high-risk game. About 97 per cent of those who trade with financial spread-betting firms make a loss, according to industry sources. The 3 per cent of winners, however, make a lot of money.

The profits are capital gains tax-free, but most punters will never see any. Furthermore, this tax advantage may disappear if a trader derives his or her sole income from spread betting.

The spreads tend to be large as they must cover the bookmaker's profit margin, expenses and dealing tax. They are becoming narrower, but spread betting remains more viable if you are betting on large share price movements, when the spreads have less impact.

Regulation

Financial spread betting is not investment, but can impinge on it and so is not immune from the powers of The Financial Services Authority which regulates most of the firms. At the time of writing, the regulator has proposed an action against Paul Davidson, also known as 'The Plumber', for his role in influencing the market through a spread bet.

Self-made millionaire and former pipe fitter Davidson had placed a £6 million bet on Cyprotex in which he already had a 35 per cent stake before the company launched an IPO on the Alternative Investment Market.

Davidson claimed that his reason for placing the bet was to buy more shares, which he otherwise would have been unable to do. He placed his bet with City Index, and it was accepted and passed through the firm's compliance department.

City Index then protected its own position by taking out a contract for difference (see Seminar 14) with Dresdner Kleinwort Wasserstein which, in its turn, backed its position by buying a substantial share stake.

It has been suggested that, given the unfavourable market conditions of the time, the IPO could not have easily happened without this spread bet and the subsequent transactions. Davidson has denied knowledge of the transactions to which his spread bet ultimately gave rise.

INFORMATION

Web sites

If you are to use a spread-betting information service, try Onewaybet.com (www.onewaybet.com). This is the independent Web site run by Angus McCrone, a journalist who writes regularly for the London _Evening Standard_, and it is reliable. The site has tables comparing spreads and sizes of bets from financial bookmakers. It has quality educational material, and is updated regularly.

Books

See Seminar 21, where I recommend a couple of books on spread betting.

Training

In my view, you do not need training in the area of spread betting. You are better off reading books and articles and, most of all, learning from practical experience. If, however, you do decide to attend one of the advertised seminars, I urge you to check out the credentials of the trainer and not to overpay. If you pay, for example, £1,500 or more for a single day's training, you are probably throwing away money, and you could be using this to actually trade.

I know of a financial fraudster who served a sentence in a young offenders' institution, and who came out and set up various financial rackets. His most recent venture is highly priced spread-betting seminars and related services.

In selling these, he produces paperwork that provides apparent evidence of his huge wins on spread betting based on his understanding of financial markets.

He obtains this evidence by placing bets through two spread-betting firms at once, each in opposite directions. If the market shifts significantly, one bet will gain, and the other lose. At this point, he will sell out of both bets, breaking even except for the costs incurred from the spreads.

He will photocopy only the paperwork representing the *winning* bet and mail this to his potential clients as apparent cast-iron evidence of his successful recent track record in financial spread betting.

He repeats the trick regularly, representing himself as a guru with the Midas touch. This fools almost everybody.

THE NEXT STEP

In the next seminar, we will look at how to trade covered warrants.

SEMINAR 15 GOLDEN RULES

▌ Spread betting is more accessible for new investors than CFDs, but less cost-effective.

▌ Start by making small bets on popular financial instruments as you get used to the market.

▌ Place your bet only when you think that the underlying financial instrument will move up or down sharply.

▌ Place daily bets only if you can constantly watch your screen.

▌ Place options-based bets as an indirect way to trade options.

▌ Use a financial bookmaker that quotes firm prices on a screen.

▎ If you close the deal by telephone, state your requirements accurately and don't expect advice. Check your contract note carefully.

▎ In placing your bet, use a guaranteed stop loss and perhaps a limit order.

▎ You could place a stop loss and a limit order simultaneously, so defining the perimeters within which you will make a profit or loss.

▎ Arbitrage is sometimes possible, but you will need accounts with several bookmakers, and to be quick off the mark.

▎ Spread-betting profits are free of capital gains tax, but this will not affect the majority of punters. The tax advantage may disappear if the trader derives his or her whole income from spread betting.

▎ Most who trade with financial bookmakers lose money, but the winners make very high gains.

▎ Check the credentials of trainers in spread betting. Do not overpay for any training course.

Seminar 16

Success in covered warrants

INTRODUCTION

Covered warrants are the latest form of highly geared derivative. They were introduced to the UK only in late 2002, after some years of popularity in continental Europe, including in Germany, where they have been going for 12 years, and in Italy and Switzerland.

In this seminar, we will look at how covered warrants work, why you should trade them, and how to go about it.

THE BASICS

Definition

A covered warrant is a financial instrument that gives the holder the right, but not the obligation, to buy or sell a share (or other asset) at the end of, or during, a given period. This is unlike a traditional warrant, for which new shares can be issued.

Both types of warrant tend to rise and fall in value with the underlying shares, on a geared basis. Let us now take a brief further look at the traditional variety.

Traditional warrants

Traditional warrants are securities that a company issues on its own shares. They are listed and traded on the London Stock Exchange, but are not part of a company's share capital and so have no voting rights.

You can use traditional warrants to buy a specified number of *new* shares in a company at a specified exercise price (also known as strike price) at a given time (or within a given period). This is often, but not always, on the basis of one share for every warrant. The warrants have different conversion dates and prices.

Do not confuse traditional warrants with options (see Seminar 17), which enable you to buy *existing* shares, and to speculate on shares going down as well as up.

Traditional warrants usually have a longer period to expiry than options, but are not so often available on large liquid companies.

Enter a new player

You will find that covered warrants offer a more protected entrée into derivatives trading than options, futures, CFDs or spread betting. For this reason, they are of potential interest for starting traders.

These instruments are listed and traded on the London Stock Exchange, as well as various international exchanges. This provides a transparent market with prices displayed openly. You will always deal through a third party, typically a stockbroker.

The gearing on covered warrants means that, for every penny that you spend, you are investing in an option on some pennies of the underlying asset. If the price of the asset rises or falls, so does the warrant in a similar percentage amount.

As time passes, the covered warrant becomes less valuable. This is reflected in a declining premium, which is how much you pay for the right to buy or sell the underlying asset at fixed price in the future.

Every covered warrant has a limited period to maturity, which is likely to be 6–12 months, but could be up to 5 years. This tends to be less than for its traditional counterpart.

The covered warrant is priced on fair value. This is unlike its traditional counterpart, where the pricing criterion is supply and demand. It has a wider range of structures, and the market is more liquid.

The warrant is 'covered' because the issuer covers its position by simultaneously buying the underlying stock or financial instrument in the market.

PLACING YOUR ORDER

Calls or puts

As a trader of covered warrants, you can buy Calls, which enable you to profit if the price of the underlying share or other instrument rises beyond the level of your premium and dealing costs, or Puts, which give you a profit if the price falls below these.

European and American style

European-style covered warrants may be exercised only on a specific date or range of dates. American-style warrants are more flexible as they may be exercised at any time up to their expiry date.

In practice, you will not normally be exercising warrants, but trading them, so the distinction is unimportant.

Spread your risk

Through covered warrants, you can spread your risk across a range of investments or markets more cheaply than by taking positions in the underlying instruments. This is invaluable for diversifying your assets.

It is possible to invest in basket warrants, which cover a group of securities, typically in a sector. You can put a covered warrant in a self-invested personal pension (SIPP), but not into an Individual Savings Account (ISA).

Dealing with your stockbroker

Find a stockbroker that will trade covered warrants. Before you deal, you will need to sign a form stating that you understand how covered warrants work. You will not, however, be required to satisfy an investor suitability test, as for options trading.

Your broker can obtain a price through the issuing banks, and trade for you this way. Or it can use an alternative quote-driven market provided by retail service providers, which represent the issuers.

Because of the market's transparency, and competition among market makers, the spread on covered warrants is quite tight.

You will pay a dealing commission that is broadly in line with what you would pay in buying or selling shares. The typical deal size is around £2,000–£3,000, indicating that this is a market for private investors.

Trades must be reported within three minutes. Electronic settlement takes place within three days through the CREST automated settlement system, and is normally for cash, although there is an alternative of physical settlement.

Purchase

Upon your purchase of covered warrants, you will pay no stamp duty. As an owner, you will receive no dividend from the underlying share. You cannot write covered warrants as you can options.

Unlike in the case of other derivatives, the most that you can lose is 100 per cent of your money. Also, if you fail to exercise your in-the-money option on a covered warrant before expiry, it will be automatically done on your behalf.

You will be liable to capital gains tax (40 per cent) on profits above the current £7,700 exemption limit.

VALUATION

The underlying asset

As part of valuing a warrant, it is important to value the underlying asset, which is typically but not always a stock. Use techniques of fundamental and technical analysis covered in this book.

The warrant structure

You will also need to check the structure of the warrant itself.

Cover ratio

Check how many warrants are needed to exercise one share, which is shown in the cover ratio. This is often one warrant for every share, which creates a cover ratio of 1:1.

A few warrants are exercisable as a number per share. For example, a cover ratio of 7:1 indicates 7 warrants exercisable for every share. To make comparison easier, restate prices as per a single warrant.

Price

A warrant's price is made up of the premium, and the intrinsic value. The premium includes the issuer's costs of hedging the transaction, and a profit margin. As we have seen, it becomes lower as the warrant moves towards the end of its life.

In a Call warrant, the intrinsic value is the price of the underlying asset, less the exercise price, which is the price at which you can exercise the warrant. If a share trades at £2.70, and a warrant gives the right to buy one share at £2.10, it will have an intrinsic value of 60p.

In a Put warrant, this works in reverse. If the warrant gives you the right to sell one share at £1.20p, and stock is trading at £1.00, it will have an intrinsic value of 20p.

If a share has intrinsic value, it is in the money. If it is neutral, it is at the money, and, if it has negative intrinsic value, it is out of the money.

Gearing

Check also the level of gearing, which is the amount of borrowing in proportion to your warrant holding. This is the underlying share or asset price divided by the price of the warrant, and multiplied by the cover ratio. The lower the figure, the better.

Black–Scholes model

How it works

You should calculate fair value for covered warrants through the Black–Scholes model, and then compare this to the market price. The model, first published in 1973 by Fischer Black and Myron Scholes, was first applied to Call and Put options on equities (see Seminar 17).

It assesses fair value, taking into account the covered warrant's value, its exercise price, its time until expiry, the risk-free interest rate, and volatility. To use the model, you will need knowledge of certain ratios that are expressed as Greek letters.

Of these, the most important is the Delta, which measures the warrant price's sensitivity to changes in the price of the underlying share. Use this to assess how quickly the warrant is likely to move, and how far. If the Delta is 1, for every 5p that the warrant moves, the share will move 5p too.

The Gamma measures how sensitive the Delta is to share price changes, and the Theta assesses how much value the premium loses as time progresses. Vega measures the warrant's price sensitivity to volatility, and Rho its price sensitivity to interest rates.

Volatility

Volatility is important except when warrants are either deeply in the money, or deeply out of the money. It may be calculated as historic or implied.

Historical volatility involves extrapolating likely future trends from the past. You calculate it as the standard deviation of a range of natural logarithms (the day's price divided by the previous day's) on price date changes over a given period. Multiply the standard deviation by the square root of the number of entries, and express the result as a percentage. There is an accuracy problem as the result varies according to the range that you select.

Implied volatility is derived from the price of the covered warrant itself and is seen as more reliable. It typically rises at the year-end, just before results are announced, so making the price of the covered warrant rise too.

As a rule of thumb, if implied volatility is more than the historical, the covered warrant is expensive.

Criticisms

The Black–Scholes model has worked over a period, and is widely relied on. But it has limitations.

The model assumes an efficient market, no jumps in volatility, and a constant risk-free rate. It also assumes no transaction costs, and no early exercising of warrants.

The price of the underlying share or other financial instrument is assumed to be lognormally distributed with constant mean and volatility.

These assumptions are not all justified, and some have seen fit to tweak Black–Scholes accordingly. Use the model only as a broad yardstick for valuation.

TRADING

General

Covered warrants are highly geared. If, for instance, you buy Calls, and they rise in value as you hope, you will make a bigger return on your money than if you had invested directly in the underlying asset.

The more volatile the warrant, the bigger the chances of a good profit, and if it is long dated, this gives you more time to make this. The price of your warrant will reflect these factors.

If you buy a short-dated warrant when volatility is low, this will cost less, and so you could make more money. But time your purchase for when the underlying share is likely to move sharply in value.

You can lose a high proportion of capital invested, so use a stop loss.

Specialist techniques

Straddle

Use a straddle if you expect the underlying stock to move significantly, but you do not know in which direction.

In a long straddle, you will buy Call and Put warrants simultaneously. You will gain if the warrant moves substantially, whether up or down. The move will need to be enough to exceed the expense of two premiums as well as the high commissions payable on a straddle.

Cash extraction

Cash extraction is when you sell your portfolio of shares and leave most of the proceeds as cash in a high-interest-bearing account. You will put the remainder in covered warrants.

Hedging

You can cover your stock position by taking an opposite position, much more cheaply due to the gearing effect, in warrants. Such hedging is as covered in Seminar 14 on CFDs, and is common to derivatives generally.

If, for example, you held some tech stocks, you could take a Put warrant on the Nasdaq, the US high-tech stock market index.

If the tech stocks should then rise, you would make money on the gain, although you would lose on your warrant. But if your tech stocks fell, your gains on the Put warrant could compensate.

INFORMATION

Web sites

You will find much information about covered warrants on the Internet.

Visit the Web sites of the issuing banks. These include Commerzbank (www.commerzbank.com), Dresdner Kleinwort Wasserstein (www.drkw.com), Goldman Sachs (www.gs.com/uk/), JP Morgan (www.jpmorganinvestor.com), Société Générale (www.warrants.com/uk/), and Trading Lab (www.tradinglab.co.uk).

Also, visit www.onvista.co.uk, and www.warrantstats.com.

THE NEXT STEP

In the next seminar, we will look at traded options, which are longer established than covered warrants, and not dissimilar, but are also riskier.

SEMINAR 16 GOLDEN RULES

▌ Do not trade covered warrants unless you can make the time to select them carefully and to watch them.

▌ You cannot lose more than 100 per cent of cash invested in a traded warrant. This provides a safety net that is not available on other derivatives.

▌ Unlike in spread betting, covered warrants are a transparent market. As a result of this, and of competition between market makers, the spreads are tight.

▌ In assessing fair value for covered warrants, use the Black–Scholes model, but only as a yardstick as not all its assumptions are valid. Also, value the underlying asset.

▌ Buy your warrant when volatility is low, but when the share price is likely to move sharply in value. Short-term warrants are cheaper than long-term.

▌ Warrants, like all derivatives, are highly geared, so it is crucial to use a stop loss.

▌ Use a straddle if you believe that the covered warrant will move significantly up or down, but you are not sure which.

Part Four

Further speculating secrets

Seminar 17

How to profit from traded options

INTRODUCTION

In this section, we will look at traded options. These are highly geared derivatives, but they are also extremely flexible. They often do well when interest rates are declining, as investors are then willing to commit cash from their deposit accounts.

HISTORY

On anecdotal evidence from the City, a maximum of only one in five of private individuals who trade options make money. Your broker is obliged to apply an investor suitability test to decide whether it can let you trade.

Despite the risks, the options market has from the 1980s experienced around 40 per cent compound annual growth. The London International Financial Futures and Options Exchange (LIFFE) (www.liffe.com) has played a large part in this.

There are always a few who deal options unscrupulously. They have been prevalent in the UK particularly in the late 1980s. In this period, I recall how one advisory options broker tried to recruit me as a salesperson. At interview, the sales director boasted of the firm's technique for hooking private investors. *Ask the client if he thinks that the market is going up or down. Whatever his reply, say that you agree with him, and sell him an option accordingly.*

This type of salesmanship was, and remains, surprisingly effective as the majority of private options traders believe that they know best, and will warm to a salesperson who offers them flattery, rather than best advice.

The salespeople who operate in this way will, for obvious reasons, not necessarily remain in their jobs. The sales director at my interview foresaw the problem. 'You're salespeople, here today, gone tomorrow,' he said. 'Use another name if you like.'

Needless to say, I declined the invitation to work for his firm. Subsequently, the sales director kept ringing me up and pleading how his firm could *use* somebody with my track record in equities dealing. His finishing line was always how much money he *knew* that I could make.

To nobody's surprise, this firm lasted several years, nimbly sidestepping disgruntled clients and hiring top lawyers to help tread a path through the legacy of loss-making trades that it was perpetually creating.

When the firm collapsed under pressure of mounting complaints, the sales director defected to the south of France where he lived in secluded luxury for a few years, chartering his own yacht.

For rip-off salespeople, employed at this and similar firms, these were the glory days. Such firms still exist, particularly but not exclusively outside the UK, but they disguise themselves a little more cleverly. Never have dealings with an actual or suspect rogue firm, as this is likely to cost you substantial money.

HOW OPTIONS WORK

The basics

Let us define the beast with which we are dealing. An option is a financial instrument that enables you to bet on the movement of individual shares, or of indices, currencies, commodities or interest rates.

The option gives you the right but not the obligation to buy or sell a security at a pre-determined price, which is the exercise price, within a specified period or, less commonly, on a specified day.

The market price that you will pay for the option is known as the premium, and is typically 10–15 per cent of the size of the option. For every buyer of an option, there is a seller, also known as a writer, but neither side has the odds intrinsically in its favour. There is no casino that rakes in the overwhelming majority of the profits.

Traditional options require you to exercise them, which means that you must buy or sell the underlying security to establish any profit or loss. Traded options, which came to the UK in 1978, are more popular as they can be traded as well as exercised.

In practice, most prefer to trade rather than to exercise an option. As options are a very liquid market, this is rarely a problem. In this seminar, we are concerned only with traded options.

Calls and puts

Call options
You can buy a _Call_ option, which gives you the right but not the obligation to buy the underlying security at the exercise price.

If the exercise price is lower than the underlying security's current market price, the option is in the money. The difference between the exercise price and the current market price represents the option's value.

If the exercise price is higher than the current market price, the Call option is out of the money.

As the buyer of a _Call_ option, you will make money if the price of the underlying share moves up so that it becomes more than the exercise price plus the premium that you have paid.

In this case, you could exercise the option by buying the underlying shares, but it is usually simpler to trade it as a profit.

Put options
You can buy a _Put_ option, which gives you the right, but not the obligation, to sell a security at the exercise price.

If the exercise price is higher than the underlying security's current market price, the option is in the money. If it is lower, the option is out of the money.

As a holder of a Put option, you will make money if the option price falls to below the level of the exercise price plus the premium that you have paid.

Intrinsic and time value

The extent to which the underlying stock's value surpasses the option's exercise price is known as intrinsic value. An option therefore only has intrinsic value when it is in the money.

The time value of an option is its total value less intrinsic value. The more time an option has until it expires, the higher this figure is likely to be, as the price of the underlying stock has corresponding time to change in the option buyer's favour.

The premium, which, as we have seen, is the market price that you pay for the option, consists of both intrinsic and time value.

Both the intrinsic and time value can change constantly as options move in and out of the money.

In and out of the money

As an option moves deeper into the money, the premium rises. Conversely, as it moves more out of the money, the premium becomes cheaper. When the exercise price is equal to the current market price, this is at the money.

When the option is in the money, its price will move largely pound for pound with the underlying share, although the increasing reduction in time value will disrupt this. When the option is out of the money, the movement of the underlying stock becomes less important than the passing of time.

A deep out-of-the-money option is called a tiny option. If the option is still out of the money shortly before expiring, the letters CAB may replace the premium. This stands for *in the cabinet*, and signifies that the option is stored out of sight because it will probably expire without any value.

Gearing

As a traded options buyer, you can trade with small amounts of money and make proportionately much higher gains than if you were investing in the underlying share or index. Conversely, if the option doesn't go as planned, you will lose your entire investment – in percentage terms enormous but, in actual terms, not necessarily much.

In these ways, the option is highly geared, rising or falling in value proportionately more sharply than the underlying security. As you should by now be aware, this is as applies to all derivatives.

The option writer

The writer – also known as seller – of the option receives from you the premium that you paid as buyer. This is his compensation for the risk of selling an option to you. As a result, the writer is under certain obligations, and must deposit collateral with his or her broker to cover these. This collateral is held as initial margin, which is recalculated daily and may require topping up.

In the case of a Call option, the writer will have to sell the shares at the exercise price if the option is exercised. You will want this only if the underlying shares rise above the level of the exercise price and premium, together with all your dealing costs.

In the case of a Put option the writer will have to buy the shares at the exercise price if the option is exercised. You will only want this if the shares fall below the level of the exercise price by at least the premium and your dealing costs. In both Call and Put options, if you do not exercise the option, you will lose the premium to the writer.

The writer makes frequent profits, by pocketing premiums from options that expire without being exercised, but his or her risks are high. Writing options is a game that you can get into too, as we shall see later in this seminar.

Contract size and price

Equity options

Equity options come in the standard contract size, which is 1,000 shares. Note that this size may vary if the underlying company is involved in a capital restructuring such as a rights issue (see Seminar 13).

On this basis, to find the cost of your option contract, multiply the option price by 1,000. If, for example, a Call option is priced at 70p, it will cost £700 per contract.

Options on LIFFE have expiry dates grouped three, six or nine months ahead. A first group of companies has the expiry dates of January, April, July and October; a second group has February, May, August and November; and a third group expires in March, June, September and December.

This way, in any given month, options for only a third of the relevant companies will expire. When, for example, a contract expires in March, a new one is created for expiry in June.

Index options

Options on stock market indices, known as index options, are essentially contracts for difference (see Seminar 14). They are riskier than equity options as they often trade for larger amounts, perhaps several thousand pounds a contract against several hundred pounds. They are also more volatile.

If, for example, you hold a 5,200 index Call option, and the index goes up to 5,300 and you exercise your option, you will gain 100 points. The indices trade at £10 a point, giving you a profit of £100 × £10, or £1,000.

As in covered warrants (see Seminar 16), index options are either American style, which you can exercise at any time until expiry, or European style, which you can exercise only on the expiry day, and so tend to have a lower premium. In practice, it rarely matters in which category your options fall, as it is normal to trade them before expiry.

VALUATION

The Black–Scholes model

When selecting traded options, you will find that they are not priced mainly on supply and demand. Traditionally, they are valued according to the Black–Scholes model, although there are now a number of variations on this method.

Black–Scholes takes into account the option's intrinsic and time value, as well as that no dividend is paid. See Seminar 16 for details on how the model works and why it is not wholly reliable.

The Long Term Capital Management (LTCM), an investment fund founded by ex-Salomon Brothers trader John Meriwether, relied partly on the Black–Scholes model to manage its assets using aggressive derivatives strategies.

Initially, LTCM worked well, offering shareholders a 42.8 per cent return in 1995, 40.8 per cent in 1996 and 17.1 per cent in 1997. But it made the mistake of assuming efficient markets. In 1998, the fund failed, and was bailed out by the US Federal Reserve.

Today too, the Black–Scholes model does not work perfectly, and options are sometimes wrongly priced on this basis. If you can find the anomalies, you can make money.

Put/Call ratios

Also, watch Put/Call ratios. When there are many buyers of *Calls* on equities, leading to a low Put/Call ratio, a reversal is likely. Conversely, when many investors are buying *Puts*, leading to a high Put/Call ratio, buyers will probably emerge and send the market soaring.

GETTING STARTED

Broker commissions and price data

Buying an option is the most common way of getting involved in this market, and is where you are likely to start. You need a broker, and should take your time choosing.

Brokers' terms vary. Some deal only by telephone, and many will require you to put up significant margin. Charges are wide-ranging, and some brokers include the commission for closing the option trade with that of the opening trade. You will pay an industry levy of £1.80 per contract.

If you lack trading experience, use an advisory broker. This type of firm will have higher charges than the execution-only broker but can save you from making expensive mistakes.

Later, when you have some trading experience, you can shop around for a broker that cuts its charges on the basis that it does not advise you. Once you are a frequent trader, such lower charges can swing the difference between an overall profit and loss.

Prices and spreads

Sometimes your broker will provide prices online. LIFFE (www.liffe.co.uk) offers you 15-minute-delayed prices. Satellite and cable TV provide 20-minute delayed prices. For a small annual subscription, Prestel (www.prestel.co.uk) provides live traded option prices and related services.

Before you trade options, check the spreads of options carefully. Published options prices are usually the mid-price, which is between the bid price at which you sell, and the offer price at which you buy. This spread can be wide. Calculate how much movement in the price is needed to cover this spread before you start moving into profit.

Margin and settlement

Once you have completed an option purchase, you will pay initial margin, which normally covers the premium. This goes to the writer of the option.

The financial settlement takes place through the London Clearing House. This is a clearing organization operated by LIFFE, which is counterparty to the trade between you as buyer, and the writer.

LIFFE guarantees settlement for the holder of the winning position. It will require you to top up your initial margin if your position declines in value to a level not covered.

STRATEGIES

General

To trade options as a *speculator*, you will need to have time to watch the market closely, and you will require a stop loss.

If you have bought an option and it is not moving, cut your losses and sell it. If you were to wait until the option is close to expiry, and it had still not moved, the premium would be worth much less.

Also use options to *hedge* your position in a share or index. This makes sense if this underlying investment is volatile. If, for instance, you believe that the market will crash, you could buy *Put* options in your stocks. If the share price crashes, you could compensate by selling the Puts for a profit.

Basic bullish strategies

Buy a Call option

If you think the underlying security or index will rise significantly in the short term, buy a *Call* option. You may foresee such a rise if, for example, the company is target of a rumoured takeover bid or you are expecting good news.

If the share price overreaches the level of the exercise price plus your premium (and dealing expenses), it will be worth while selling your option on the market, and taking a profit. If you believe that the share price will rise higher, the better strategy is to wait and sell later for a higher profit. As an alternative, you can exercise the option.

Write a Put option

As a riskier alternative to buying a *Call* option, you can become the writer of a *Put* option. This way, you will receive the premium from the buyer, which is the main attraction of the deal.

If, as usually happens, the *Put* expires worthless, you will keep the premium without having to buy the underlying stock.

But if the share price falls below the exercise price, your profits will decrease and, once they have declined by the value of the premium (plus the buyer's dealing costs), you will be vulnerable. The option is then likely to be exercised; in which case you must buy shares at the exercise price, which is above the market value of the stock.

As an options writer, you will never lose more than the value of the underlying share, as its price cannot fall below 0 pence. Despite this, City professionals avoid writing *Put* options due to unfortunate experience. I know of one young female trader who lost a fortune this way during the initial market correction of high-tech stocks in March and April 2000.

Basic bearish strategies

Buy a Put option

Buying a put option is also your simplest strategy when you think that a share price or index will plummet. This is very likely to be in a bear market. If the share price falls below the level of the exercise price plus your premium (plus dealing costs), you will make a profit from selling the option. Of course, if you think the price will continue to fall, you may do better to wait with a view to trading later, or to exercising.

In a similar speculative spirit, if, in buying a Put option, you have misjudged the stock's direction, and the share price soars, you can sell it for less than you paid, taking a loss. Otherwise, you can continue to hold in the hope that the share price will fall back before the option expires.

Write a Call option

As a parallel bear strategy, you could write a *Call* option. If so, you will take a premium from the buyer, and will retain it only if the option is not exercised. This should happen only if the share price fails to rise above the exercise price plus premium (and dealing costs) before the option expires.

If you write a *naked* Call option, you do not own the shares that you are selling. This carries additional risk. If the option is exercised against you, you will have to buy shares at the prevailing market price to sell them at the lower exercise price.

Under these circumstances, your loss will be the difference between the exercise price and the prevailing share price, plus all dealing expenses. This is offset by the premium that you will have received, and will keep.

In theory, as a naked Call writer, your risk is theoretically unlimited. In practice, the risk is limited by time, and also by the fact that stock prices do not soar to infinity.

Advanced strategies

The Buy write

To implement Buy write strategy, you will buy a stock and simultaneously either buy or write an option on it. By this strategy, you can reduce or increase your risk, and, with it, your reward potential.

For example, if you buy a stock and a put option on it, and the share price falls, you will make money on the option as compensation.

You can be bolder. If you buy a stock and a call option on it, and the share price rises, you will make money twice: first on the stock, and, second, through the option. But if the stock price falls, you will lose money twice.

A favoured variation is to buy a stock and simultaneously to write a Call option on it with an exercise price of, say, 10 per cent above the stock price. If the share price rises, but not above the exercise price plus premium (and option buyer's dealing expenses), you will keep the premium. If it does overreach this level, you will be forced to provide the shares at exercise price. But you will have made a 10 per cent profit on the underlying shares, and will keep the premium.

The straddle

Use a straddle if you expect the underlying stock to move significantly, but you do not know in which direction.

In a long straddle, you will simultaneously buy a Call option and a Put option each at an identical exercise price and expiration dates

If you are to make a profit on the trade, the share price will need to move up or down enough to exceed the expense of two premiums as well as the high commissions payable on a straddle.

The spread

A spread is when you buy an option and write one simultaneously on the same stock. These two options should each be at a different expiry date (calendar spread) or exercise price.

STOCK MARKET SPECULATORS' HALL OF FAME

Member No 6 – Nick Leeson

Nick Leeson has achieved worldwide notoriety as the working-class lad who bust Barings, the investment bank, by illicit gambling on derivatives. The event demonstrated to the world how risky derivatives are.

As a 28-year-old from Watford who had notoriously failed his maths A level, Leeson started out as a settlement clerk at Barings. By 1993, he had become general manager and star trader in the bank's Singapore office.

Leeson's trading strategies were largely based on arbitrage, which means profiting from often minute price differentials between the same securities on different markets.

In January 1995, Barings started writing Put and Call options on the Nikkei 225 index at the same exercise price. This created a straddle – the simultaneous purchase of a *Call* option and *Put* option at an identical strike price and expiration dates.

As the options writer, Barings would have kept the premiums only if the index stayed within the 19,000–21,000 trading range. On January 17, Kobe and Osaka were hit by a huge earthquake and the Nikkei 225 fell below the 19,000 level, putting Barings' profits at risk. On 23 January, the index was down to 17,950.

Leeson started buying March and June 95 futures contracts, which were a bet on an improvement in the market. But the Index deteriorated further, and eventually Barings had lost more than £800m, which was more than its capital.

The Bank of England did not bail out Barings as some had expected and, eventually, Dutch insurer ING acquired the bust bank.

Nick Leeson was jailed for his role in the bank's demise, and he wrote a fascinating book about his experiences, *Rogue Trader*, which was later made into a film.

Use a spread when you expect the price of the underlying stock to move only slightly, without overreaching the exercise prices of the two options.

The spread costs less than a straddle because the premium that you receive from writing the option at least partly offsets that which you pay.

Turbo charging

This is when you buy two Calls or Puts that are similar but with different exercise prices. If the options then move in your favour, you stand to make more than if you had bought one option. You also risk losing more.

Butterfly spread

If you want to limit your risk, you can create a butterfly spread. To achieve this, buy four different options at three exercise prices, so limiting risk. The price that you will pay is that you limit profit.

Other risk limitation strategies

The Christmas tree spread similarly limits risk and reward. It requires you to buy six options using four strike prices.

The Condor spread – also known as the top hat spread – has the same effect. This involves buying one Call, selling two others and buying a fourth, at different strike prices.

The Cylinder involves buying an option and simultaneously writing one for the same amount but at a different exercise price. This way, you can offset the premium received on writing one option against the purchase cost of the other. This minimizes your financial outlay.

By another technique, a Boston, you can avoid paying the premium on an option purchased until the exercise date.

Other strategies worth investigating include the pyramid, the tarantula, and the carousel. For details on how these work, see Seminar 18, which covers futures.

FURTHER RESEARCH

Education counts

If you want to explore traded options further, I urge you to visit The Chicago Board Options Exchange (www.cboe.com). This site gives you a sound and lively course on options. Do not be put off by the US focus, as the underlying principles are the same.

Otherwise, LIFFE offers a good online course on options at its Web site (www.liffe.co.uk). For a useful overview, visit the site of Shaeffersresearch. com (www.shaeffersresearch.com). Among brokers, Berkeley Futures (www.bfi.co.uk) has a useful starter guide: *Everything you need to know about futures and options, but were afraid to ask.*

Take advantage of free software that shows how options are structured and priced, For this purpose, download Optimum software free from the Web site of Nigel Webb Software at www.warp9.org/nwsoft.

THE NEXT STEP

In the next seminar, we will take a look at futures. These are the wilder cousins of options and a market mainly for professionals.

SEMINAR 17 GOLDEN RULES

▌ When interest rates decline, investors seek to put cash on deposit elsewhere, which can benefit the options market.

▌ Neither the buyer nor the writer of a traded option has the odds intrinsically in its favour.

▌ As the option moves deeper into the money, the premium rises.

▌ You can make money from trading options that have been mispriced on the basis of the Black–Scholes model.

▌ When the Put/Call ratio is low, expect sellers to emerge, and, when it is high, buyers.

▌ If you are starting out, an advisory broker can save you from some expensive mistakes.

▌ Check the spread of an option before you buy, as this can be wide.

▌ If you have bought an option and it is not moving, cut your losses and sell before the passing of time erodes its value further.

▌ To protect your position, write covered rather than naked Calls.

▌ Use a straddle if you expect the underlying stock to move significantly, but you are not sure in which direction.

▌ Use a spread when you expect the price of the underlying stock to move only slightly, without overreaching the strike price of the two options.

▌ To keep the delta at zero, buy and sell securities and options on them appropriately.

▌ To limit risk, create a Butterfly spread, a Christmas tree spread, or a Condor spread.

▌ Conduct further research into options, starting with the Chicago Board Options Exchange at www.cboe.com.

Seminar 18

How to win at trading futures

INTRODUCTION

Futures are a high-risk form of derivative that is becoming increasingly accessible to the private speculator. They can be on either commodities or financial instruments such as shares. In this seminar, we will look at how the futures market started and how it works.

THE BASICS

History

In the early to mid-19th century, mid-West farmers were visiting Chicago to sell their future crops at a fixed price, and this gave rise to the earliest form of commodity futures. This way, the farmers had a guaranteed sale and so could lock into a certain profit. If they had retained their crop instead of selling it, they would have taken the risk of the price of their crops moving against them.

The traders who bought from the farmers were speculators. They hoped that the crops would be worth more on the sell date than they had paid. Futures still work on this principle today.

Types

Commodity futures are a binding agreement to buy or sell a given quantity of an asset at today's price on a specified future date. This could be, for instance, cocoa, sugar or wheat.

In the 1970s, financial futures started to appear. These are based on a financial instrument such as a share, index, interest rate or currency. In their case, the defining agreement is to exchange a cash sum that reflects the difference between the initial price of the underlying asset and its price on settlement.

How futures work

Gearing and margin

Like all derivatives, futures are highly geared. Similarly, whether you go long or short on a contract, you will initially put up only a part payment as initial margin. In the usual way, you will need to top this up if you are to hold open your position should the value of your contract have moved too far against you. Your broker will keep you informed of the daily-adjusted profit or loss in your position.

Trading

In theory, you can run your futures contract to expiry. In practice, you are likely to trade it, in which case, if you have bought a contract, you will sell it, or if you have sold, you will buy.

By trading before expiry in this way, you can avoid, for instance, physical delivery of the cocoa or sugar on commodity futures. You can also sell short.

Trading is possible because futures contracts are standardized. The delivery date and the amount of the underlying asset are both stated. As promoters of futures have put it, the price at which you buy or sell reflects fair value, and there are no hidden charges. As with other derivatives, you will not pay stamp duty on your purchase.

Price

The price of commodity futures is directly linked to the cash or spot price, which is that of the underlying commodity. Delivery can be in September, December, March and June.

The futures price on the earliest of these months, called the front month contract, is closest to the spot price. It will be slightly more, however, to include interest, dealing charges, and, where relevant, the cost of storing the underlying commodity.

If the gap between the futures price on the front month contract and the spot price were too wide, arbitrageurs would reduce it.

LIFFE

Futures are traded on a regulated exchange, where prices are placed in a central order book. In the UK, this is the London International Futures and Options Exchange (LIFFE) (www.liffe.com). See Seminar 17 for the Exchange's role in options.

Trading of futures on LIFFE is electronic, unlike in the past, when traders in coloured jackets shouted at each other on the floor. On this basis, trading is liquid and transparent. The Exchange publishes the prices and the number of futures contracts traded, as well as the open interest, which shows contracts that have not yet been closed out.

As for options trading, LIFFE sets the rules for futures. The London Clearing House takes the margin payments from buyers and sellers. On this basis, it guarantees all trades and open contracts against defaulting.

Range

The range of commodity futures traded on LIFFE is substantial. Among the most popular are Robusta coffee and No 5 white sugar, as well as BIFFEX, which enables ship owners to hedge against volatility of shipping rates.

You will also find a variety of financial futures here. Among these are Universal Stock Futures (USFs), which are on shares in large individual companies. The contract is based on 1,000 shares in the case of UK companies, but on 100 shares for continental European or US companies.

As a trader in USFs, your profit or loss will be the applicable number of shares multiplied by the share price movement. Such trades have in the past marginally outperformed CFDs and spread bets, according to a LIFFE survey.

You can also trade index futures. If you are a private speculator on limited resources, the Mini FTSE-100 index futures are designed to appeal. Trading at three-month intervals, these are valued at only £2.00 per index point, which will limit your gains but also your exposure.

Other financial futures are on interest rates or currencies. You can trade, for instance, short-term sterling interest rates. The relevant contract trades at a discount to 100. If the market expects rates of 3 per cent at the time of delivery, the contract will trade at 97 (100 less 3).

Futures are also available on bonds. In contracts on long-term government bonds, the price reflects the perceived likely price of a notional government bond with a specified coupon and maturity rate.

TRADING

Success rate

Only one in ten at most of those who trade futures makes a profit, according to unrefuted anecdotal evidence.

How can you increase your chances of success? Successful stock market speculators agree that you need a plan. First, find a suitable broker.

Your broker

In the UK, only paid-up members of LIFFE can trade futures. Your broker must have access to these members if it is to offer futures dealing services to the public.

As in the case of options, if you are starting out as a speculator in futures, you are best off using an advisory broker.

Such a firm may make misplaced recommendations or become over-zealous but it may also protect you from major losses. It will charge higher commissions than execution-only firms, but this could be a small price to pay.

If you are a beginner, find a broker with no minimum charges, as this means that you can trade in small amounts with impunity.

When you open an account, you must send in a deposit, and sign both a client agreement letter and a risk warning form. Read the documentation carefully. As you will be ultimately responsible for your own gains and losses, do not trade until you understand what you are doing.

Avoid the sharks

At this point, I must give you a warning, which will be familiar to my clients, students, and readers. Learn to recognize and avoid the shark futures traders.

Professionals who have years of experience in fleecing the public of its money manage these bucket shops. As we have seen elsewhere in this book, the firm may also be selling shares or options. It will claim to specialize in anything that it can represent as an investment, including modern art, fine wines and whisky.

The end result is always the same. The sharks will effectively steal your money, laundering it through obscure offshore financial institutions, and you will never see a penny of it again, no matter what reassurances they give you.

The futures dealers who work in these firms all support each other and it can be hard for the client on the other end of the telephone to detect their lack of integrity.

The lifestyle that these white-collar bandits enjoy from their ill-gotten gains is lavish. I know of a sales manager of one such futures dealing firm who lives in a £3 million London house for which he has paid outright. He sends his children to top private schools, and has incredible holidays abroad. In addition, he has a small fortune in offshore savings.

This character is one of a kind and he runs his dealing floor ruthlessly. If he sees any of his dealers sitting down during the day, he lumbers towards them and bawls: 'What's this? Bear Corner. Chairs are for bears. Stand up.' He dismisses constant under-performers.

As a client of such a firm, you may hear such shouting in the background as you speak with your dealer on the phone. The brokers may appear too plausible and, no matter how they might disguise it, too pushy.

Such a bucket shop may make it suspiciously easy for you to become a client. It may welcome even the smallest trade, knowing that the next step, or the one after that, could be to fleece you of all that you have.

Be selective

Once you have sidestepped such pitfalls and selected a *suitable* broker, you will need to concentrate on the transaction.

If you are starting out, go for financial futures. These are traded more often than commodity futures, and relevant information is more widely available. This helps to create a more predictable market.

Once you have some experience, consider commodity futures. Trading these can be highly profitable, but you must understand the characteristics of the underlying asset. This way, you can make an informed guess about how the futures will perform in reaction to world events. For example, it is political factors that influence the price of oil or gold, but climactic changes that impact grain.

To keep your risk low without sacrificing potential reward, trade in countries that are familiar to you.

Use technical analysis

Professional futures traders tend to use technical analysis, and you would be wise not to turn your back on this.

Many trade on familiar chart patterns, and it can often be profitable to follow suit. In particular, watch support and resistance levels, and trading volume.

We cover technical analysis in detail in Seminars 7–11, and also 19–20.

SPECIALIST TRADING TECHNIQUES

Pyramid trading

Use pyramid trading as a way to average down. You will be buying new contracts similar to what you already hold as the price drops. This way, you will reduce your average price paid.

Once the contract rises above the average level that you have paid for the contract plus all dealing costs, you will be showing a profit.

Tarantula trading

For tarantula trading, you will need a number of futures contracts, long and short, which compensate for each other and all have the same delivery date.

These contracts are the legs of your tarantula. Each contract purchase starts at the furthermost part of the leg. It ends in the spider's body.

When any long contract shows a loss, the spider's leg is broken, but it will heal if the contract turns to profit. You can start a long contract again, at a different price.

Carousel

The Carousel has any number of contracts. The inner horse represents a new crop or production, and the outer horse represents the old.

As the carousel spins, this marks the passing of time. You should let the profitable relationships between the horses run, but cut the losses short.

Three-dimensional chess

Three-dimensional chess enables you to set up contracts with a variety of delivery dates. You may close out a futures contract on a central chessboard. You can then set up similar contracts with a longer delivery date on a longer chessboard, or with a shorter delivery date on a shorter chessboard.

FUTURES TRADERS

Futures are high risk, due to their volatility and high gearing. You can lose 100 per cent of your money or more very quickly. They are most suitable for sophisticated traders.

Many of these are large companies. They will use futures in interest rates or currencies for hedging purposes. Manufacturers use commodity futures to ensure that farmers deliver raw material such as sugar or wheat when required, and at a fixed price.

There are ways to trade futures with small sums of money, including through the spread-betting firms. Only trade with money that you can afford to lose, and apply basic principles of trading and money management (see Seminars 3 and 4).

THE NEXT STEP

In the next seminar, it is time to return to technical analysis. We will look at Fibonacci numbers and Elliott Wave theory.

SEMINAR 18 GOLDEN RULES

▌ Start by trading financial futures. These are more predictable than commodity futures.

▌ If you are a private speculator on limited resources, consider Mini FTSE-100 index futures on LIFFE.

▌ As a beginner, you are best off using an advisory broker.

▌ Learn to recognize and to avoid the shark futures traders. A pushy dealer or background shouting is a tell-tale sign.

▌ Before you trade commodity futures, understand the unique characteristics of the underlying asset.

▌ Use pyramid trading to reduce the average cost of your contracts.

Seminar 19

Fibonacci and Elliott Wave

INTRODUCTION

In this seminar, we will examine the theories of Leonardo Fibonacci, an Italian mathematician. We will then look at Wave theory in general.

FIBONACCI

Early days

The mathematician now known as Leonardo Fibonacci was born in about 1170 as humble Leonardo. On his father's side, he was a descendant of one Bonacci – in Latin, *filius Bonacci*, which means son of Bonacci. This perhaps gave rise to the name Fibonacci.

As a child, Leonardo moved to live with his father, a public notary in the customs at Bugia, now Bejaia, a town in northeast Algeria. Here, the boy developed his interest in mathematics. He came to see that the Hindu-Arabic system of positioning decimals was often simpler and more effective than using Roman numerals.

Subsequently, Fibonacci returned to Pisa. In 1202, at the age of 32, he produced his masterpiece, *Liber Abaci*, which translates as *Book of Accounting*.

In this, he explained how to use Hindu-Arabic decimal positioning in business, applying examples to profit calculations, weight assessment and currencies. His system became popular throughout Europe.

In 1225, Frederick II, the Holy Roman Emperor, invited the middle-aged Fibonacci to take part in a mathematics tournament. Fibonacci distinguished himself, which gave a further boost to his reputation.

Sequence of numbers

Fibonacci is now famous not so much for his decimal numbering system as for his sequence of numbers. In _Liber Abaci_, Fibonacci evolved his numbers sequence theory as a way of determining a mathematical puzzle: if a pair of rabbits was to give birth to another pair, how could a population of rabbits develop?

On the major assumption that no rabbits would die, and that they would be born in pairs, Fibonacci calculated the running total as follows. A first pair of rabbits would give birth to a second, and then, the next month, to a third. The following month, the original and its firstborn pair would each give birth to another pair.

If every pair of rabbits could give birth to another in its second month of life, and if first births took place in January, by April there would be 8 pairs, and by May, as many as 13 pairs.

Taking its cue, the Fibonacci number sequence starts with 1, 1, 2, 3, 5, 8, and 13. Any two numbers added together are equal to the next highest number (for example, 5 + 8 = 13). The sequence continues in this vein theoretically to infinity. In his book _Investors Chronicle Guide to Charting_ (see Seminar 21), journalist Alistair Blair describes this principle as a 'lip-smacking version of compound interest'.

The Fibonacci numbers have further interrelationships. After the first four numbers, any number's ratio to its next highest is about 0.618, which mathematicians call phi. The ratio of any number to its next lowest is about 1.618. In addition, alternate numbers have a ratio of either 2.168, or 0.382, which is its inverse. Broadly speaking, the higher the number, the more precisely the ratios are adhered to.

Golden mean

Although Fibonacci is famous for this number sequence, he was not the first to discover the basics of it. Mathematicians of the ancient world knew about the ratio of 0.618 or 1.618, expressed by the Greek letter phi. In ancient Greece, this was known as the golden mean. Both the mathematician Pythagoras and the philosopher Plato discussed it, and builders used it to construct the Parthenon.

In ancient Egypt, the equivalent was the golden ratio. Architects used it to construct the Great Pyramid of Giza, whose inclining sides were each 1.618 times the size of half the bottom.

The ratio between a small section of a given length and a larger one is identical to that between the larger section and the entire length, according to the golden ratio.

The logarithmic spiral

Any spiral is based on a geometric expansion derived from multiplying a number by a constant ratio, which in the Fibonacci sequence is 1.618. Fibonacci followers claim that a logarithmic spiral based on the golden ratio is constant in all areas of nature.

Along this spiral, all points are mathematically related to each other. In the human frame, for instance, the distance from the navel to the top of the head is about 0.618 of that from the feet to the navel.

This spiral is created from arcs drawn between the corners of squares within a so-called golden rectangle constructed from the golden mean. The squares have infinite capacity for expansion and contraction.

The sunflower demonstrates the logarithmic spiral based on the golden ratio in action. The flower has 89 curves, and this is a Fibonacci number. Of the curves, 34 turn in one direction and 55 in another, both of which numbers are also in the Fibonacci sequence.

You will find the logarithmic spiral also in the web of the epeira spider, in the growth of bacteria, and in whirlpools. The spiral within makes infinite movement in any direction, and this incorporates growth and decay. What has this got to do with financial markets?

Financial markets – retracements and fan lines

The most popular application of the Fibonacci numbers in financial markets is through Fibonacci retracements. These are based on the observation that corrective waves have in the past retraced the prior wave by 38.2 per cent (significant but not sharp), 50 per cent (sharp), or 61.8 per cent (extremely sharp).

Fibonacci fan lines are a variation on the theme. They include three trend lines, the fan lines in question, from the first point and through the vertical line. These will be at 38.2 per cent, 50 per cent and 61.8 per cent.

As share prices pass these fan lines, apparent resistance and support levels at the intersection can provide clues for the analyst as to future trend reversals.

The Fibonacci retracements may be combined with the fan lines to indicate the support and resistance levels still more strongly.

Arcs and time zones

Fibonacci arcs are similar to fan lines. They include three arcs – in fact half circles – that intersect a trend line, again at Fibonacci levels of 38.2 per cent, 50 per cent and 61.8 per cent.

As the share price passes the arcs, analysts can detect support and resistance, based on which they can attempt to forecast trend reversals.

Where the arcs and the fan lines cross, any support or resistance is likely to be stronger.

In addition, there are Fibonacci Time Zones. These take the form of vertical lines that are separated in accordance with Fibonacci numbers. If, for instance, the market takes a week to complete an upward movement, a pullback might take 38.2 per cent of this time.

Theory of cycles

As we shall see, some pioneers in the history of technical analysis have adapted Fibonacci numbers to their own theories. Among these was Ralph Nelson Elliott, who founded Elliott Wave theory.

In their book *Elliott Wave Principle* (see Seminar 21), A J Frost and Robert Prechter (see box later in this seminar) argue that if phi is the growth force in the universe, it might govern man's productive capacity, which the stock market measures.

If so, it should be possible to make broad predictions of future cycles based on the premise that they will repeat a pattern, based on Fibonacci numbers. It could be the previous cycle, or an amalgamation of previous ones.

As part of this logic, cycles of different time scales fit into each other, according to technical analysis guru Tony Plummer. The Juglar, Berry, and Strauss and How cycles are examples of this multifit, although their origins and purpose vary. In 1862, Clement Juglar found a 7–11-year cycle that reflected investment in the economy. In 1991, Brian Berry found a 25–35-year cycle based on infrastructure development. On a longer-term basis, in 1991, William Strauss and Neil How argued for an 85–99-year cycle reflecting crisis.

The Kondratieff and Kuznets cycles do not fit with the above three cycles, and to that extent are outsiders, according to Plummer. In 1926, Nikolai Kondratieff (see box below) discovered a 40–60-year commodity price cycle. In 1930, Simon Kuznets reported a 15–25-year cycle based on demographic issues.

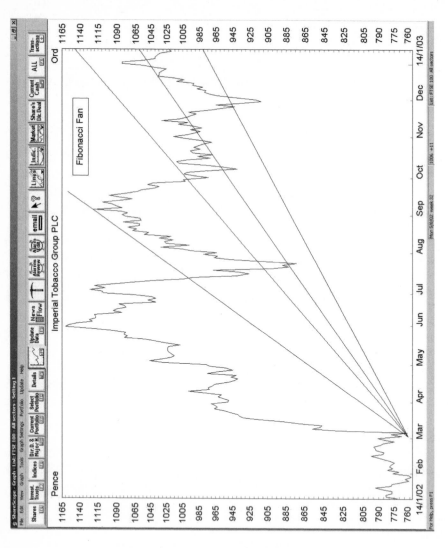

Figure 19.1   Fibonacci fan lines

STOCK MARKET SPECULATORS' HALL OF FAME

Member No 7 – Nikolai D Kondratieff

Nikolai D Kondratieff was born in 1898 in Russia. He worked as an economist in Stalin's Agricultural Academy and Business Research Institute. In the 1920s, most economists were interested in cycles of up to 15 years but he was investigating a longer-term approach.

In developing his theories, Kondratieff studied prices and interest rates between 1879 and 1926. He found that in capitalist economies, long-term cycles of boom and bust last 50–60 years. The cycles have impact on stocks, commodities and other markets as well as on interest rates.

Kondratieff further observed that the economy passes through four phases: inflationary growth, stagflation, deflationary growth and depression. Others have compared these to the four seasons.

Unfortunately, Kondratieff was born in the wrong period in Russia's history. At only 40 years old, he died in a Siberian labour camp, a martyr to what the Russian government considered a dangerous view of Capitalist economies.

Kondratieff has been quietly influential in the small world of Wave theorists. I have noticed that his books are periodically promoted to private stock market investors at a very high price. It is reading for the dedicated.

Each of the Juglar, Berry, and Strauss and How cycles incorporates three stages or sub-cycles, which are logically related to each other, Plummer says. The first sub-cycle is reacting to a crisis, and the second acknowledges a change in circumstances, while the third is fearful and destructive.

Cycle lows come at an expected time. Cycle highs often arrive early, in which case they are called a left translation, or late, which is a right translation. In every case, a lower cycle is influenced by a higher-level cycle, which depends itself on fundamental trends.

The cycles can represent stock markets, in which case they tend to anticipate a similar set of cycles representing economic trends, according to Plummer.

Elliott Wave theory provides a framework, based on Fibonacci figures, that encompasses the concept of interrelated cycles. We will spend the rest of this seminar looking at it in more detail.

ELLIOTT WAVE THEORY

Ralph Nelson Elliott

Ralph Nelson Elliott, the founder of Elliott Wave theory, was born in 1871, and lived in San Antonio, Texas. In 1896, he became an accountant, and for the next 25 years, he worked for mainly railroad companies in Central and South America, and Mexico.

In this main part of his working life, he specialized in restructuring. He became acquainted with the extremes of rich and poor lifestyles in the primitive society of Latin America, which, according to Elliott Wave guru Robert Prechter (see box later in this seminar), may have served him well when in later life he focused his talents on the no less volatile stock market.

In the early 1920s, Elliott developed a line of work as business consultant to tea rooms and restaurants in New York, and, in 1924, he became a staff writer for *Tea Room and Gift Shop*, a magazine published in the city to cater for the new fad.

In his editorials, Elliott applauded keeping records to guide future action, expressed preference for 'graphic explanation' and argued that business fads could be overdone. In his stated view, it was often better to make the wrong decision than none at all. Such views from the future founder of Elliott Wave theory seem in retrospect both in character and formative.

In 1925, Elliott became the chief accountant for the country of Nicaragua, which the US marines were controlling. He later moved to Guatemala City, and became general auditor of the International Railway of Central America. He wrote a book, *Tea Room and Cafeteria Management*, in which he made some reference to business cycles. He also wrote a book on Latin American social problems, *The Future of Latin America*, which was never published.

Elliott returned to the USA as a management consultant, partly to obtain hospital treatment in New York as he was suffering from a disease contracted in South America that affected his alimentary tract.

By 1927, he had moved to Los Angeles to build up his consultancy business, but his illness became worse. He became fascinated with the stock market, which in the 1920s was going through a particularly bullish phase. He started developing the Elliott Wave theory.

Elliott corresponded about his theory with Detroit-based financial expert Charles Collins, who was founder and editor of a stock market newsletter. Initially sceptical, Collins became interested in Elliott's theory. He was impressed with an accurate forecast that Elliott made by telegram on 13 March 1935 that the Dow Jones Averages were making a final bottom.

For the next two years, Collins subscribed to an advisory service of Elliott, and together they worked on a book, *The Wave Principle*, which was published in August 1938.

In 1939, Elliott wrote a series of highly regarded articles in the magazine *Financial World*. In these, he explained the basics of Elliott Wave theory, in which he identified three main facets. The first was wave patterns; the second was the ratio between waves; and the third was time.

Q: Elliott Wave theory seems complicated. Is it worth the effort of mastering?

A: Opinions differ. Elliott Wave is useful as a way to recognize patterns. But the wave structure is complicated, and makes forecasting difficult.

Some find that the simple rules work for them. If you accept that the five-wave rise is followed by the three-wave decline on a regular basis, it enables forecasting on this basis.

Others remain cynical. One friend of mine, who has worked for years as a technical analyst for a high-profile firm (sorry I cannot name it) grins whenever I mention Elliott Wave and describes it as a 'bit of a con'. In his experience Elliott Wave makes money for advisers and gurus, but not for traders.

You will need to make up your own mind. If you want to explore Elliott Wave theory further in detail before putting it into practice, the clearest explanation that I have ever seen is in the book *Fibonacci Applications and Strategies* by Robert Fisher (John Wiley). See also Seminar 21 for further reading.

In 1946, Elliott's definitive work on Elliott Wave theory, *Nature's Law – The Secret of the Universe*, was published. In this book, Elliott applied his theory to the Dow Jones Industrial Average. He intended that it should be used in situations where mass psychology applied. These included the stock market but not individual stocks.

The legacy

In 1948, Elliott died, but his theory lived after him. In 1960, Hamilton Bolton wrote a book, *Elliott Wave Principle – A Critical Appraisal*.

Today, Elliott Wave theory is applied not just to the Dow Jones Industrial Average but also to other stock market indices, as well as to commodities, currencies and bonds. How far it works remains controversial.

Market gossip has it that there are only three people in the world who really understand Elliott Wave theory. One is Robert Prechter; another is Bob Beckman; and a third is dead.

This is manifestly an exaggeration. Some stock market speculators have taken up the gauntlet, albeit with mixed results. It took Bill Adlard, technical analyst for data provider Hemscott.net, on his own admission, about a year to grasp Elliott Wave theory.

Adlard has described Elliott Wave as the 'most difficult, but most important', part of his own stock analysis. He sees the theory's multifaceted structure as a strength, enabling its component parts to 'fit together in layers like an onion'.

Elliott Wave theory can be applied to any time scale from a few hours to hundreds of years. On this basis, its promoters say that it is useful for traders as well as investors. Prechter maintains that the difference between trading and investing is simply the size of the trend.

In Prechter's view, Elliott Wave is a science, but that is not the whole story.

'That being said, it probably takes an artistic mind to do it well, because the market draws pictures, and you must decide if they are positioned correctly,' he has said.

STOCK MARKET SPECULATORS' HALL OF FAME

Member No 8 – Robert Prechter

Robert Prechter is a Yale graduate who originally worked as an accountant. He also put in time as a rock drummer and as a technical analyst at Merrill Lynch.

He developed a modified version of Elliott Wave theory and, for some years, he published a related newsletter that achieved a modest success.

By the 1980s, Prechter had achieved the status of a world-renowned stock market guru. Through his presence on TV and in the press, he became known even to those who never invested. His popularity received a boost perhaps from his claims that pop music and other social trends helped to forecast future stock market movements.

Like all gurus, Prechter eventually faltered. Shortly before the 1987 crash, he appeared to issue conflicting advice, and his disciples were unclear on whether to buy or to sell. He became a temporary target of resentment as the market crashed, although there is also a case that he had predicted it.

Today, Prechter is acknowledged as probably the world's leading expert on Elliott Wave theory, and his book *Conquer the Crash* (John Wiley), with its bearish prognosis and advice on how to cope in a market downturn, hit the bestseller list in 2002.

Prechter believes that Elliott Wave theory gives investors and traders a phenomenal advantage, and he explains how it works on his Web site (www.elliottwave.com).

The theory

Elliott Wave theory finds patterns in price fluctuations, and that these take the same form, no matter what the scale. In this respect, the theory has similarities to fractal geometry. In this area, Benoit Mandelbrot had discovered that fluctuations in nature are similar, whether large or small. Unlike in Elliott Wave theory, he did not see them as patterns.

In Elliott Wave theory, an advance in a five-wave movement, known as **Wave 1**, is followed by a decline in a three-wave movement, known as **Wave 2**. The wave image evokes the sea, echoing references to tides and waves in the literature of Dow theory (see seminar 7), whose three trends are compatible with, although taking place earlier than, the initial five waves in Elliott Wave.

The advance consists of *Wave (1)* up, followed by *Wave (2)* down, then *Wave (3)* up, followed by *Wave (4)* down, then *Wave (5)* up.

Wave 2 follows, taking the form of *Wave (a)* down, *Wave (b)* up, and *Wave (c)* down.

Wave (1), *Wave (3)* and *Wave (5)*, being rising, are called impulsive waves. *Wave (2)* and *Wave (4)* are called corrective waves. They are all part of **Wave 1**. *Wave (a)*, *Wave (b)* and *Wave (c)* are also called corrective waves, but in this case they are part of an overall correction, in the form of **Wave 2**.

In this way, a market cycle amounts to an overall eight waves. The three-wave decline will never fully retrace the previous five-wave upturn, according to the theory.

Elliott himself advised that these patterns had forecasting value, and that when the five-wave rise had been completed, a three-wave decline would follow, and vice versa.

Further divisions

Wave (1), *Wave (2)*, and *Wave (5)* each divide further into five waves on the basis that they are moving with the trend set by a larger rising wave, **Wave 1**. *Wave (2)* and *Wave (4)* each divide into only three waves, on the basis that they are moving against the trend set by **Wave 1**.

Wave (a) and *Wave (c)* are moving down with the declining trend set by **Wave 2**, and so each splits into five waves. In contrast, *Wave (b)* splits into three waves as it is moving up against the broader downward trend.

These relationships illustrate that five waves never constitute a correction.

If a trend line is drawn under *Wave (1)* and *Wave (2)* as a support level, and another above *Wave (1)* as a resistance level, this provides a functioning channel. It may need adjustment as the pattern progresses. Generally, *Wave (4)* often functions as a support level.

Elliott described the broad five-three pattern of **Wave 1** and **Wave 2** in sequence as a law of nature, although, according to Tony Plummer, it is the derivative of a more fundamental three-three pattern, which is itself the law of nature. Either way, Elliott Wave is a theory of growth.

Under Elliott Wave theory, there are nine varieties of the eight-wave (five plus three) cycle, each of which has its own time span. The largest is the grand super cycle, which lasts between 150 and 200 years and consists of five super cycles.

Every super cycle consists of five cycles, each of which breaks down into five primary waves. Every primary wave has five intermediates, each of which lasts about one or two years and has five minors.

Each minor lasts between three and five months and breaks up into five minutes. Every minute consists of five minuettes, each of which has five sub-minuettes. Each sub-minuette may last only a few hours.

Doing the splits

Every wave splits into smaller ones, as well as belonging to the next larger one, according to Elliott Wave. As we have already seen, one wave is sub-divided into five or three. In addition, a larger wave may be subdivided into eight smaller waves, which can then be split into 34 still smaller ones, and, from there, into 144.

The proportional relationship of the waves is linked to Fibonacci numbers. Key numbers such as 3, 5, 8, 34, 144 are in the Fibonacci sequence.

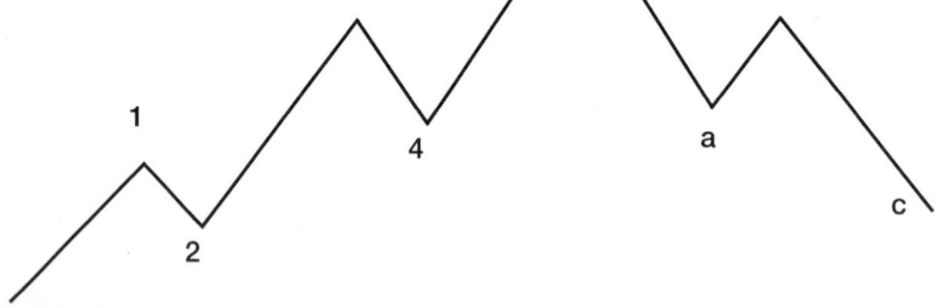

Elliot Wave Movement

Figure 19.2   Elliott Wave movement

The rule of alternation

Under the rule of alternation, the market does not repeat itself. If one wave is simple, the one that follows is likely to be complex, and vice versa. Bear markets and bull markets alternate. In terms of detail, you know only what *not* to expect. The rule of alternation is probable but not certain, according to Prechter.

FURTHER SECRETS OF THE WAVES

The five-wave rise

In the initial five-wave rise that constitutes **Wave 1**, *Wave (1)* is the shortest, and the least thrusting. It is similar to the Dow's initial phase.

Wave (2) typically retraces most, but not all, of *Wave (1)*, and may create a double bottom (see Seminar 9).

Wave (3) is typically longer than the rest, and, according to Elliott, will never be the shortest. It has the heaviest trading volume and often exceeds price targets set by those who are not Elliott Wave followers. It is said to have fantastic profit potential.

If *Wave (1)* has not already overreached the rally in the previous day's down trend, *Wave (3)* should do so. At this point, trend followers tend to jump in and buy the shares.

Wave (4) is corrective, but in a different way from *Wave (2)*, and may create a triangle (see Seminar 9). The bottom of *Wave (4)* should never fall below the peak of *Wave (1)*. If a bear market should later happen, *Wave (4)* often serves as a support level.

Wave (5) is typically less powerful than *Wave (3)*, and sometimes will not overreach it. If it rises on bullish news, this may not be backed by trading volume, or technical indicators (see Seminar 11), and so could prove short-lived.

In *Wave (5)*, a Wedge (see Seminar 9) may occur. If this is rising, it is a bullish sign and if it is falling, this is bearish. Included in the Wedge, which will not last long, are five waves, each of which splits into three.

Wave extension

Within the five impulse waves, *Wave (3)*, or sometimes *Wave (1)* or *(5)*, may extend into five further waves. In this way, the overall impulse pattern will consist of nine waves instead of five.

The three-wave correction

Let us look at the process in more detail. The three-wave correction that follows a five-wave rise looks like a pullback from the upward trend. If *Wave (a)* can be split into five waves, this is a sign of a possible incipient bear trend, particularly if it is accompanied by enhanced trading volume.

Wave (b) comes as a rally. This gives you an opportunity to sell out, or sell short. The downturn comes quickly and is typically accompanied by low trading volume. *Wave (c)* will very likely fall below the bottom of *Wave (a)*.

The three-wave correction may appear in a zigzag form, expressed as a 5–3–5 pattern. Alternatively, it may be a flat, which is a 3–3–5 pattern that consolidates into a rectangle.

Otherwise, a double three may occur, which is when two a–b–c sequences combine to create seven waves. This indicates a sideways moving market. A triple three, which is when three such sequences make eleven waves, enhances the effect.

Price objectives and retracements

As a user of Elliott Wave theory, you can set price objectives using Fibonacci ratios. For example, if you multiply *Wave (1)* by 1.618, and trace the total from the bottom of *Wave (2)*, this will give you a targeted length for *Wave (3)*.

You can also use Fibonacci numbers to forecast percentage retracements. In a strong trend, the minimum retracement will be 38 per cent, but in a weak trend, as high as 62 per cent. Otherwise, it may be 50 per cent. Bear in mind that all these percentages are approximate.

You can also use Fibonacci figures to set time targets from a trend change on the chart. Count the subsequent trading days, and expect the next big reversal on a Fibonacci day. You can apply the technique over a longer time period than mere days.

The critics

Neither Elliott nor his many disciples have ever even attempted to explain the theory behind Elliott Wave. For Elliott, it is simply a law of nature. If so, this law does not appear elsewhere, except in Fibonacci numbers.

The theory was originally applied only to the Dow Jones Industrial Average. Traders have found problems in applying it to certain markets such as commodities and foreign exchange. It can work particularly badly when applied to individual shares, for which it was never designed.

Elliot Wave theory is complicated and little understood.

Martin Pring, one of the world's leading technical analysts, has concluded that Elliott Wave is a highly subjective tool, due to problems of interpretation. In his view, the value of its interpretations should probably be downplayed.

THE NEXT STEP

Fibonacci numbers influenced William D Gann, whom many have hailed as a great trader. In the next seminar, we will look at his life and work.

SEMINAR 19 GOLDEN RULES

▮ In the Fibonacci sequence, any two numbers added together are equal to the next highest number.

▮ In the Fibonacci sequence, after the first four numbers, any number's ratio to its next highest is about 0.618, and to its next lowest about 1.618.

▮ Fibonacci retracements are based on the observation that corrective waves tend to retrace the prior wave by 38.2%, 50% or 61.8%.

▮ Fibonacci fan lines are three trend lines at 38.2%, 50% and 61.8%. They indicate support resistance levels.

▮ Fibonacci arcs are a variation on the theme of the fan lines.

▮ Under Elliott Wave theory, the proportionate relationship of the waves is linked to Fibonacci numbers.

▮ Elliott Wave finds patterns in price fluctuations, and these take the same form on any time scale.

▮ Under Elliott Wave theory, the market cycle has a five-part advancing wave, followed by a three-part corrective wave.

▮ There are nine such eight-wave cycles. Every wave splits into smaller ones, and belongs to the next larger wave.

▮ The rule of alternation says that the market does not repeat itself. This rule is probable but not certain.

▮ Elliott Wave theory works less well for individual shares than for the broad index. It has given rise to interpretation problems.

Seminar 20

Secrets of William Gann and financial astrology

INTRODUCTION

In this section, we will look at the influential theories of William D Gann, a great trader. He dabbled in financial astrology, and we shall glance at this too.

WILLIAM D GANN

Myths and reality

William D Gann is dubbed by some promoters of his trading methods as the greatest trader of stocks and commodities who ever lived. Others are sometimes more cautious.

The guru's beginnings were not auspicious. Gann was born in 1878 to a family that lived on a farm seven miles from Lufkin, Texas. He had eight brothers and two sisters. The house had no indoor plumbing and, from an early age, William was required to work on the farm.

This experience, coupled with his Baptist upbringing, gave the young Gann an appetite for hard work that was to serve him well. He did not smoke or drink, and was frugal in his spending habits.

As an adult, Gann became a broker, attending business school in the evenings, and, when he was 25 years old, he moved to New York. He married twice and fathered two children.

In 1919, when he was 41 years old, Gann set up his own business. He published a newsletter, the *Supply and Demand Letter*, that forecast stock and commodity prices, particularly on an annual basis. In the 1920s, his forecasts were said to be 85 per cent accurate.

He later published an influential early book on technical analysis, *Truth of the Stock Tape*. His novel, *Tunnel through the Air*, forecast that Japan would attack the USA, and was well received.

Like other gurus before him, Gann made money from writing and selling courses, but not as much from trading stocks and commodities as some that promote his theories have suggested. When he died from stomach cancer in 1955, Gann was not wealthy.

Trading techniques

Gann invented and operated his own trading system based on geometrical and other mathematical principles, and their relationship with an intuitive market.

Like Elliott, Gann relied on Fibonacci numbers, and believed that market upturns are greater than the downturns.

In other respects, Gann differed from Elliott. He considered trading volume significant. In his view, the longer a market move lasted, the more significant it was.

Gann was a closet astrologer, and, at one point, he had studied Indian sidereal astrology in India. He believed that share prices moved in cycles according to universal laws, including astrology. He included astrological symbols on his charts.

Highs and lows

For Gann, highs and lows have a special significance. This becomes apparent from his trend indicator lines. These plot a trend line against a price line on a weekly chart.

If the price reaches both a higher high and a higher low than in the previous week, the trend indicator line will rise to the new high.

Conversely, if the price achieves a lower high and a lower low, the line will move down to the new low.

Support and resistance

Gann placed great emphasis on support and resistance levels. He believed that past highs created a resistance line that, if breached, became support, and that past lows created a support line that, if breached, became resistance.

To determine prospective resistance and support levels, Gann invented the cardinal square. This consists of rows and columns that intersect each other within a square, subdividing its space into smaller squares.

Gann recorded the all-time low of a share price in the centre square, and each price increment clockwise in the nearest surrounding squares.

There are variations. Sometimes Gann would insert an all-time high, in which case the sequence of numbers inserted clockwise would decline. There is also an anti-clockwise version.

The outcome is the same. The numbers within the directly vertical and horizontal lines that pass through the centre square are the most likely resistance or support levels. These two lines are called the cardinal cross. The diagonal lines include further resistance and support levels.

Key numbers

Gann believed that specified numbers had particular significance. This was not only in share prices, but also in share price movements, and dates.

One year was an important watershed after which a future key point could be broadly identified, according to Gann. He attached similar significance to 18 months and two years.

The number seven is significant as it represents the number of days in the week, according to Gann theory. Multiples of this, particularly 49, also matter. Gann saw anniversaries of highs and lows as important and paid a lot of attention to percentages.

If a price rises 100 per cent, Gann theory indicates that the move is probably complete, and that any fall will be thwarted at the 0 per cent level. The next most important percentage is 50 per cent, and others that are significant include 12.5 per cent, 25 per cent, 37.5 per cent, 62.5 per cent, and 75 per cent. These are percentage equivalents of multiples of one-eighth, into which Gann divided price action. He used a third in a similar way, which makes percentages such as 33 per cent and 67 per cent significant.

Gann found the 360 degrees in a circle significant, and he compared this with the 365 days in a year. Turns of 30, 90, or 120 degrees and similar indicate a potential change in market conditions. Gann theory sometimes represents the degrees of a circle in pence. On this basis, 90p or 360p are *natural* levels of resistance and support.

Gann's most significant trend line is at 45 degrees, which represents an absolute balance between price and time. If prices are above the line, there is a bull market, and if below it, a bear market. To breach the line means to reverse the trend.

Gann fan lines

Gann believed that price and time were proportionally related. On this basis, how long it takes a price to be reached is in proportion to the price itself. For instance, two units of price might match one unit of time.

To find tops and bottoms, Gann squared price and time. He represented these relationships as fan lines, which are usually developed from major highs and lows.

Immortal status

By the time he died in 1955, Gann had set out all his trading methods in his books and other writings. Today, he has a cult following, and a number of firms promote his methods.

Gann was undeniably able to impress and persuade others, partly because of the mathematical logic underlying the connections that he makes. In practice, how well his trading methods worked, or still do, is subject of dispute. Many a novice trader has lost money following Gann.

The disciples should heed their master. In his book _How to Make Profits Trading in Commodities_, Gann wrote: 'When you make one to three trades that show losses, whether they be large or small, something is wrong with you and not the market. Your trend may have changed. My rule is to get out and wait. Study the reason for your losses.'

ASTROLOGY

Today's market

William D Gann's support has given a lift to the pseudo-science of astrology. There is no shortage of astrologists who forecast stock prices and market movements. Some make a good living from it. What then is the essence of their art?

Astrology has it that economic growth and recession are linked to the planetary cycles. Individual investors are said to achieve success on their stock market strictly in accordance with their astrological profile.

There are more general indicators. The planet Uranus is said to look kindly on speculators, while Jupiter signifies good luck. Neptune is the planet of illusion and should warn you against making an investment error.

The Chinese have their own version. In their case, the elements symbolize stock market trends. The earth represents stability and wood is growth. Water symbolizes bottoming, and metal is contraction.

Although there is no evidence that astrology works, there is a market for this tosh. The astrologers drum up apparent support from a few greats of the past. J P Morgan, founder of the Morgan Bank, reportedly said: 'Anyone can be a millionaire, but, to become a billionaire, you need astrology.'

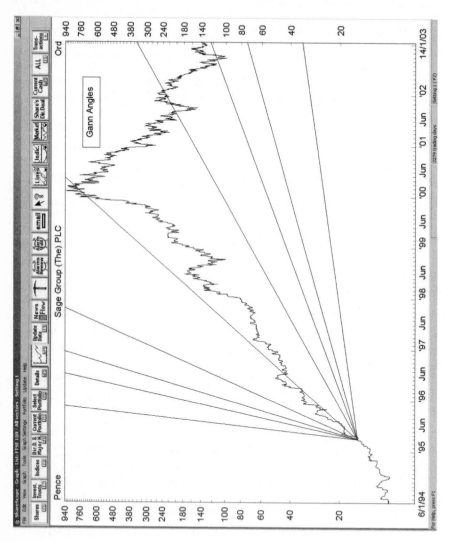

Figure 20.1 Gann lines

STOCK MARKET SPECULATORS' HALL OF FAME

Member No 9 – George Bayer

George Bayer was a stock market astrologer who lived in the early 20th century. Unlike Gann, he was open about his techniques.

He found significance in biblical numbers. In a passage of Revelation 12: 14, for instance, Bayer read that a woman is given the wings of an eagle to fly from the serpent into a place where she is nourished 'for a time, and times, and half a time'.

This period, on Bayer's reckoning, may be 10 plus 20 plus 5, which equals 35. Bayer therefore concluded that share and commodity prices might move in units of 35. He divided 35 into 8 parts, and, on this basis, developed a theory of numbers.

In his day, Bayer had appeal for the superstitious. In his book *Turning Four Hundred Years of Astrology to Practical Use and Other Matters*, he referred to the temporary closure of US stock markets in 1914.

Historians attribute this to the advent of the First World War. Bayer had a more inspired interpretation. He considered that the darkness arose because of an eclipse of the sun that had taken place almost exactly 122 years earlier, on 15 September 1792. In his own words, the stock market light was extinguished.

If you are interested in Bayer, you will find both courses and software available to cater for your taste. They do not all come cheap. If you are a member of the Society of Technical Analysts (www.sta-uk.org), you may borrow free from its library Bayer's *Complete Course in Astrology: Erection and interpretation of horoscopes for natives as well as for stocks* (1937).

Stock market astrologers admit that their methods are not infallible. But, like chartists, they retrospectively claim great foresight. Some are convinced that they alone had forecast the 1929 stock market crash.

Be wary. Not all promoters of astrology systems believe in what they are doing. Recently, a wealthy businessman was selling an astrology stock market forecasting system by direct mail. To stimulate interest, he made every purchaser sign a declaration saying that he or she would not reveal the system's methods to anybody else.

This gimmick boosted the mystique and so the sales of a product in which the promoter, on his own admission, had no personal faith.

To find out more about financial astrology, browse the Internet. A free course is on offer at www.astroecon.com. An interesting site is that of best-

selling astrologer Timothy Curley (www.myspiritualastrologer.com). Also
visit the International Association of Business Astrologers at www.business
astrologers.com.

THE NEXT STEP

In the course to date, we have now covered the basic knowledge that you
need for speculating on the stock market. In the next seminar, I will
recommend books that you could read to consolidate and extend your
knowledge.

SEMINAR 20 GOLDEN RULES

- Do not follow Gann blindly. His chart theory, despite its mathematical
  logic, does not always work.
- There is no evidence that financial astrology works.

Seminar 21

The speculator's guide to reading

INTRODUCTION

To read or not to read

Can investment books help you? In principle, yes. One good idea that you learn from a book can repay its cover price, and, more importantly, your time invested in reading it, many times over.

But be selective. Professionals in the industry write more valuable books than journalists, for obvious reasons. The best books are often expensive. They are, in most cases, published by only a few houses, including Kogan Page, John Wiley, Financial Times/Pearson, McGraw-Hill and the New York Institute of Finance.

Ordinary bookshops are often inadequately stocked with investment books. I prefer online outlets. If you buy from Global-investor.com (www.global-investor.com), my favourite bookshop, the price is often discounted. Ordering by telephone is simple, and there are also postal or online options. Delivery is prompt and reliable.

Amazon is also a useful source of business books, although it is not my first choice as it has made occasional delivery errors. The Web site (www.amazon.co.uk) offers informative reviews, but watch for biases in the author's favour.

BEGINNER'S BOOKS

Flawed is often best

First, you need to understand the basics. The primers that teach you the most are the fruit of individual minds, and this makes them as flawed as they are fascinating. One such book is *The Motley Fool UK Investment Guide* by David Berger and James Carlisle (Boxtree), which I am pleased to see is now in its third edition.

If you get along with the facetious style, this book offers useful ideas on how to plan your stock market portfolio. But do not follow the advice blindly. The approach, reflecting the approach of the Motley Fool Web site (www.fool.co.uk), is not particularly sympathetic to penny shares, where many speculators have made money. It is unenthusiastic about trading and technical analysis, which puts it at odds with the book that you are reading now. It warms towards tracker funds, which at the time of writing have suffered some decline.

If you want technical analysis as part of a broader approach, read *The Armchair Investor, A Do-it-yourself guide for amateur investors* by Bernice Cohen (Orion). The author is a self-made private investor and she presents her text in a chatty style.

For a stock-picking approach based on both fundamental value and growth potential combined, read the books of Jim Slater, who is Britain's best-known stock market guru for private investors. For beginners, he wrote *Investment Made Easy* (Orion). I prefer his slightly more advanced first book, *The Zulu Principle* (Orion), which is highly readable, and has sold well over 40,000 copies.

For novices, I have written *The 10-Week Flexible Investment Plan. A Beginner's Guide to Stock Market Success* (Kogan Page). You will find here an explanation of methods that my City colleagues and I have used over the years to make money trading on the stock market.

Also read *The Intelligent Guide to Stock Market Investment*, by Kevin Keasey, Robert Hudson and Kevin Littler (John Wiley). This gives you an objective overview of the stock market. Complex analytical techniques are covered simply and clearly.

For easy reference, use *How to Read the Financial Pages* by Michael Brett (Century Business). The book is recommended reading on some prestigious City courses. There is none that explains the basics better.

GENERAL

Read *The Global-Investor Book of Investing Rules* (global-investor.com), edited by Philip Jenks and Stephen Eckett. It presents investing rules from 150 investors in a succinct form.

The rules in the book sometimes contradict each other, but this is part of what makes stock market trading so individual. I declare an interest, as I am one of the contributors.

What Works On Wall Street (McGraw-Hill) by James O'Shaughnessy reveals the stock ratios that have worked best over decades. A low PE ratio comes out as a strong indicator of value. One tip sheet editor that I know was so impressed with this book that he has worked its theories into his stock selection procedures.

You can learn a lot from funny books that have an underlying serious-ness. The best is *Where Are the Customers' Yachts?* by Fred Schwed Jr (John Wiley). This book, first published in 1940, offers a tongue-in-cheek analysis of how Wall Street works.

Do not miss *The Buck Stops Here* by Jim Parton (Simon & Schuster). It will give you a no-holds-barred and simultaneously comic description of the inner workings of an investment bank from a junior salesman's perspective. It represents stockbrokers as ignorant and overpaid idlers.

A no less flattering portrait of investment bankers appears in *Monkey Business*, by John Rolfe and Peter Troobe (Warner Business Books). This exposé has many lessons for would-be traders.

In a similar spirit, *Mrs Moneypenny: Survival in the City* by Mrs Money-penny (Piatkus) is worth reading. It demonstrates some of the pressures on women who work in the City.

For a less anecdotal overview on how the City works, I find *The Money Machine, How The City Works*, by Philip Coggan (Penguin), a worthy read, although it can be a little concentrated. *How the City of London Works, An introduction to its financial markets* by William Clarke (Sweet & Maxwell) is on the author's admission a child's guide, although it has great value in setting out the basics simply. *The Death of Gentlemanly Capitalism* by Philip Augar (Penguin) provides a useful critical history. The limitation on these books and others of their kind is that they would benefit from updating almost as soon as they are published.

How about some ranting? I continually return to the books of 1980s stock market guru and Elliott Wave theorist Robert Beckman. His theories about boom-to-bust long-term cycles in our economy are interesting, and all his comments provocative.

Here is a taster from his bestseller *The Downwave* (Milestone Publica-tions). 'In the beginning God made morons. He did that for practice. Then he got down to the serious task of making total imbeciles.'

TRADING

An overview

Make a Million in Twelve Months, by James Hipwell and Anil Bhoyrul (John Blake), is a useful light read. The authors, two former *Daily Mirror* journalists, show you streetwise ways to make a quick profit from trading shares, with help from the Internet.

For helpful warnings, read *How to Make Your Million from the Internet*, by Jonathan Maitland (Hodder & Stoughton). The author is a TV broadcaster who mortgaged his house for £50,000 and tried unsuccessfully to turn this sum into £1m over 12 months through day trading.

For a technological approach, read *Stephen Eckett on Online Investing* by Stephen Eckett (Harriman House). This book, developed from a regular column in *Investors Chronicle*, is exceptionally helpful.

Day trading

Understand Day Trading in a Day, by Ian Bruce (Take That), will give you a brief how-to course, inclusive of some technical analysis. Read for an overview before you tackle a more comprehensive book.

If you are considering trading the US market, read *Day Trade Online* by Christopher Farrell (John Wiley). This book explains how to exploit the spread on share price quotes.

Compleat Guide to Day Trading Stocks by Jake Bernstein (McGraw-Hill) presents the author's interesting theories of market cycles, and is well worth reading.

Selling short

Evil's Good by Simon Cawkwell (t1ps.com) has the lowdown on taking a short position and, despite the easy style, is no beginners' guide. The author, also known as Evil Knievel, is Britain's best-known private investor who specializes in short selling (see Seminar 13).

Also read *Make A Million from the Falling Market* by Anil Bhoyrul (Metro Publishing), who now writes for the *Sunday Express*. This is a cheeky book that focuses on selling short. It is full of useful rule-of-thumb valuation methods.

Master practitioners

Do not miss *Reminiscences of a Stock Operator*, by Edwin Lefevre (John Wiley). This is a thinly disguised account of the life of legendary share trader Jesse Livermore, and demonstrates how, as a trader, you should not fight the market. The book is required reading for novices on some City and Wall Street trading floors.

Covering the same theme in a more modern style is *Jesse Livermore, World's Greatest Stock Trader* by Richard Smitten (John Wiley).

Also, read *Trader Vic – Methods of a Wall Street Master* by Victor Sperandeo (with T Sullivan Brown) (John Wiley). The book portrays in an entertaining and idiosyncratic way how a proven successful trader operates.

Another classic worth reading is *Stock Market Wizards* by Jack D Schwager (John Wiley). This book contains interviews with top stock traders on their widely varying techniques.

A personal favourite is *Practical Speculation* by Victor Niederhoffer and Laurel Kenner (John Wiley). This is a fantastic and deeply cynical book that exposes much of the flim-flam surrounding stock performance forecasting. Although it makes shocking and uncomfortable reading, it does what so many others do not. It applies rigorous standards of testing, and it tells the truth. All this from a great speculator. Niederhoffer has been a great hedge fund manager, but has also experienced going bust from ill-timed stock trades. Read this book, even if it is the only one you do.

FUNDAMENTAL ANALYSIS

Interpretation of financial statements

To learn about a company report and accounts, read *Understanding Company Financial Statements* by R H Parker (Penguin Business). The book focuses on analysis and interpretation rather than practical accounting techniques, which suits your purpose as a speculator on the stock market. The text is a little concentrated, but will provide you with an overview.

The most useful of the more comprehensive books remains *Interpreting Company Reports and Accounts*, by Geoffrey Holmes, Alan Sugden and Paul Gee (Prentice Hall/Woodhead-Faulkner). Obtain the latest (eighth) edition as accounting is always changing.

For reference, I recommend *Guide to Analysing Companies* (The Economist Books) by Bob Vause. Be sure to get the latest (second) edition. It is logically organized and fully indexed.

Unlocking Company Reports & Accounts by Wendy McKenzie (Financial Times/Prentice Hall) takes you through the basics of interpreting accounts to quite a high level. The text is recommended reading for part of the Securities Institute Diploma.

Some years ago, I took this book with me on a holiday to St Petersburg and read it from cover to cover. I thought then that it was one of the best books on basic accounts analysis that I have read (and there have been many).

For a view on how accounting excesses can mislead investors, read *Investing in a Post-Enron World* by Paul Jorion (McGraw-Hill).

Ratio analysis

On interpreting the numbers, read *Security Analysis on Wall Street* by Jeffrey C Hooke (John Wiley). It offers a broad overview of the securities analyst's craft, and a structured framework for your own analysis. There are brief sections on sectors such as insurance and technology in which analysts use specialized techniques.

For reference purposes, I recommend *Magic Numbers* by Peter Temple (John Wiley). The book includes 33 key ratios, and shows you what they mean, how to calculate them, and how they interrelate.

To set ratio analysis within a practical perspective, read *The Super Analysts*, by Andrew Lemming (John Wiley). The book consists of interviews with top analysts who throw light on the intricacies of their craft.

Value investing

On value investing, try *John Neff on Investing* by John Neff (John Wiley). The book explains how the author, as a US-based portfolio manager for Vanguard's Windsor and Gemini Funds, beat the market in 22 out of 31 years.

As an easy way to get to grips with the theories of Benjamin Graham, the father of value investing, try *Value Investing Made Easy* (McGraw-Hill), by Janet Lowe. After reading this, Graham's own masterpieces, *The Intelligent Investor* and *Security Analysis* (Harper & Row), will seem less daunting.

There are many books about Warren Buffett, Graham's disciple and the world's most successful living investor. The best of these, in my view, is *The Midas Touch*, by John Train, which was reissued in 1993 in a smart new edition by Harriman House. John Train tells us how Buffett operates, and what we can learn from this. He doesn't oversimplify, exaggerate, or bore with excessive detail.

I also like *Buffettology* by Mary Buffett and David Clark (Pocket Books). For a fun read, also try *Warren Buffett Speaks* by Janet Lowe (John Wiley), which is a compendium of quotations from the master.

Corporate finance

The Penguin Guide to Finance by Hugo Dixon (Penguin Books) offers an excellent overview of corporate finance. The author's back-of-the-envelope approach to calculation is ideal for those who want a broad-brush understanding of the subject.

Also, try *Introduction to Corporate Finance, Workbook 8*, edited by D C Gardner (FT Pitman Publishing). This workbook steers you through the basics, and provides a clear explanation of the Capital Asset Pricing Model.

On capital markets, and how fund managers operate, read *The City: Inside the great expectation machine* by Tony Golding (Financial Times/Prentice Hall). It is a dense but well-informed read.

TECHNICAL ANALYSIS

Beginners' guides

Want to discover more about technical analysis?

My favourite basic guide is *Charters on Charting*, by David Charters (Rushmere Wynne). The author is an independent technical analyst.

I'll tell you why I love this book. First, the author describes complex concepts in language that a child could understand. Second, it is organized logically. Third, it is written from a practitioner's perspective. Fourth, and most importantly, the author's enthusiasm for his subject shines through.

Unfortunately, the book has for some years been out of print. An equities trader suggested to me that a good substitute is the *Investors Chronicle Guide to Charting, An Analysis for the Intelligent Investor*, by Alistair Blair (Financial Times/Prentice Hall).

I bought the book, and it made me laugh aloud. The author takes such a detached look at technical analysis, balancing his cynicism with a determination to be fair.

The book includes a plethora of worked examples, and is particularly good on point and figure charting. But at the end of the day it has limited value for me because it is written by an unrepentant sceptic.

Otherwise, *The Technical Analysis Course: A Winning Program for Investors and Traders*, by Thomas A Meyers (McGraw-Hill Education), is clearly set out, and highly readable. Each chapter is short, and ends with a simple quiz. In its first two editions, it has deservedly sold more than 36,000 copies.

Also read *Getting Started in Technical Analysis*, by Jack Schwager (John Wiley). This gives you an excellent understanding of the basics, and is a favourite of rookies on the trading floor of some Wall Street firms.

Advanced guides

To get to grips with technical analysis in detail, read *Technical Analysis of the Financial Markets: A Comprehensive Guide to Trading Methods and Applications* by John J Murphy (New York Institute of Finance). This is the main core text on the diploma course of the Society of Technical Analysts. To test yourself as you go along, buy *Study Guide for Technical Analysis of the Financial Markets* by John Murphy (New York Institute of Finance).

This book is the best overall guide to technical analysis. It is far more accessible and tightly written and modern, in my view, than its two main rivals, *Technical Analysis of Stock Trends* by Robert Edwards and John Magee (New York Institute of Finance) – acknowledged by aficionados to be the ultimate word in chart reading – and *Technical Analysis Explained* by Martin Pring (McGraw-Hill). But why not do what so many do? Buy all three books and consult them. They explain the same thing in different words, and there are some healthy contradictions. Be sure, however, to get up-to-date versions.

The Master Swing Trader: Tools and Techniques to Profit from Outstanding Short-Term Trading Opportunities by Alan S Farley (McGraw-Hill Education) will show you underlying concepts that you can exploit in short-term trading situations.

I recommend *Big Trends in Trading* by Price Headley (John Wiley). The author demonstrates proven trading methods based on technical analysis that are ideal for volatile markets. He discusses his favourite indicators, including the equity put/call ratio.

If you are interested in cycles, read *Channels & Cycles: A Tribute to J.M. Hurst* by Brian J Millard (Traders Press). J M Hurst, the subject of this book, was a mathematical analyst with an aerospace engineering background, who helped a small group of investors in the 1960s in California to research the stock market by analysing computerized data. They used mainframe computers on a rented basis.

Millard's book explains Hurst's theory that trades are more profitable over a short than a long duration. In the author's view, the optimal period is 50–100 days.

Japanese candlesticks

If you are a beginner to Japanese candlesticks and like to test yourself as you go along, I recommend *The Candlestick Course* by Steve Nison (John Wiley). This book provides an accessible introduction. It has tests at the end of every chapter, with comprehensive answers that reinforce what you have learnt.

Otherwise, read the classic in the field, which is *Japanese Candlestick Charting Techniques: A Contemporary Guide to the Ancient Investment Techniques of the Far East* by Steve Nison (Prentice Hall Press).

Point and figure charting

For a basic understanding, I recommend *Point & Figure: Commodity & Stock Trading Techniques*, by Kermit C Zieg (Traders Press). The text aims to teach you to become proficient at the craft within a few minutes.

To discover more, read *Point & Figure Charting: the Essential Applications for Forecasting and Tracking Market Prices* by Thomas Dorsey (Wiley Trading).

Fibonacci numbers

For a basic guide, read *Fascinating Fibonaccis: Mystery and Magic in Numbers* by Trudi H Garland (Dale Seymour Publications).

For a more specialized approach, I recommend *The New Fibonacci Trader: Tools and Strategies for Trading Success* by Robert Fischer and Jens Fischer (John Wiley). The book comes with a CD-ROM. Areas covered include Fibonacci summation series, PHI-channels, and time goal analysis.

Elliott Wave

R.N. Elliott's Masterworks: The Definitive Collection, edited by Robert Prechter (New Classics Library), is a mixed, but fascinating, compendium of Elliott's own writings. It includes a biography of the master.

Otherwise, read *Elliott Wave Principle* by Robert Prechter Jr and A J Frost (John Wiley).

A lighter alternative is *Conquer the Crash: You Can Survive and Prosper in a Deflationary Depression* by Robert Prechter Jr (John Wiley).

Robert Beckman has written not especially accessible books about Elliott Wave theory, including *Supertiming* (Milestone Publications).

Master technicians at work

Read *Winning on Wall Street* by Martin Zweig (Warner Books). The author, a renowned stock picker, discusses his favourite technical indicators. This is not a simple read, but the author has made serious money from his system, and his passion is infectious.

How to Make Money in Stocks by William O'Neil (McGraw-Hill) is another essential read. The author offers a proven stock market investing system that relies partly on technical analysis.

Also read *Long-Term Secrets to Short-Term Trading* by Larry Williams (John Wiley). The author discusses share price patterns, broad influences on stock markets, and money management. He is one of the best traders in the world.

Psychology

Read *Forecasting Financial Markets: The Psychology of Successful Investing* by Tony Plummer (4th edition) (Kogan Page). This book, which is core reading on the diploma course of the Society of Technical Analysts, serves as a fascinating introduction to technical analysis, and attempts to address why you should use it in the first place. The author's theory is that crowd psychology dictates markets, and this provides a basis for predicting performance of stock prices, indices and the economy generally.

Also, read *The Disciplined Trader* by Mark Douglas (New York Institute of Finance), which offers insights into market psychology. The author advises that the stock market is boundless, pitiless, and can take everything from you as it teases you with the prospect of unlimited gains. Damn it, do not miss this book. It is truly fantastic.

Read *Trading for a Living* by Dr Alexander Elder (John Wiley). The author, a US psychiatrist born in Russia, looks at share trading from the vantage point of the psychiatrist's couch. It is one of the most successful books on trading ever published, and furthers the case for using technical analysis in trading.

Criticism of technical analysis

One of the best-known critics of technical analysis is fund manager John Train. In his bestselling book *The Money Masters* (HarperBusiness), he denounces the entire concept as fakery.

Burton G Malkiel presents the case against technical analysis in more detail in his investment classic *A Random Walk down Wall Street* (W.W. Norton).

In *A Mathematician Plays the Market* (Penguin), John Allen Paulos, a professor of mathematics, applies his theory about the random nature of patterns to stock prices. He dismisses most of technical analysis as illogical.

GROWTH INVESTING

General

One Up on Wall Street by Peter Lynch (Penguin) offers inspiring insights on how to use your ordinary life experience to give you the edge in selecting growth stocks. The author's enthusiasm is infectious. Buy and enjoy. You are in the hands of a master.

Investing Common Stocks and Uncommon Profits by Philip A Fisher (John Wiley) offers some useful qualitative criteria for selecting growth stocks. Again the author is a master of investing.

High-tech stocks

On high-tech stocks, I particularly like *The Big Tech Score* by Mike Kwatinetz, with Danielle Kwatinetz Wood (John Wiley). The author, a Wall Street investment analyst, explains sophisticated valuation methods in an accessible style.

A must-read is *Super Stocks*, by Kenneth Fisher (IRWIN Professional Publishing). This classic shows you how to use the price/sales ratio, among others, to select bargain-basement high-tech stocks. It has had significant influence on the stock selection techniques used by Conor McCarthy, founding editor of *Techinvest*, a successful tip sheet that specializes in high-tech stocks. Do not miss this book.

Penny shares

If you intend to dabble in penny shares, read *How to Make a Killing in Penny Shares*, by Michael Walters (Laddingford Books). The book is sometimes superficial, but it is readable and the author understands this market.

ECONOMICS

The basics

Until now, there have been too few books on economics for UK investors. I am relieved that Peter Temple has plugged the gap with *First Steps in Economic Indicators* (FT Prentice Hall).

For a still broader beginner's guide, read *Free Lunch*, by David Smith (Profile Books). You will be delighted at how interesting he makes the subject.

How to Lie With Statistics by Darrell Huff (Penguin) offers insight into how statistics are manipulated. The style is humorous, but the underlying content is serious.

DERIVATIVES

General

As this book was going to press I managed to get my hands on Peter Temple's latest book, *The Investor's Toolbox* (global-investor), and it is a real winner. The book provides a practical but analytical guide to using spread betting, CFDs, options, warrants and exchange-traded funds.

The book is set out on thick glossy paper, and includes colour reproductions of Web pages, as well as useful tables and Web addresses. Besides the basics, there are sections on trading strategies, and an entertaining history of derivatives. It is the best of its kind (and a serious rival to this one).

Spread betting

The most up-to-date book on spread betting is *How to Win at Spread Betting*, by Charles Vintcent (Financial Times/Prentice Hall). It covers the basics thoroughly, but is short and, in places, too general.

A book that I like better is *Spread Betting* by Andrew Burke (Aesculus Press). This is written in an inspirational style and is seriously well informed, although, at the time of writing, it needs updating.

Covered warrants

There is only one major book so far on covered warrants. This is *Andrew McHattie on Covered Warrants: New Opportunities in an Exciting New Market*, by Andrew McHattie (Harriman House).

When this book was first published in October 2002, I rushed to buy it. The author is a known expert on conventional warrants. In his book, he discusses the new covered variety in far more depth, and more objectively, than much of the marketing-inspired journalism that surrounded the launch of these products in London in late 2002.

Options

The book that I like best on traded options is *Investing in Traded Options: Market Strategies* by Robert Linggard (Take That). The author takes you clearly and systematically through the basics.

Otherwise, I like *Getting Started in Options* by Michael Thomsett (John Wiley). This US-published book has you thinking like a successful trader.

A third readable alternative is *Traded Options: A Private Investor's Guide* by Peter Temple (Financial Times/Prentice Hall).

SCAMS

Make sure that you read about how stock market scams work. I have seen tens of thousands of small investors fleeced, and it is ironically these very victims who are most likely to get caught again. Get wise in this area.

For a good overview, read *Fraud! How to Protect Yourself from Schemes, Scams and Swindles* by Marsha Bertrand (AMACOM).

Also read my own first book, *The City Share Pushers* (Scope Books). This is a full exposé of how the more dubious share promoters work. For a fictionalized account, read my novel *Stock Market Rollercoaster* (John Wiley). These books will demonstrate wisdom that I learnt in the market, and, if you read them seriously, will be worth more to you than most other reading.

My earlier novel *The Survivors* (Scope Books) presents a picture of stock market fraud from a different angle. It is entertainment.

EMERGING MARKETS

If you are interested in investing in emerging markets, read *Adventure Capitalist* by Jim Rogers (John Wiley). The author explains in this book how he took off round esoteric parts of the world in a custom-built yellow Mercedes, staying in countries like China, Mongolia and Russia. As a former associate of legendary hedge fund trader George Soros, Rogers looks at these countries from the perspective of a master investor.

For preserving assets in various parts of the world for tax reasons, as well as investing tips, I recommend you read _PT_ by W G Hill (Scope International). It is becoming increasingly hard to get hold of this underground classic, but it makes riveting reading. The author explains how you can preserve your earnings from the tax man. The author's methods are not quite what your average accountant would recommend.

MOTIVATIONAL

Read _Think and Grow Rich_, by Napoleon Hill (Random House), and it could change your life, and with it, your trading experience. The author explains how material success is largely an attitude of mind, and offers tested techniques for achieving wealth and happiness

Similarly inspiring is _The Instant Millionaire_ by Mark Fisher (New World Library). Here is a fictionalized account of how an ordinary young man visits his millionaire uncle and receives practical lessons in the art of growing rich.

I recommend _Rich Dad's Prophecy_ by Robert Kiyosaki with Sharon L Lechter, CPA (Warner Business Books). The authors advise on how to build _your personal financial ark_ to stay afloat when the stock market eventually crashes. The approach is strong on the broad picture, but weak on detail.

If you feel guilty about speculating on the stock market, set your mind at rest by reading _How I Found Freedom in an Unfree World_, by Harry Brown (Avon Books).

THE NEXT STEP

We are at the end of the course, but your future as a stock market speculator lies ahead of you.

Please turn to the next section where I will explain how you can develop your knowledge of trading and investment techniques further.

SEMINAR 21 GOLDEN RULES

▎ Time and money invested in reading about investment is amply repaid.

▎ Great investors often write more valuable books than professional journalists.

▌ Global-investor.com is the leading online business and investment bookshop. It offers good discounts and a reliable service.

▌ Read not only on how to make money trading on the stock market, but also on how to avoid losing it through scams.

A final word

In this book we have come a long way. I have taken you through all the basic skills that you need to get started as a stock market speculator, including tricky areas such as short selling, and recent developments in the UK such as covered warrants.

When I embarked on this project, I knew that my task was as impossible as it was exciting. The subject of stock market speculation is vast.

I have, of course, been selective. There is a body of 'must-have' knowledge, including the basics of fundamental and technical analysis, of money management and trading techniques, of stockbroker and software selection, that I have tried to impart.

If you are starting out, or are in the early stages, of your career as a stock market speculator, this book should have boosted your skills and confidence, and given you vital knowledge.

As an experienced City share dealer, I wanted to give you a little more than a journalistic trot through the mechanics of stock market speculation. In the 1980s, I was a fundamentalist. I wanted to understand companies before I invested and traded, and gave the financial statements priority.

Subsequently, I have become more favourably disposed towards technical analysis. I have seen it save investors from ruin and even make them money, particularly in the bear market that followed the collapse of high-tech stocks in March 2000.

How to Win as a Stock Market Speculator reflects this development in my thinking. It also includes details of regulatory developments in the City and the impact that they will have on your trading.

Remember that not every trading method works for everybody, and that much of trading successfully involves bluffing.

To take the learning process further, read some of the books recommended in Seminar 21, and explore some of the Web sites listed in the appendix. Above all, practise trading yourself.

Should you have queries, please contact me via my Web site at www.flex invest.co.uk, or directly at info@flexinvest.co.uk.

Until then, happy speculating.

Alexander Davidson
London, December 2003

Appendix:
useful Web sites

Here follows a list of Web sites that you may find useful as a stock market speculator. Please note that some of these charge a subscription fee for access to the best content.

Alternative Investment Market (AIM)

BDO Stoy Hayward – accountancy firm specializing in AIM
www.bdo.co.uk

Graham H Wills & Company – a stockbroker that offers IPOs in OFEX and AIM stocks
www.ghw.co.uk

Newsletter Publishing Ltd – relevant tip sheets
www.redskyresearch.com

Analysis

Analyst – financial analysis for private investors
www.analystinvestor.com

Beeson Gregory – research on small- and medium-sized companies in Europe
www.beeson-gregory.co.uk

Charles Schwab – US-based analyst centre
www.schwab.com

Equity Development – analysts' reports commissioned by companies
www.equity-development.co.uk

Equityinvestigator – independent analysts' research on high-tech stocks
www.equityinvestigator.com

FirstCall Research Direct
www.firstcall.com

hemscott – high but expensive quality tips, analysis and data
www.hemscott.com/equities/index.htm

IDEAGLobal – former investment banking analysts' independent research covering
US markets
www.ideaglobal.com

Institutional Investor – lists top analysts and their track record
www.iimagazine.com

Merrill Lynch HSBC
www.mlhsbc.com

Moneyguru – own analysts
www.moneyguru.com

Multex Investor
www.multexinvestor.com

Peel Hunt – small company research and video interviews
www.peelhunt.com

Salomon Smith Barney
www.salomonsmithbarney.com

SG Cowen – technology-driven investment bank
www.sgcowen.com

ShareScope.com
www.ShareScope.com.

UBS Warburg
www.ubswarburg.com

Books

Global-investor – an excellent large online seller of investment books. Try here
first for discounted range and highly reliable delivery service.
www.global-investor.com

Amazon – cut-price books, and online reviews
www.amazon.co.uk

Books.co.uk – price surveys and other comparisons of online bookshops
www.books.co.uk

Contracts for difference

How they work

Copperchip
www.copperchip.co.uk

IGIndex Direct
www.igshares.com

Sucden UK
www.equitycfd.co.uk

Dealers

Berkeley Futures
www.bfl.co.uk

Blue Index
www.Blueindexuk.com

Cantor Index
www.cantorindexcfd.com

City Index
www.cityindex.co.uk

Client2Client
www.client2client.com

Deal4free
www.deal4free.com/cfd

E*Trade
www.etrade.com

GNI
www.gni.co.uk

Halewood International Futures
www.hifutures.com

Hargreaves Lansdown
www.h-l.co.uk

idealing
www.idealing.com

IFX
www.ifx.com

IG Index
www.igindex.co.uk

ManDirect
www.mandirect.co.uk

Refco Market Access
www.refcoinvestors.com

Sucden Equities CFDs
www.equitycfd.co.uk

Union CAL
www.unioncal.com/equities.html

Complaints

The Financial Services Authority
www.fsa.gov.uk

Covered warrants – information and/or dealing

ADVFN
www.advfn.com

Comdirect
www.comdirect.co.uk

Commerzbank
www.warrants.commerzbank.com

Dresdner Kleinwort Wasserstein
www.warrants.dresdner.com

Durlacher
www.durlacher.co.uk

Goldman Sachs
www.gs-warrants.co.uk

JP Morgan
www.jpmorganinvestor.com

The London Stock Exchange
www.londonstockexchange.com

SG Warrants
www.warrants.com

TD Waterhouse
www.tdwaterhouse.co.uk

TradingLab
www.tradinglab.co.uk

Derivatives

Chicago Board of Traded Options Exchange – probably the best educational
material on traded options available on the Internet
www.cboe.com

The London International Financial Futures and Options Exchange – useful
educational material
www.liffe.com

Prestel – live traded options prices
www.finexprestel.co.uk

Warrants Alert – a newsletter on warrants, and an introductory guide
www.tipsheets.co.uk.

Directors' dealings

Citywire
www.citywire.co.uk

Digitallook
www.digitallook.com

Discount brokers (financial services)

Aisa direct
www.aisa.co.uk

Alder Broker Group
www.abgltd.co.uk

Bestinvest
www.bestinvest.co.uk

Chartwell
www.chartwell-investment.co.uk

Cheapfunds.co.uk
www.cheapfunds.co.uk

Chelsea Financial Services
www.chelseafs.co.uk

Direct investor
www.direct-investor.com

Discount Investments Ltd
www.discount-investments.co.uk

Garrison Investment Analysis
www.garrison.co.uk

Hargreaves Lansdown
www.hargreaveslansdown.co.uk

Heritage Financial Services
www.heritage-financial.co.uk

Investment Discount House
www.idh.co.uk

Investment Discounts On-Line UK
www.theidol.co.uk

SAVED
www.isaved.co.uk

Max Value
www.maxvalue.co.uk

Moneyworld-ifa
www.moneyworld-ifa.co.uk

PEP-TopTen.com
www.pep-topten.com

quickdiscounts.com
www.quickdiscounts.com

Seymour Sinclair Investments
www.seymoursinclair.co.uk

Exchanges

London Stock Exchange
www.londonstockexchange.com

NASDAQ – the US high-tech market
www.Nasdaq.co.uk

Fantasy trading

DLJdirect – excellent demo
www.tdwaterhouse.co.uk

Hollywood Stock Exchange – fantasy trading in film stars and musician as practice
for stock market trading.
www.hsx.com

Selftrade – very good demo
www.europeanbrokerno1.com

Foreign exchange

News and research
Trend Analysis
www.trend-analysis.com

Dealers
Berkeley Futures
www.bfl.co.uk

Cantorindex
www.cantorindex.com

City Index
www.cityindex.co.uk

CMC deal4free
www.cmcplc.com

ED&F Man
www.edfman.com

GAIN Capital
www.gaincapital.com

Global Forex
www.globalforex.com

GNI
www.gni.co.uk

IFX Markets
www.ifxmarkets.com

IG Markets
www.igforex.com

Kyte Group
www.kytegroup.com

Lind-Waldock (a US firm)
www.lindwaldock.com

MG Financial Group
www.forex-mg.com

Refc Market Access
www.refcoinvestors.com

Spreadex
www.spreadexfinancials.com

Sucden
www.sucden.co.uk

Free samples (of financial newsletters)

www.financial-freebies.com

www.thefreestuffgallery.com

Futures dealers

Easy2Trade
www.easy2trade.com

See also under **Options and /or futures dealers**

General

Flexible Investment Strategies – critical and unconstrained investment education
(owned by the author of this book)
www.flexinvest.co.uk

itruffle – for the small cap sector
www.itruffle.com

mrscohen.co.uk – general for the private investor
www.mrscohen.co.uk.

The Motley Fool UK – educational, news and model portfolios (sometimes under-performing) for the private investor
www.fool.co.uk

High tech stocks

Durlacher – the investment boutique
www.durlacher.co.uk./research

Richard Holway Ltd
www.holway.com

Silicon Investor
www.techstocks.com

International investing

JP Morgan's ADR Web site – useful on ADRs
www.adr.com

Renaissance Capital – good research material on Russian equities
www.rencap.com

Investment clubs

Proshare
www.proshare.org

Investment courses/educational

Basic guide to options
www.tradebasics.com

Investor's Business Daily – free course online (including technical analysis) from US guru William O'Neil
www.investors.com

Martin Cole's four-day futures trading course on the Costa del Sol
www.learningtotrade.com

Sharecrazy.com
www.sharecrazy.com

The Siroc site – educational on futures and options
www.siroc.co.uk

Message boards

DigitalLook.com – bulletin board comments roundup
www.digitallook.com,

The Motley Fool UK
www.fool.co.uk

The Motley Fool US
www.fool.com

Raging Bull
www.ragingbull.com

Silicon Investor – subscription-based but high quality
www.siliconinvestor.com

Web page providing links to message boards of Market Eye, Hem Scott, UK Shares, and Ample (formerly Interactive Investor International)
www.freeyellow.com/members6/scottit/page7.html

New issues

Financial News – a leading publication about new issues of shares and other financial instruments on capital markets. Mainly for professionals
www.efinancialnews.com

issues direct – a Web site specializing in new issues
www.issuesdirect.com

OFEX

Equities Direct – online broker dealing in OFEX stocks
www.equities-direct.co.uk

OFEX Web site
www.OFEX.co.uk

unquoted.co.uk – news, information, interviews and message boards on OFEX companies
www.unquoted.co.uk

Options and/or futures dealers

ADM Investor Services – advisory service on options
www.admisi.com

Berkeley Futures
www.bfi.co.uk

BWD Rensburg
www.bwdrensburg.com

Cannon Bridge Corporation
www.cannonbridge.com

Charles Stanley
www.charles-stanley.co.uk

Cheviot Capital
www.cheviot.co.uk

Easy2trade
www.easy2trade.com

Fyshe Horton Finney
www.fyshe.co.uk

GNItouch Futures
www.gni.co.uk

Goy Harris Cartwright
www.ghcl.co.uk

Halewood International
www.hifutures.com

James Brearley
www.brearley.co.uk

Kyte Group
www.kytegroup.com

Man Direct
www.mandirect.com

Monument Securities
www.monumentsecurities.com

Mybroker
www.mybroker.com

ODL Securities
www.odlsecurities.com

Philip J Milton
www.miltonpj.net

Reco Market Access
www.refcoinvestors.com

Redmayne Bentley
www.redmayne.co.uk

Seymour Pierce Bell
www.seymourpierce.com

Thomas Grant
www.thomas-grant.com

Sucden
www.sucden.co.uk

Voltrex Options
www.voltrex.net

Penny Shares

Use these sites for background information and perspectives. If you want to buy, I advise you to do your own research.

City Equities – UK penny share dealer
www.cityequities.com

Penny Investor.com
www.pennyinvestor.com

Penny Shares Ltd.com – an online tipsheet
www.pennysharesltd.com

Pennystockinsider.com
www.pennystockinsider.com

Penny Stocks.net – advice on US pink sheets stocks
www.penny-stocks.net

Rollercoaster Stocks
www.rollercoasterstocks.com

Professional charting programs

Indexia
www.indexia.co.uk

Omnitrader
www.omnitrader.com

ShareScope
www.ShareScope.co.uk

Synergy
www.synergy.com

Updata
www.updata.com

Research (on companies)

Corporate reports
www.corpreports.co.uk

FinancialWeb – US news, research, Securities & Exchange Commission filings, and company reports
www.financialweb.com

Hemscott.net
www.hemscott.net

Hoover's Online – online details of more than 15,000 companies worldwide
www.hoovers.com

Investor-relations
www.investor-relations.co.uk.

Dr Ed Yardeni's Economics Network – US economics and stock market research
from the chief global economist of Deutsche Bank Securities in New York
www.prudential.com

Zacks.com – brokers' reports and news (US site)
www.zacks.com

Search engines (our favourites)

Google
www.google.com

Yahoo
www.yahoo.com

Share price quotes

Teletext
www.teletext.co.uk

Spread betting

General
Onewaybet.com
www.onewaybet.com

The Internet Sporting Club
www.internetsportingclub.co.uk

spreadbets.net
www.spreadbets.net

spreadbetting explained
www.spreadbettingexplained.com

Financial bookmakers
Cantor Index
www.cantorindex.com

City Index
www.cityindex.co.uk

CMC Spreadbet
www.deal4free.com

Financial Spreads
www.finspreads.com

IG Index
www.igindex.co.uk

Spreadex
www.spreadex.co.uk

TradIndex
www.tradindex.com

idealing
www.idealing.com

Stockbrokers
General
The Association of Private Client Investment Managers and Stockbrokers – a list of brokers (online and otherwise)
www.apcims.co.uk

Money extra – online brokers compared
www.moneyextra.com

Motley Fool UK – a table comparing costs of online brokers, and related message boards
www.fool.co.uk

Online brokers
Abbey National Sharedealing Service
E-mail: Nick.crabb@abbeynational.co.uk

Barclays Stockbrokers
www.barclays-stockbrokers.co.uk

Berkeley Futures
www.bfl.co.uk

James Brearley & Sons
www.jbrearley.co.uk

Cave & Sons Limited
www.caves.co.uk

Charles Schwab
www.schwab-europe.com

City Deal Services
www.citydeal.co.uk

Comdirect
www.comdirect.co.uk

Davy Stockbrokers
www.davy.ie

DLJ Direct
www.dljdirect.co.uk

Durlacher Ltd
www.durlacher.com

e-cortal
www.e-cortal.com

egg
www.egg.com

E*Trade
www.etrade.com

Fastrade
www.fastrade.co.uk

Goy Harris Cartright
E-mail: customerservice@ghcl.co.uk

Halifax
E-mail: www.halifax-online.co.uk

Hargreaves Landsdown
www.h-l.co.uk

Hoodless Brennan
www.hoodlessbrennan.com

idealing
www.idealing.com

Interactive Brokers
www.interactivebrokers.co.uk

INVESTeLINK
www.investelink.co.uk

Jarvis ShareDeal Active
www.sharedealactive.co.uk

LloydsTSB Sharedeal Direct
www.lloydstsb.com

Murray Beith Murray Asset Management
E-mail: asset@murraybeith.co.uk

MyBroker
E-mail: info@mybroker.co.uk

NatWest Shareview
www.natwest.co.uk

Norwich & Peterborough
www.npss.co.uk

Redmayne Bentley
E-mail: info@redmayne.co.uk

Refco Market Access
www.refcoinvestors.com

SAGA Share Direct
www.saga.co.uk

Self Trade UK Ltd
www.selftrade.co.uk
E-mail: info@selftrade.co.uk

The Share Centre
E-mail: info@shareco.uk

Share people
www.sharepeople.co.uk

Stocktrade
E-mail: sharedealing@stocktrade.co.uk

TD Waterhouse
www.tdwaterhouse.co.uk

Teather & Greenwood
www.teathers.com

Torrie & Co
www.torrie.co.uk

Virgin Money
www.virginmoney.com

Walker, Crips, Weddle, Beck
E-mail: clientservices@wcwb.co.uk

Xest
www.xest.com

Stock market news

Bloomberg
www.bloomberg.co.uk

DigitalLook – e-mail news alerts on your stock portfolio
www.digitallook.com

Electronic Telegraph
www.telegraph.co.uk

Evening Standard online
www.thisislondon.com

The Financial Times
www.ft.com

Fleet Street Publications – Britain's largest investment newsletter publisher
www.fleetstreetpublications.co.uk

Forbes – US business magazine
www.forbes.com

Guardian Unlimited
www.guardian.co.uk

Investors Chronicle
www.investorschronicle.co.uk

Newsletter Publishing – how to subscribe to The AIM Newsletter (and sister publications). Sample copies provided online.
www.newsletters.co.uk

News review – summary of weekend City press
www.news-review.co.uk

Red Herring magazine – US high tech company developments
www.redherring.com

This Is Money – news archives of *Daily Mail*, *Mail on Sunday*, and *Evening Standard*
www.thisismoney.co.uk

Tipsheets.co.uk – details of leading tipsheets on the market
www.tipsheets.co.uk

Tax

Blythens – tax advice
www.blythens.co.uk

Deloitte & Touche – tax advice
www.deloitte.co.uk

Details of tax rates
www.glazers.co.uk

Inland Revenue
www.inlandrevenue.gov.uk/home.htm

Technical analysis

Candlecharts.com – a site packed with valuable educational material on candlesticks, run by world authority Steve Nison
www.candlecharts.com

DecisionPoint.com – material on charting, some free, the rest for subscribers only
www.decisionpoint.com

Digitallook – access to charts
www.digitallook.com

FTMarketWatch – an excellent charting facility available
www.ftmarket-watch.com

murphymorris.com – leading market technician John Murphy addresses subscribers
www.murphymorris.com

mytrack program – if you want to draw your own trend lines
www.mytrack.com

Society of Technical Analysts – news of interest to technical analysts. Definitions of technical analysis, and details of educational courses, books stocked in the Society's library and an invitation to become a member of the Society
www.sta-uk.org

StockCharts.com – excellent general site on charting, with valuable educational material on point and figure charts
www.stockcharts.com

Technical Analysis from A to Z – highly informative
www.equis.com/free/taaz

Trading shares

Career DayTrader.com – useful articles and interviews on day trading
www.careerdaytrader.com

Cyberinvest – information and links for home-based traders
www.cyberinvest.com

DayTraders.com
www.daytraders.com

Robert Miner's Web site – useful advice
www.dynamictraders.com

Unconventional financial advice

Eden Press – California-based seller of unconventional tax haven books
www.edenpress.com

The offshore secrets network – a glimpse into unconventional offshore investing
www.offshoresecrets.com

The Sovereign Society – unconventional tax haven advice
www.sovereignsociety.com

Index